Measuring the Business Value of Information Technology

IT Best Practices Series

IT Best Practices Series

This book is published as a part of the IT Best Practices Series at Intel Press. Books in this series focus on managing information technology investments to produce measured business value. Business value indicators include financial metrics such as return on investment, operational metrics such as inventory turns, and productivity metrics such as reduced time to complete tasks.

Information technology investments include network and server infrastructure, business systems, engineering systems, and personal productivity systems. Business value can be obtained when mature technologies are deployed thoughtfully and also when new technologies emerge that provide new capabilities.

This series primarily reflects the experiences of Intel's IT organization, which are complemented with experiences of other IT organizations. Examples and case studies are included to show how business value manifests itself in different companies and industries.

For detailed information about these and other books, as well as announcements of forthcoming books in the series, visit the Intel Press Web site: *www.intel.com/intelpress.*

Measuring the Business Value of Information Technology

Practical Strategies for IT and Business Managers

David S. Sward

ISBN 0-9764832-7-0

Publisher: Richard Bowles

Managing Editor: David King

Program Manager: Stuart Douglas

Text Design & Composition: PhoebusGroup, LLP

Graphic Art: Rick Eberly

Library of Congress Cataloging in Publication Data:

Printed in China

10 9 8 7 6 5 4 3 2

Second printing: December 2006
First printing: June 2006

To Karla.

Contents

5   Measuring the Impacts of IT   111

6   Launching a Business Value Program   147

Foreword

It is with great pleasure that I introduce David Sward's book, *Measuring the Business Value of Information Technology*. This is the second book in the emerging series from Intel Press based on IT thought leadership and best practices. In this book David Sward, based on his experience in running the Intel IT Business Value program, operationalizes much of the IT capability maturity framework for value introduced in my book, *Managing Information Technology for Business Value*.

As IT organizations are most often measured on service excellence, many CIOs can forget that this has to be accompanied by usage excellence on behalf of the user community to fully exploit a portfolio of IT solutions and applications. In this book, David draws upon his human factors engineering and psychology background as he introduces an empirical science approach to enable better measurement and quantification of the business value that IT delivers. Using experimental techniques, activity logs, and attentive observation, David had developed methods for understanding and estimating productivity improvements, particularly using a user-centered lens.

Productivity has always been a key promise of IT systems. A human mind assisted by the processing, storage, indexing, visualization and communication capabilities of information systems cannot help but be more productive. In fact, as Moore's law has evolved, IT has become the steam engine of our emerging information society, and yet somehow quantifying the productivity benefits of IT has remained elusive. Enter David Sward, whose rigorous methods provide a solution for quantifying IT enabled productivity benefits on an individual IT investment level.

Measuring the Business Value of Information Technology is most certainly based on experiences at Intel. At the same time, David has included examples from other organizations, including interesting results from a small manufacturing company in India that participated in Intel's SMB program. Lessons learned at New Swan Autocomp. Pvt. Ltd. demonstrates that the payoffs of measuring business value can be found in smaller companies as well.

In the past few years I have spoken to hundreds if not thousands of CIOs and just a handful have been able to specifically talk about the average return from their IT investments when asked. David, in particular, focuses on building better IT investment business cases and designing them for better value realization. One of the most common business problems associated with building business cases is how to identify and particularly assign a monetary value to benefits enabled through an IT investment—the value dial concept that David describes is a breakthrough approach which significantly lowers the barrier for building and quantifying better quality business cases.

I suggest that David Sward provides another important lesson when he shows how important it is to turn business value measurement projects into a program of continuous improvement. While specific projects can evaluate new opportunities, such as the opportunity to broaden deployment of wireless systems to better support mobile computing, the business value program approach should in fact become part of the *modus operandi* of any IT organization.

In summary, I would like to borrow a perspective that Intel's Doug Busch offered in his foreword to my book, *Managing Information Technology for Business Value*. Doug said, with adaptation, "There is a long road between today's practices and a mature discipline of information technology management. *Measuring the Business Value of Information Technology* is a significant milestone on that journey." I think you will enjoy reading David's pragmatic and data-driven book.

Martin Curley, Director, IT Innovation and Research

Acknowledgments

First and foremost, I want to thank my loving wife Karla. She has shown me that all things are possible. In many ways writing this book has been more of a sacrifice for her than for me. She has had to put up with my constant traveling, my late hours, and my working on weekends. Karla, thank you for your love and support during this endeavor and in all things in life.

My parents, Janet and Leon, taught me the value of a solid work ethic and instilled in me a can-do attitude. My siblings, Tim, Denis, Steve, and Jen have challenged me throughout my life to do my best. I want to thank Bill and Linda for bringing Karla into my life. They raised a caring and wonderful person. A loving family is an amazing gift and one for which I am eternally grateful.

My name is on the book. The credit is not mine to take. I achieved this accomplishment through the incredible efforts of many other dedicated individuals. Many within Intel, the IT industry, and academia contributed content and ideas. There are hundreds of unnamed IT professionals within Intel that have worked diligently to document the business value of solutions they deploy and these individuals have made the program an ongoing success. It is their hard-won lessons collected over the years that have given the program the breadth represented in this book.

This book was written to expand on a subset of concepts developed in a book by Martin Curley, called *Managing IT for Business Value*. His early support and guidance was critical in getting this book done. Martin has been a mentor and trusted advisor during this endeavor. He never stops generating great ideas and continues to drive the IT discipline forward on several important fronts. I greatly appreciate the professional guidance and personal support provided by Brian Gorman. Brian documented the history of the program. His business acumen and extensive financial knowledge proved invaluable throughout the program and when writing this book. Intel's Cynthia Morgan was instrumental in pushing this project forward. It was her drive and enthusiasm that got this book into print. I am grateful to her for all her support during this process and throughout the years.

The original IT Business Value Team deservers most of the credit for the success of the program. The ideas in the book are a result of this team's hard work; each person contributed significantly to the program that is presented in this book. The team included Katie Haas, Brian Gorman, Ann Barefield, Steve Graves, Majorkumar Govindaraju, Rick Lansford, Julia Alsberg, Caleb Rabinowitz, Angela Cox, Meredith Wharton, and Russ Sype. Katie drove the program from the start and her vitality and enthusiasm spills into everything she does. Working with her was one of the most enjoyable periods during my career. The program's early success was due to her leadership.

The team reused as much work as possible while filling in the areas that didn't satisfy our needs. We started with a similar Intel effort within our e-Business Group. Tom Pope provided process information and created the original business value dials. Champ Merrick was also instrumental in running the program in eBG, as was Jeff Ely. The team drew heavily from concepts in human factors engineering, finance, experimental design, and performance measurement.

The management review committee (MRC) run by Bryan Pruden oversaw the program and contributed many great ideas. The MRC provided a healthy tension between the tactical concerns of the program team and the long term vision. It included John Johnson (VP and CIO of Intel IT), Maureen Glynn, Don Turner, Martin Curley, Bob Welch, Theresa Baudier, Brian Gorman, Joe McAvoy, and Nick Montoya. It was Doug Busch, Intel's CIO at the time, who had the vision to drive this idea.

Majorkumar Govindaraju and Steve Graves deserve special recognition. They worked tirelessly developing new ideas and techniques to measure employee productivity. Ann Barefield and Tovi Abello drove the finance side of the program making many contributions. Malvina Nisman reviewed and updated the Business Value Index, providing the most recent information. Ajay Sharma, Jimmy Wai, and Bee Peng Eo provided material and support for the New Swan Autocomp. Pvt. Ltd. case study. Qua Veda summarized Intel's approach to user segmentation. Kraig Finstad reviewed Intel's current efforts on measuring user experience.

Aviv Lichtman provided background materials and supported the broadband case study. Intel's Jim Kenneally provided the standard finance descriptions. Randy Sieffert and I have worked closely developing ideas in User Experience Design, along with Michael Flores, Andrew Sweany, Wei Xu, and Daniel Hardy from Arizona State University Polytechnic. Rick Lansford worked to provide information on the business value process and developed the database. Julia Alsberg provided a summary of the current spreadsheet used by the ITBV program.

Robert Laubacher at the MIT Sloan School of Management co-authored the final chapter. My thinking in a number of areas has been heavily influenced by our joint efforts. Rob also provide helpful feedback on early drafts of the manuscript.

I want to thank Roger Schvaneveldt at Arizona State University Polytechnic for early reviews of the manuscript and suggesting many good ideas. He has been a long time friend and colleague.

Intel's Katie Haas, Brian Gorman, Leigh Dragoon, Janie DeJoode, Jim Kenneally, Rick Lansford, and Janice Lopez, provided insightful comments on early versions. Chuck House, Katie Haas, Steve Graves, and Majorkumar Govindarajur provide feedback on the final version.

I owe a great deal to David and Susan King from PhoebusGroup. Their critical eyes, helpful suggestions, and careful editing have improved the book greatly. Rick Eberly created the graphics and Bob Allen reviewed the manuscript in detail. Along the way, I received helpful suggestions from Alan Morrison, Roger Peterson, and Chuck House.

Thanks to Rich Bowles, Intel Press publisher, and his team. Stuart Douglas, Mark Budzinski, and Wayne Jones assisted with marketing, project management, printing, and distribution.

I want to thank the individuals from St. Vincent's Hospital who agreed to share a great case study, Tim Stettheimer CIO and Theresa Z. Meadows RN. Gary York, founder of Awarix, was critical in getting this case study in the book. Without his support it would have not been possible. I also want to thank Intel's Joseph Dalton who facilitated the introductions.

Bill Bruno from Stratigent LLC introduced me to one of the best measurement techniques I have seen in recent years and worked hard to ensure that the book benefited from including their approach. Finally, thanks to Ian Campbell from Nucleus Research for sharing his conversion efficiency estimates.

David Sward
May, 2006

Chapter 1

Introduction

If you can't measure IT, you can't manage IT.
—Modified from Andy Grove, Chairman Emeritus, Intel Corporation

Organizations large and small face the same dilemma: scarce resources. Choosing and deploying the right solution to maximize an organization's performance, to satisfy customers, and to make and maintain a profit has never been more critical. Information technology, in particular, often loses its significance as a major contributing success factor in an organization's strategic objectives because it is predominantly considered a function within an organization that is not integral to achieving business objectives. Consequently, budgets are squeezed year after year as IT organizations inevitability drift towards the "cost center" perception, and not toward being the competitive differentiator that IT has the potential to be.

As a Human Factors Engineer (HFE) and someone who has worked in the IT industry for many years, I consider this a myopic and potentially dangerous notion for any organization. It is critical for IT organizations to alter their thinking and identify not only the cost, but the value that IT brings to the enterprise. How can this be done? Measure the bottom-line impact of information technology to reveal its true value and enable allocation of resources in the most essential areas.

> **Human Factors Engineering**
>
> Human Factors Engineering is an applied discipline that seeks to optimize human interaction and safe operation with technology by applying what is known about human capabilities and limitations to the design, use, maintenance, and removal of both simple and complex systems.
>
> In an earlier era, some of this work was the domain of industrial engineers leading time-and-motion studies on the assembly line. However, most office environments and the work processes performed in those environments, do not easily lend themselves to traditional time-and-motion measurement. HFE professionals fill an important role with their specialized training in the subtleties of the knowledge workplace.

Audiences For This Book

I wrote this book with several audiences in mind.

- Project managers who have a potential IT solution in mind that will benefit their organizations. Finance will not approve deployment without solid data demonstrating business value to the company. This book will provide project managers with ideas, methods, and examples of how to systematically collect data on the business value of the solution.

- Managers of IT organizations who want to determine the best way to maximize the value delivered to their company, defend their current budgets, and argue successfully for increased funding that will help grow the business. This book provides techniques for measuring business value for a portfolio of IT investments.

- Product managers at companies that develop and deliver IT solutions. The sales and marketing organization needs to develop objective and credible case studies on how the company's IT products and services impact the customer's bottom line. This book explains how to develop credible and empirically sound case studies demonstrating information technology's business value (ITBV).

- CEOs of companies who want to grow their businesses and who have asked all business units to develop alternatives, including the

IT department. This book provides rational and systematic ways to choose which investments in information technology impact the bottom line.

■ Lecturers in MBA programs who want to illustrate the importance of informed business decision making for IT investments. In addition to explaining how to frame the conversation on informed decision making and ITBV, this book provides a business-school style case study to support classroom discussion.

■ IT professionals who want to complement their technical skills with the ability to use metrics and methods to demonstrate the business value of their IT initiatives. This book provides IT professionals with better metrics that quantify the widespread soft benefits of IT and links those soft benefits to the enterprise bottom line.

■ IT solution providers serving small and medium-size businesses (SMBs) where extensive financial and HFE analyses are usually unfeasible. For those who serve SMBs, this book provides examples that can serve as benchmarks supporting investment decisions or recommendations.

In today's fiercely competitive business climate, IT organizations face increasing pressure to prove the business value of information technology investments. Interest in the valuation process is widespread because ITBV affects the entire enterprise. Doing a credible job of measuring ITBV has never been an easy task.

IT Cost vs. IT Benefit

IT is often viewed as a cost center, and a result of this perspective is sustained focus on total cost of ownership (TCO). While this is an important and necessary approach to IT management, used in isolation it does nothing to demonstrate the impact IT has on the profitability of the company it supports. When a department is viewed solely as a cost center, budgets are squeezed year over year as competition continually erodes budgetary resources. As a result, it is difficult for IT organizations to enable the long-term competitive advantage senior management demands. Corporations operate in a complex mix of markets on a global

> ### Customer, Stakeholder, and End-User
>
> ■ The *customer* is the person or organization investing in the IT solution. Customer orientation vs. technology orientation indicates that IT is being run like a business.
>
> ■ *Stakeholders* have a vested business interest in the IT solution, are not directly funding the project, and should be able to influence the project.
>
> ■ *End users* are the individuals who use an IT solution to perform their work. These people press the keys, click the mouse, input information, and respond to output from the IT solution to accomplish business objectives.
>
> It is critical to involve end-users and stakeholders in the development process to ensure that the IT solution satisfies their needs as well as the needs of the customer.

scale that is changing at ever-increasing speed. Users have never been so sophisticated or demanding with respect to the IT services they require in this highly competitive environment. This book explores one way IT can move from being perceived as a cost center to becoming a strategic partner that contributes to organizational objectives and enables a competitive advantage for the organization. To do this, the IT organization must change from being techno-centric to user-centric.

As shown in Figure 1.1, when user experience design (UED) brings together business objectives, user requirements, and IT capabilities, then the IT organization is in position to leverage these three inputs into a significantly large amount of measured business value. IT organizations that successfully bridge the gap between end-users and business objectives will create a competitive advantage with IT investments that impact the company's bottom line.

This book is about the processes and tools implemented within Intel and in other organizations that measure the business value of information technology. The ideas and methods that comprise Intel's ITBV program are heavily influenced by finance concepts and by the discipline of Human Factors Engineering, which is my primary discipline. HFE is the scientific discipline that develops and applies the principles of what is known about human capabilities and limitations to the design, use, maintenance, and removal of simple and complex systems.

I led an Intel HFE team that brought scientific rigor to a new ITBV program that measured and improved business value contributions

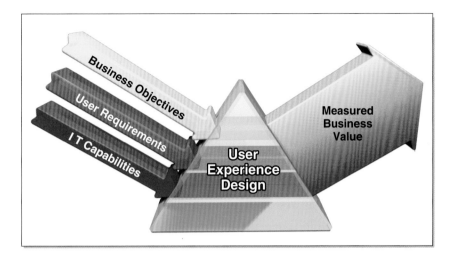

Figure 1.1 Driving Greater Business Value

driven by IT investments. HFE provided the right level of objectivity to a number of outcomes that are typically difficult to measure. Specifically, HFE provides an excellent way to measure IT impact on employee productivity. Individuals with formal training in HFE have a skill set that enables them to tackle many of the difficult issues around quantifying so-called *soft* benefits.

An Intel finance team was also at the nucleus of the ITBV program from the onset to ensure that proper financial methods were woven into the program. While we both clearly understand that other skill sets play a part in developing an ITBV program, it was representatives from finance and HFE that set the foundation for framing the overall structure and processes Intel used.

Combining finance, HFE, and other methods into a unified systematic approach is the key to success when defining, measuring, and tracking the business value of IT. Many methods discussed in this book are drawn from a variety of disciplines and are in use in many enterprises. Applying methods with successful track records to an ITBV program can only add to its overall quality.

Information Technology and Business Value Defined

Throughout the book, I define information technology as the products, services, or solutions that are deployed to store, retrieve, transport, or process information in the course of a business unit or end-user accomplishing a goal. While adding the aspect of a business unit or end-user to the definition goes beyond the typical definition, it is critical to understand that businesses deploy IT to assist employees in getting their jobs done.

An IT organization is any group, department, or division, either internal or external to the company, that is responsible for developing or deploying information technology to the users they support. These IT organizations may support an accounting firm, a parts manufacturer, an office supply store, an on-line retailer, a marketing group, or a high-tech company.

Business value is the benefit for business units and the enterprise as a whole, represented in dollar terms, that is a result of IT solutions or services, as evidenced by one or more of the following:

- Direct contribution to the corporation's market position or revenue
- Deliverables and results that support solving customer business needs and challenges
- Customer cost savings or financial benefits
- Examples of technology investment that advance the industry

Information Technology and Business Value

In the last 20 years there have been incredible changes in information technology. People work through Internet-connected high powered workstations, notebook computers with integrated wireless, servers, personal digital assistants (PDAs), pagers, and dozens of other smart devices. Continued advances in hardware and software are changing the speed and shape of how business gets done. While there is a general assumption that IT increases productivity, companies are increasingly demanding that IT investments demonstrate measurable results (Harvard Business School 1999).

The academic community has been divided for years on whether IT provides business value. In the 1980s, Robert Solow, professor at MIT Sloan, summarized his thinking by saying, "I see computers everywhere except in the productivity statistics."

In recent years, researchers have shown the connection between IT and productivity. Using a production function approach to compare business-value outputs (*i.e.*, revenue, stock price) with and inputs (*i.e.*, capitol, labor) Brynjolfsson and Hitt (2002) found a positive return on IT investments. In 2002, Dedrick, Gurbaxani, and Kraemer concluded that greater investment in IT is associated with greater productivity growth at the company and country level. Research by Tallon, Kraemer, and Gurbaxani (2000) based on executive perspectives concluded that the degree of alignment between the IT strategy and the firm's business strategy was important and that investment alone was not enough. These studies substantiate the relationship between IT and business value.

As consensus among economists was developing on the role of IT in improving productivity, Nicholas Carr published an article called "IT Doesn't Matter." In that article, Carr argued that IT was becoming a routine input, a commodity, that could no longer enable firms to achieve a strategic advantage and continued investment in IT is a poor strategy (Carr, 2003). The response from gurus in the IT field was immediate. Individuals like Paul Strassmann, John Seely Brown, and Chris Langdon, along with numerous business school professors, responded, as did several leading CIOs. These individuals outlined counter-arguments that were powerful, articulate, and persuasive. There was one downside. The responses were targeted for IT professionals, whereas Carr wrote his original article for CEOs (House, 2004).

The seeming disagreement between Carr and the economists is largely a matter of their differing perspectives. Economic research provides evidence that IT creates value when examining data across hundreds of firms or an entire economy. Carr and other strategic management writers are interested in the ability of IT to enable a sustainable competitive advantage for a firm. Given the difference in perspectives, the actual disagreements are less than they appear.

IT investment alone is not guaranteed to improve productivity. In addition to investing in IT, the enterprise must also manage the IT ecosystem and business process. Brynjolfsson, Hitt, and Yang (2002) found that firms that invest in IT without making the requisite organizational investments do worse than firms that stand pat. Smith and Fingar (2003) wrote in a book rebutting Carr's claims, "IT doesn't matter—business processes do."

There are many approaches for quantifying IT payoffs, ranging from highly scientific to the purely subjective (Wen and Sylla, 1999). A case can be made that the more traditional valuation methods that focus solely on costs and tangible benefits quantifiable at a firm level are incomplete. It is important to objectivity measure all aspects of business value for specific IT solutions and the changes that result. I believe determining the business value of improvements in individual worker performance helps facilitates alignment between IT initiatives and business objectives.

Intel's IT Business Value Program

At the end of 2001, Intel challenged its IT organization to measure the bottom-line impact—the business value—of their IT solutions. Delivering IT solutions in a technology company compounded the challenge and intensified the scrutiny when data-driven proof was made a requirement.

To meet this challenge, IT implemented the IT Business Value program to assess both the forecasted value of an IT solution and the actual business value delivered to our customers and to Intel Corporation as a whole. The ITBV program developed the following:

- A standard set of financial measurements of business value, which we call *business value dials*, that serve as a common language throughout the company and are based on customer business objectives.

- A standard measurement methodology to determine the impact of IT solutions.

- A common valuation process with finance acting as independent auditors.

- A business-value portfolio of the forecasted and delivered results determined by customer-generated critical success indicators.

- A set of ground rules used to define the program's operation and to drive accountability for the business value realized by our customers.

The ITBV team also added an organizational performance evaluation metric to Intel's employee bonus (EB) program to ensure motivation and to encourage everyone to work toward the same end.

Before the ITBV program, Intel's IT organization measured success, like many IT organizations, in terms of higher network availability, server uptime, and number of calls answered, and so forth. The ITBV program significantly expanded the metrics being tracked to include those related to an improved bottom-line, such as time to market for Intel products, increased revenue, capital purchase avoidance, and measured improvements in employee productivity.

The ITBV program team worked with business units across Intel to develop and apply standard metrics and methods for capturing the forecasted and actual value of information technology products, services, and solutions. Whether in the factory, among design engineers, or in the standard office setting, the team quantified IT's impact, developing methods for tracing benefits and forging a closer partnership between our internal customers and IT.

- In 2002 the ITBV program set a goal of $100 million and successfully documented over $180 million in new business value that Intel's IT delivered to the corporation. In 2003, the goal was raised to $250 million, and the program documented $419 million in new business value.

- In 2002 and 2003 ITBV capped the maximum value any one program could contribute to the goal, at $20 million and $40 million respectively. This was done to prevent any one project from accounting for the majority of the business value goal for that year.

- In 2004 the employee incentive connection was removed, as well as the cap on programs, and the goal was set at $400 million. In 2004 the program documented $479 million in new business value. In the end, we documented over $1 billion in new business value in those three years.

Formalizing the measurement of business value has changed the corporate attitude toward the value of investing in information technology. Project owners are more willing and more equipped to document, measure and objectively demonstrate the value of their projects in customer terms.

I believe that it is critical for IT organizations to adopt metrics and measures of information technology's value as part of their approval, development, and implementation processes. Focusing on data and keeping the customer involved encourages the line-of-business owners to invest the time to evaluate their project's impact on the company's bottom line.

Managing Information Technology

In 2004 Martin Curley published *Managing IT for Business Value*. His book covers many of the processes used within Intel and elsewhere to maximize the business value that the IT organization delivers to the corporation. Researchers at the Software Engineering Institute (SEI) at Carnegie Mellon University had developed the idea of a capability maturity model (CMM) when looking at ways to improve the software development process. Curley applied the concept to business processes

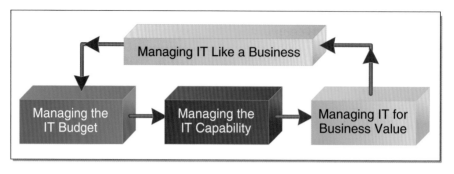

Figure 1.2 CMF Strategies

Source: Curley 2006

instead of software development and placed these processes within an IT Capability Maturity Framework (CMF). The IT CMF suggests that as the IT discipline continues to coalesce, it will continue to develop systematic approaches to managing and measuring business value. A fundamental idea within the IT CMF is that investment decisions require repeatable processes describing practices that an IT organization should use to effectively manage information technology to maximize the business value delivered to the company.

This book, *Measuring the Business Value of Information Technology,* is designed to expand on a subset of concepts contained within Curley's book and provide a blueprint of processes and methodologies that can be used to establish an IT Business Value program within your organization. I will review the metrics, studies, and processes developed as a part of our ITBV program.

IT Capability Maturity Framework Overview

At Intel, we view IT management as a production function, as shown in Figure 1.2. The *IT Budget* provides the essential input to the production process. The budget drives *IT Capability* which, in turn, produces *IT Value* as the output. *Managing IT Like a Business* is the feedback mechanism for adjusting the budget, capability, and value to optimize the outputs. The entire production system describes IT governance, which is the overall management, decision making, and accountability needed to maximize value within given constraints (*e.g.*, acceptable levels of risk, regulatory compliance). In this model the IT budget is used to not only fund the envisioning, development, operations, and provisioning of IT solutions, but also to develop the IT capability, the underlying assets, and to strengthen the IT value chain.

The maturity of each of these functions is described by five stages, or levels, as shown in Figure 1.3. Initially, these functions are *ad hoc*, which means that the IT organization is barely managed at all. At the second stage, basic processes have been identified and can be repeated. In the case of the IT budget, for example, budget performance has become predictable. Level three is marked by sharper process definitions. In the case of the IT business value function, attention shifts from total cost of ownership to a more precise definition of return on investment (ROI). The fourth level is marked by improved process management. In terms of IT capability, the shift to level 4 is attained when the IT organization provides more than technology expertise and becomes a strategic business partner for the enterprise as a whole. The fifth and final level is marked by process optimization. The IT budget is sustainable, IT

Figure 1.3 IT Capability Maturity Frameworks

Source: Curley 2006

capability is a core competency for the enterprise, business value is optimized, and the IT organization is viewed as a value center (vs. a cost center).

As capabilities mature within a firm, the IT organization will climb the maturity staircases in parallel. Creating world-class practices around managing IT for business value without the IT capability to deliver value is clearly not an optimized situation. It is more common and effective for an organization to achieve level-3 capabilities across the board and then to focus on moving ahead to level 4 for all four capabilities.

I recommend that IT organizations routinely perform an IT Business Value maturity assessment to verify progress against previous measures and to identify what improvement actions to take next. Only through concerted, coordinated action will the overall business value delivered through IT be improved and ultimately reflected in business performance.

Establishing an ITBV program is one of the most important initiatives an IT organization can engage in to drive towards higher levels of the IT CMF. Launching an ITBV program helps to ensure that the value IT aims to deliver is aligned with customer or end-user needs, to document forecasted and actual business value delivered systematically, and to communicate this bottom-line impact in the customer's language. The ITBV team directly supports the business plan for the IT organization and creates the processes that measure and maximize the business value that IT is delivering.

IT organizations must demonstrate their bottom-line impact as they continue to battle for limited budgetary resources, and must enable a competitive advantage for their firm by expanding their focus to new key processes, such as user experience design. As companies start to realize the value that can be achieved by delivering compelling and innovative user experiences, they will look to IT organizations to deliver on this front. Is your IT organization capable and up to the challenge?

How to Use this Book

Core chapters of this book build one upon another beginning with business value measurement in Chapter 2 and ending with the ITBV program in Chapter 6. These chapters are best read in sequence. Appendices and remaining chapters can be sampled at any time.

This book is organized in a layered architecture, as shown in Figure 1.4. Basic concepts provide a foundation for conducting ITBV studies and a collection of systematic studies constitutes an ITBV program. Here is how the story unfolds:

■ Chapter 1 is an introductory chapter that identifies the overall goals for this book, defines basic terms, and establishes the relationship between IT and business value. It also offers a production-system model along with capability maturity frameworks that are the basis for identifying and maximizing business value contributions from IT investments.

■ Chapter 2 enriches the concept of business value and introduces business value dials, which is Intel's way of describing the indica-

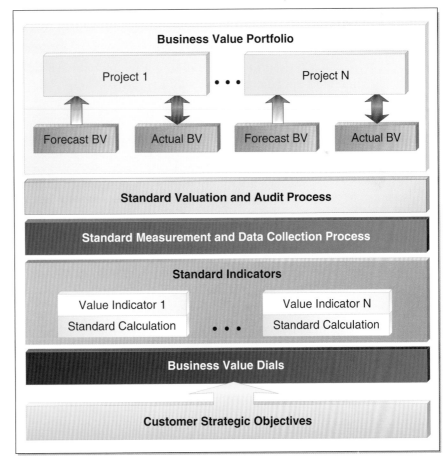

Figure 1.4 Business Value Architecture

tors that measure value contributions. Chapter 2 introduces the overall measurement framework and provides a 13-step overview of the business value process.

■ Chapter 3 examines business value from a financial point of view. ROI and its relationship to the time value of money is one of several financial ratios presented. The business value concept is instantiated with a multitude of examples.

■ Chapter 4 describes how to measure the impact of IT on employee productivity. Often described as a soft benefit, productivity can be measured using tools drawn from human factors engineering, statistics, and experimental design.

■ Chapter 5 explains the design of an ITBV study and pulls together the financial and productivity tools developed previously. Readers will find this chapter to be the turning point as the entire ITBV process comes to life.

■ Chapter 6 describes in detail how to launch an ITBV program and includes specifications for staffing and skill sets. A key concern is how ITBV is integrated into the enterprise as a whole.

■ In Chapter 7 we describe how Intel's ITBV program was launched. This insider's view will be especially valuable to IT strategists in larger corporations.

■ Chapter 8 looks ahead to summarize academic work and evaluate its utility to ITBV practitioners. We discuss ongoing research at Intel and speculate how user experience design will improve the business value of IT.

■ Appendix A provides business-school style case study of a health care provider's use of innovative technology to create business value. The case explores the innovative use of IT to improve patient throughput at St. Vincent's hospital.

■ Appendix B contains two examples of business value studies. They include the quantification of enterprise software deployment for team collaboration and the deployment of technology into manufacturing.

■ Appendix C provides additional details about the tools and processes required to implement and run a program.

Summary

Implementing an innovative approach to determine the business value of information technology is an enormous task, but the payoff for the IT organization and the enterprise as a whole is worth the effort. The ITBV program developed processes and metrics that quantified $1.39 billion in bottom-line impact from information technology over the first three years.

The tools and methodologies produced by an ITBV program easily fit within other common management practices. As Martin Curley has shown, ITBV process improvement is well supported by capability maturity frameworks as IT organizations uncover and define processes, measure and optimize metrics, and build sustainable excellence in four management domains, IT budget, IT capability, IT business value, and IT as a business.

From research done to build the program, we have concluded that to create a world-class IT organization that clearly demonstrates bottom-line impact for the company, the culture must shift from techno-centric to user-centric thinking. IT strategists will need to develop and systematically implement a uniform business value language. The firm will need to establish a dedicated team that is supported by upper management, charter this team to define rules which govern program, and develop and systematically use a standard measurement and valuation process.

An ITBV perspective is often a new mind set for IT professionals and the corporation. Measured results instill a belief that IT can and should help create a competitive advantage and increase shareholder value by not just deploying information technology, but deploying the right information technology.

Chapter **2**

Business Value

Price is what you pay. Value is what you get.
—Warren Buffet

An ongoing challenge for many IT organizations today is deciding how to compare various IT investments. If this task wasn't hard enough to begin with, it is typically done across departments or distinct IT functions. Imagine the meeting when multiple IT groups are all competing for limited resources, each presenting their projects with supporting data and arguing over whose project has merit. Sound familiar? Independent of how this is done or the tools used, there tends to be a common theme that cuts across efforts. How do you get to an *apples-to-apples* comparison? This chapter sets the foundation for this work by covering the basic concepts of an IT Business Value program. Namely, developing a common language of business value and a agreeing on a business value process. Getting these in place will help facilitate managing IT for business value.

Fully comprehending the business problem a proposed IT solution addresses is key to determining the value of an IT solution. Too often, techno-centric IT solution providers miss the real business value of information technology by simply asking "Can I?" instead of asking the more thoughtful question, "Should I?" when considering making an IT investment.

Determining the business sense of making an IT investment requires a high level of objectivity. By collaborating with partners who saw the benefits and measurements in an independent light—*i.e.*, partners who were not directly vested in a particular result—we found we were able to make decisions that achieved accurate and credible results.

This chapter lays the groundwork for later chapters by examining the concept of business value, discussing how to make the concept operational, describing a measurement framework for assessing the impact of IT solutions, and outlining the steps that comprise the business value process.

Developing a Common Language

At Intel, we believe that the cornerstone of any IT Business Value program is the creation of a common language of business value.

Employees in areas such as IT and applications development groups usually don't think in terms of profit-and-loss (P&L) statements and general ledger codes. Technical and engineering people need to be able to use terminology that their financial partners can translate into cash inflows and cash outflows.

Using this common language, IT groups can effectively communicate the value they deliver through IT solutions. The language helps IT put into proper perspective the business problem, the necessary business and financial modeling, and the necessary discussions for making a good business decision. Without a common business-value vocabulary, people tend to justify IT programs with vague phrases like "efficiency gains" or "strategic in nature."

Creating a common language for discussing business value begins with two basic steps. First, you must come to agreement on a clear definition of what the term "business value" means. Next, you must establish precise ways of describing success in achieving business value from an IT investment and learn to express these metrics in the customer's language.

Defining Business Value

IT shops have typically thought of the value of an IT solution in terms of performance improvements such as higher network availability, increased server uptime, a greater number of trouble calls answered, and so forth. Today, however, *better, faster, cheaper* arguments such as these are too vague to justify new IT spending. A far more compelling argument for investing in an IT solution would be one that effectively demonstrates how a particular solution can be expected to directly impact the organization's bottom line.

To define business value, you need to know what is seen as valuable through the eyes of your end-users, your customer, and your company. Is it bottom-line impact, top-line growth, or using IT to open new markets? Only after you clearly understand what has value to your company, can you agree upon a definition of business value that expresses it.

At Intel, we agreed on the following definition of business value.

Business Value

The benefit for business groups, represented in dollar terms, that is a result of Information Technology solutions or services, as evidenced by one or more of the following:

- Direct contribution to the corporation's market position or revenue

- Deliverables and results that support solving customer business needs and challenges

- Financial improvements derived from customer cost savings or benefits

- Examples of technology investment that advance the industry

---

Establishing Metrics

When your company has formed a definition of business value, your IT managers must learn to think differently about how they evaluate successful IT investments. What, specifically does the customer hope to achieve? How will they know when they have achieved it? The answers to these questions should be stated in the language of the customer, and they should become new metrics for measuring the financial success of IT investments. When you have determined that a customer wants an IT solution that produces faster time-to-market, increased revenue, or improvements in employee productivity, you have achieved concrete objectives that can be observed and quantified.

Business Value Dials

A business value dial is Intel's term for a standardized indicator of business value. As shown in Figure 2.1, these dials are like gauges or instruments. When deploying IT solutions, our intention is to influence these business value dials.

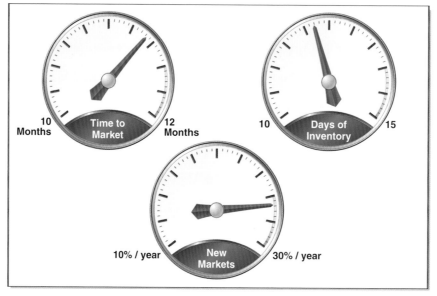

Figure 2.1 Business Value Dials

After an extensive evaluation of potential sources of business value at Intel done by Tom Pope, 18 business value dials were initially defined. These business value dials have been updated by other teams, and the most recent set is presented in this chapter. Defining these dials is an important part of the common language used to describe specific observable and quantifiable elements of business goals. We have worked hard at Intel to stabilize these dials so that we can chart progress over years.

In working with the business value dials we have made three types of modifications to our dials when they were need. These modifications have included:

- Creating a new dial because a new IT solution involves business value that is not covered in the existing set. (This is rare.)

- Splitting an existing dial into two dials to better account for the business value.

- Combining two value dials because the distinction between them is no longer relevant. For example, unit cost and other cost avoidance were originally separate business value dials, but over time we determined that the separation was not necessary and the two could be combined into a single business value dial.

For IT organizations setting up an ITBV program we suggest that developing and refining business value dials is absolutely necessary. Each organization implementing a similar program should review the business value dials and add to them as they see fit, filling in gaps in the existing set with respect to their line of business. For example, if your IT organization supports the health care sector, an appropriate value dial might be "patient satisfaction."

Business Value Dials in Health Care

A business value analysis at Birmingham, Alabama-based St. Vincent's Hospital studied the value of integrating RFID and display technologies to make relevant data immediately available to hospital staff. (See the case study on Improved Throughput at St. Vincent's Hospital in Appendix A.) A field study identified several hospital activities that could be improved with more readily available data. The business value measures of success included the following:

- Increased utilization of the hospital's resources—a key indicator of patient throughput

- Increased discharges by noon—a second key indicator of patient throughput

- Reduction in *diversions*, that is, patients turned away due to perceived lack of resources

- Improved patient and staff satisfaction

We found that looking at projects in terms of business value dials changes the way IT managers view the benefits of new investments. After launching the program, we saw that proposed projects were increasingly based on bottom-line impacts, such as increased revenue, risk avoidance, employee productivity, increased factory yield, and so on.

Business Value Dial Calculations

The business value dials provide common definitions, context, and focus on where IT solutions are delivering value. They also provide a framework for IT professionals to understand how to quantify the business benefits of IT. They can even be used as an educational tool for showing how IT can have both direct and indirect influence on the bottom line. However, for business dials to be really useful, you need to develop a set of generic calculations.

From 2002-2004 we reviewed over 350 IT projects and measured more than 60 in detail. Some projects spanned the entire enterprise, some focused on specific manufacturing processes, and others spearheaded the improvement of Intel's own products. Each delivered business value, each had metrics, each had equations that financially quantified the value, and each was explained within the context of the business value dials.

With the concept of business value dials, we really reach the *meat* of the ITBV program. Paired with the discipline of objective human performance measurement from Human Factors Engineering, the value dials represent the core of our new ability to translate IT-driven productivity or operational gains into clear cash-flow results.

Each business value dial used at Intel is defined and explained with examples and sample calculations in the following section. Again, all of these definitions represent fairly standard financial concepts, but we found that laying them out in clear, business specific, language was critical in re-aligning the IT mind set toward specific types of value delivery, and also in making our assertion of value delivery clear and crisp.

There are business value dials for monitoring and controlling four categories that impact a firm's bottom line: headcount management, expense avoidance, working capital, and revenue increases. These business dials are not intended to be an exhaustive inventory, and the appropriate dials will vary depending on the enterprise.

These four category of business value dials are detailed in the following sections.

Headcount Growth

Concept: Solutions that enable reduction in human resources or absorb business growth without growing headcount. The company can either move employees to areas of greater return (with job-search time and support provided for eligible employees) or put teams on new projects.

Table 2.1   Business Value Dials Related to Headcount Management

BV Dial	Definition
Headcount Growth	Solutions that enable reduction in human resources or absorb business growth without growing headcount. The company can either move employees to areas of greater return (with job-search time and support provided for eligible employees) or put teams on new projects.
	Sample Calculation: (Number of headcount reduced or avoided) x (Average burden rate for region and job type)
Employee Turnover	Solutions that reduce undesired employee turnover. Significant cost savings are realized when hiring, training, and interviewing are avoided.
	Sample Calculation: (35% of annual burden rate and region and job type) x (number of headcount turnover avoided)
Employee Productivity	Gains in headcount efficiencies or effectiveness. Headcount is expected to produce more through these gains due to the additional time-based efficiencies.
	Sample Calculation: (Number of employees affected) x (time) x (average burden rate) x (50%)

This happens when IT solutions replace or augment core job tasks that individuals perform. In growth areas, the solution can let each individual perform more job tasks in a given timeframe, enabling the company to avoid paying additional people to accomplish the same business result. In declining areas, the solution may result in actual headcount reductions in that part of the business.

When using this value dial, watch out for the pitfall of adding automation that does not actually reduce the number of personnel or increase the amount of work accomplished in the same unit of time with the same number of employees. Actual reductions in total headcount are, of course, the most reliable indicator in this area, but embedding indicators that lead to accountability, such as invoices handled per clerk, manufacturing line items per planner, calls handled by support staff, and orders per customer analyst can also be used.

Example: Implementing an electronic accounts payable process to verify invoices and relay payments can eliminate the need for accounts payable clerks. Moving a variety of planning methodologies to a single, standard process on standard systems can eliminate or decrease the need for factory planners. Self-help applications that let customers place their own orders can reduce the number of order-takers needed.

It is important to have a solid model of *average burden rates* per employee, including non-salary related components of the cost per employee, such as benefits, facilities and other shared-services charges. These will likely include fixed and variable components, some of which may not be reduced at the time of headcount reduction. There will also be variability by region and impacted job type. Pragmatically, for modeling purposes some of this detail may require more data gathering work than is justified for the ITBV measurement task, and simplifying assumptions are often justifiable in this context.

Productivity Improvement due to Workflow Changes in a Call Center

The productivity of a proposed IT solution can be measured by the improvement in efficiency with which the user can perform tasks. The ITBV team performed a study to measure the impact of reducing the number of steps in a business process workflow and how it impacted task completion times.

A field study was conducted in a customer support call center with five support specialists, involving 11 tasks to evaluate a proposed workflow. Each user performed the 11 tasks and the task completion times for each user were averaged. The objective of the study was to compare the time to complete the tasks in the current workflow with that in the revised workflow, and to evaluate the savings in task completion time and headcount.

As IT customer support is a highly structured and routine office environment, any time savings at the level of tasks can be aggregated into daily time savings. It was found that the headcount needed to support the proposed system could be reduced by 85 percent, and the employees could be reassigned to higher value areas.

Employee Turnover

Concept: Solutions that reduce undesired employee turnover. Significant cost savings are realized when hiring, training, and interviewing are avoided. Some jobs entail a high percentage of low-satisfaction activities, resulting in high turnover rates, creating an undesirable financial impact on the organization. Such roles are prime candidates for IT solutions and process redesign that can minimize repetitive and unpleasant job elements and thus reduce turnover.

Examples: Many jobs within an organization involve data-reconciliation or analysis tasks that produce little real value-add for the company. For example, planners that manually refresh demand triggers and build plans each new business cycle. Changing to centralized planning information that guides build-plan options through automated business rules minimizes the tedium for the people involved. Other similar examples involve budget and inventory reconciliation tasks.

Turnover rates must be studied in groups before and after implementation, a solid partnership with staffing and human resources groups is always a good idea. Our experience indicates that an average cost for rehiring, training, interviewing, advertising, lost productivity and relocation is about 35 percent of the annual salary and benefits for that job. The U.S. Department of Labor estimates that the cost to an organization to replace an employee averages 33 percent of the new hire's salary (Brannick, 1999). However, some estimates place this value as high as 1.5 times the annual salary and benefits, citing that many approaches fail to take all relevant costs into account and therefore consistently underestimate the impact to the organization (Fitz-Enz, 1997).

Employee Productivity

Concept: Gains in efficiencies or effectiveness where the employee is expected to produce more through these gains due to the additional time-based efficiencies. Many IT solutions have a direct or indirect impact on employees, and therefore will potentially impact employee productivity. Some IT solutions result in outright automation of jobs or major portions of jobs, and are covered above. The employee productivity business value dial applies in the rest of these cases—when people are going to become more efficient in some way, a job task will be removed through automation, or done in less time, or will require fewer steps.

Often this impact is on non-core or administrative tasks, such as managing ones own benefits and employment-related information, obtaining work-related information such as management or HR policies and administering other forms required in the workplace. These and similar tasks tend to interrupt core activities or cause annoyances in the workplace.

Examples: Human resources or employee-facing applications tend to generate employee productivity benefits. Web-based managers' reference manuals, self-help benefits administration tools, online employee information forms, and searchable databases of company polices are all administrative tools that can reduce employee time on non-core tasks. Employee productivity benefits are also often seen with office automation tools that make it easier to obtain needed data for analysis, or with mobility and remote work capabilities that enable employees to do useful work while traveling.

Financial Tips: Determining the value of employee productivity gains can be especially challenging. The intuitive high-level approach is to take and employee's burden rate and to multiply it by the number of hours saved. Unfortunately, most IT solutions don't save large units of time, and it has historically proven quite difficult to correlate the deployment of specific employee productivity tools to changes in macro-scale productivity measures such as revenue per employee. This lack of perceived correlation helps to feed skepticism concerning the true enterprise impact of small gains of employee productivity associated with discrete implementations of IT solutions.

To partially counter this skepticism, we discount the value of the time saved by 50 percent in most cases. Be aware that this discounting factor was not viewed as the *right* answer, and there was considerable debate on this during the decision-making process, most notably between IT Finance and Human Factors Engineering representatives.

The discount process consistently generates considerable debate. We believe that discounting helps set reasonable priorities for employee productivity studies, especially in contrast to other studies with more certain outcomes. As measurement methodologies improve, we would like nothing better than to assemble a compelling case for reducing or removing the discount factor in this category.

System End-of-Life (EOL)

Concept: Removing unnecessary IT support and maintenance costs as a result of a new system upgrade or consolidation of multiple systems. The gross benefits of removal are included in this business value dial. In many cases, deployment of a new IT solution provides a company with the opportunity to remove one or several other solutions from the environment. In some cases, moving to a simpler or more standardized application environment enables a company to replace dozens of servers and solutions with fewer high performance servers and a single solution.

Table 2.2 Business Value Dials Related to Expense Avoidance

BV Dial	Definition
System End-of-Life	Removing unnecessary IT support and maintenance costs as a result of a new system upgrade or consolidation of multiple systems. The gross benefits of this removal are included in this dial.
	Sample Calculation: (Full-time-equivalent headcount support x average burden rate) + (ongoing software license and maintenance costs) + (cash avoidance credit for equipment salvaged for future use)
Materials Discounts	Solutions that result in strategic advantages for material purchasing process that both the company and the supplier can use.
	Sample Calculation: (Prior material pricing) − (Current pricing)
Risk Avoidance	Process controls or business continuity and security controls that minimize costly errors or double payments or ensure that the business is constantly running without data or production loss. Some risk can impact a public company's ability to operate, which would impact shareholder value.
	Sample Calculation: (Cash impact of negative event) x (Probability of occurrence)
Scrap Reduction	Solutions that reduce scrap or waste in product manufacturing or development. Scrap is usually due to errors, waste, or planning processes.
	Sample Calculation: (Total value of scrap reduced or avoided) + (Increased profit due to incremental unit sales)
Capital HW/SW Avoidance	Avoiding purchases in hardware or software as a result of strategic decisions or consolidations.
	Sample Calculation: (Full-time-equivalent headcount support x Average burden rate) + (Ongoing software license and maintenance costs) + (Cash avoidance credit for equipment salvaged for future use)
Factory Uptime	Solutions that keep the factory machinery up and running more hours of the day. Focus is on optimization, not factory downtime avoidance. Goal is to increase productive factory hours. Value of uptime varies, based on production process, whether assembly test manufacturing or fabrication, and whether factory is running at capacity.
	Sample Calculation (Contribution margin of product) x (Forecast volume increase)
Unit and Other Cost Avoidance	Unit cost focuses on lower cost manufacturing features or per-unit production cost. Other cost avoidances are those that may take place but are not captured in the other dials.
	Sample Calculation: (Cost per unit of the avoided services) x (Unit volumes) or Total cost of the avoided contract

Examples: It is not uncommon for companies to use a number of materials-procurement applications, each one meeting the localized needs of specific departments or groups. A standard materials-procurement application can replace all others. Ending support for multiple applications in favor of deploying fewer applications results in considerable savings. Companies that have grown from one or more acquisitions are prime candidates for this type of savings.

Financial Tips: It could be argued that this business value dial is a hybrid of the headcount reduction and hardware and software capital avoidance value dials, and that might be correct. When a company stops using old systems, the people, hardware and software that supported the related business processes normally go away. Experience shows that it is important to place focus on EOL as a specific business value dial by separately calling it out. The additional focus usually results in a documented "plan of record" to actually stop an application's use in the environment. This approach helps provide the justification needed to make sure legacy applications do indeed go away, and enhances tracking applications targeted for EOL.

Note that equipment used for an existing application can often be salvaged and re-used for a new purpose, but there may be compelling arguments in terms of reliability or support costs to simply dispose of the old equipment entirely. This is an example of an area where good financial modeling is important to ensure that the incentive created by ITBV measurement does not get in the way of good decision-making.

Materials Discounts

Concept: Solutions that result in strategic advantages for the material purchasing process that both the organization and supplier can use. Paying less for materials or reducing the cost of the procurement process achieves savings.

Examples:

- Direct contractual discounts—Establishing automation that makes it easier for a company's suppliers to do business can help in negotiation for favorable customer pricing agreements.

- Discounts for early payments—Automation and contract clause tracking can highlight specific suppliers or special contracts that provide favorable discounts for early payment.

- New methods of buying—Automation can create reverse auctions or make volume pricing in electronic marketplaces possible.

- Data analysis—Standardizing formats and common data locations can simplify analysis of spending behaviors and highlight opportunities for supplier aggregation volume discounts, reduction of off-contract "maverick buying" aggregation through purchasing catalogs, and so forth. Analysis can also ensure that contractual terms are fully enforced, for example by comparing actual prices charged with contracted terms.

Financial Tips: In assessing the business value derived by applying these methods, it's important to use a realistic cost basis for the materials in question. For example, a good procurement team seldom pays the materials supplier's opening price. Real savings, are found in the difference between the actual procurement price and the price normally obtained after the procurement team's negotiations.

When taking advantage of discounts for early payments, make sure to offset this discount by the opportunity value of the cash you are foregoing early. It's important to align policy in this area with the organization's working capital policy.

Risk Avoidance

Concept: Process controls or business continuity and security controls that minimize costly errors or double payments or ensure the company's business is constantly running without data or production loss. Some risks can impact the firm's ability to operate within the rules and regulations for publicly held companies, which would impact shareholder value. It also includes business processes supported by control systems that can provide checks and balances to find errors, highlight potential fraud, and assure the accuracy of the firm's reporting.

Examples:

Threats to business operations may be avoided with measures aimed at thwarting or mitigating external threats such as virus attacks, or with system upgrades that reduce the likelihood of business interruptions or data loss/corruption in critical areas such as factory operations, sales order processing, or financial reporting.

■ Business process risk avoidance—Automated controls can monitor day-to-day payments and processes and may be verified by audit activity. Examples include reducing the risk of lost receipts and double payments to suppliers or customers. For example, many companies offer bonus or rebate programs for products sold, or even reimbursements for cooperative advertising programs. Centralized, automated claims processes not only helps the claimant submit a claim, they also create record and completeness assurances that prevent payment of erroneous, fraudulent, or double-submitted claims.

■ Business continuity and risk avoidance—Consider a firm that has grown rapidly by expanding its core business as well as through multiple acquisitions. At some point, the financial consolidation and reporting processes founded on a general ledger system become unsustainable under the broad scope of the larger enterprise and its larger transaction load. If this situation is left unchecked, the company might become unable to accurately generate financial statements. By re-engineering the consolidation process and upgrading the general ledger, the firm reduces the risk of errors and avoids a potentially costly loss of investor trust and confidence.

■ Factory Isolation—Under extreme situations, such as a prolonged virus attack on the network, it might be beneficial to create self-sufficient factory networks capable of running all necessary business operations in a disconnected-from-net state. In doing so, any potential loss in production capability is avoided.

Financial Tips: To value an implementation of a business process risk avoidance measure, use an *expected value* formula based on results from a manual audit. Audit results should indicate the percentage of erroneous payments, the average dollar impact of each erroneous payment, and the total number of transactions conducted per year. This information is sufficient for an estimate of the expected value of implementing the new controls. However, be careful when calculating the average dollar impact, as some errors can work in favor of the firm and must be traced through the business process to see the real impact. For example, when customers catch all these errors, they may drive up call-center problem resolution costs, but not cash payment costs.

The valuation of business continuity risk-avoidance can be very difficult to quantify. Risk-creating events, such as factory downtime due to a virus attack, can encompass a huge range of potential impacts with each event having a highly uncertain likelihood. A full valuation of such events will generally prove elusive, as will the estimations of likelihood of each event. Solid statistical methodology is important in this area, but many of the larger quantitative inputs required for value calculation are likely to be based on expert opinion. In general, this is an area where Intel's ITBV program has been satisfied with underreporting our likely total value delivered, preferring to maintain our reputation for credibility rather than the option of basing a huge risk avoidance valuation on the mitigation of catastrophic events.

This remains an area where ongoing methodological research and improvement is called for. Absent solid valuation data, this area becomes subject to significant amounts of human judgment, potentially resulting in large amounts of under- or over-investment. The ITBV program can retain basic credibility by underreporting, but does not fulfill its larger missions of guiding investments and of providing a full accounting of actual value delivered.

Scrap Reduction

Concept: Solutions that allow scrap avoidance or waste in product manufacturing or development. Scrap is usually due to errors, waste, or planning processes. IT solutions help avoid scrap when they enable a company to do better production planning to match demand at a product and stock-keeping unit (SKU) mix level, or when IT solutions better convey product information and orders to assure correct builds. This can also include any IT solution that allows better monitoring of the manufacturing process and avoids scrap due to tool down time, conformance to specifications, incorrect raw materials, and other issues related to product that is scrapped due to quality control issues during the manufacturing process.

Examples: Sometimes an organization can build the right amount of inventory in total, but with the wrong product SKU mix, due to bad input from the demand forecast system. By modifying the business process so that it is based on a central system, with reduced data latency, fewer judgment points, and shorter cycle times, a firm can incorporate the latest detailed SKU-level information into its build plans.

An IT solution that enables faster notification of *tool down* in specific areas of the manufacturing process can increase the success rate of technicians who must take immediate action to save products from being destroyed within a very short time window.

When working with one or more contract manufacturing outsourcers, errors can occur when relaying build instructions through the phone, fax or a paper document. For example, some component products require specific, complex markings or identifiers for them to be accepted into the customer's manufacturing process. Errors in communication or manual data entry transcription may result in scrapping otherwise good product. A new IT solution that electronically relays the build order and markings directly to the contract manufacturer's automated system eliminates such costly errors.

Financial Tips: An organization that builds the wrong product faces multiple problems. It must carry unnecessary inventory for some period of time. It might need to deeply discount the product price to move the unwanted inventory, spend administrative resources to obtain customer waivers on the product and earn a sale, or scrap the units as a complete write-off. Worse, if factory capacity is constrained, the wrongly built units may have displaced production of units which could have generated profit. The end result is often some combination of these concerns. When assessing the valuation of scrap reduction, review the market dynamics for the products in question. Value the scrap reduction appropriately as some type of weighted average of the resolutions mentioned above. When doing this, it is important not to double-count business value with other value dials, as there are often overlaps in this category of activity.

Capital, Hardware, and Software Avoidance.

Concept: Avoiding purchases in hardware or software as a result of strategic decisions or consolidations. Modifying methods or systems can reduce, avoid or delay the need for installing new hardware and software.

Examples: After a merger or acquisition, integrating systems across units can eliminate duplicate infrastructure installations and avoid renewing dissimilar or unwanted enterprise software licenses and their associated maintenance requirements. By optimizing the combined environment, a firm can avoid hardware-related upgrades or shrink the environment through server consolidation.

By networking systems in a computation-intensive design environment, users can share compute cycles between existing high-cost workstations, avoiding or postponing new workstation purchases.

Financial Tips: Server and infrastructure consolidation can yield significant cost avoidance going forward. Be sure to value this cost avoidance while being wary of overvaluing decommissioned systems. The price paid for these systems has generally decreased and their true value is therefore reduced to their resale value. Also, when a company realizes these types of hardware and software consolidation and avoidance savings, it often sees savings through headcount reductions, headcount growth, and employee productivity.

Factory Uptime

Concept: Solutions that keep factory machinery up and running more hours of the day. Focus is on optimization, not factory downtime avoidance, the goal is to increase productive factory hours. This value dial comprises several different process changes that let a factory produce more products within the same or even less time, thereby increasing output, productive uptime, and/or yield. These changes can include extending the minutes that automation is up and running, increasing the speed of throughput (or beat-rate) for production, optimizing automation and even decreasing lead times for materials. The value of uptime varies, based on production process and whether the factory is running at capacity.

Examples:

- Factory automation, factory loading and manufacturing resource planning (MRP) systems require maintenance. Reducing this maintenance time can provide more hours of production.

- Down-the-wire factory diagnostic systems and cockpit system monitors can efficiently spot and reset production automation problems. They can also identify production that is trending toward specification limits.

- Tool-allocation analysis systems and equipment-performance support systems can analyze loadings to yield and optimal workflow and mix across the production environment.

- Materials procurement and inventory systems can streamline materials flow, eliminating production delays caused by excessive lead times.

Financial Tips: Factory uptime savings must be valued differently depending on current business conditions; the primary consideration here is whether the factory is at capacity. When the factory is working at its limit, foregoing extra capacity means losing additional sales (valued at the product margin over variable cost, fixed cost will not go up). When the factory is not constrained, however, the cost of downtime may be zero. These considerations should be taken into account when projecting forward and analyzing the long-term demand forecast in relation to any long-term capacity plans.

Unit (and other) Cost Avoidance

Concept: Unit cost focuses on lower cost manufacturing features or per-unit production cost. Other cost avoidances are those that may take place but are not captured in the other business value dials. Items in this category tend to be one of two types. Most often, they are non-factory uptime items that are absorbed into other cost-of-sales areas, such as freight savings. At other times, they are reductions in the cost of outsourced services that occur infrequently enough to not have their own specific value dial.

Examples:

- Non-factory uptime unit-cost avoidance—Processes that track product shipments, and correctly target certain shipments for expedited services and other for standard freight, can save significant dollars in freight billings. A company can achieve similar savings through planning systems that let it produce products in a geographic location near its customer base.

- Collaborative product development efforts that engage suppliers, product engineers and manufacturing engineers in a coordinated design effort can lower the cost of manufacturing products.

- Other cost avoidance—Web based marketing, technical sales and post sales product support tools can help customers find their own answers without involving the enterprise's call centers or help desk. Increasing the amount of question resolution through the Web can significantly lower support costs.

- IT departments that have "down-the-wire" diagnostic capability can troubleshoot a client PC from a central location without dispatching a technician to the client's location. This ability can reduce outsourced technical support costs or internal IT costs.

Financial Tips: This business value dial is most often used when reducing or avoiding an outsourced service fee. When reducing or avoiding an internal cost, the savings tend to land in another value dial, such as employee productivity. It is possible to separate this dial into two—unit-cost reduction and outsourced cost reduction—but most organizations will not have enough activity in this dial to warrant the split.

Table 2.3 Business Value Dials Related to Revenue Increases

BV Dial	Definition
Time to Market	Focused on ensuring and accelerating the company's technology leadership in the market-place by making sure products get to market first or ahead of scheduled road map. A premium earned by selling first-to-market products at a higher price is one of many business value dial definitions that fits here. Increased market share is another measure.
	Sample Calculation: (Early adopter price premium) x (Number of units) or (Incremental units) x (Gross margin) x (Duration of market share improvement)
Optimize Existing Markets	Solutions focused on increasing or adding revenue or units shipped to current market segment share.
	Sample Calculation: (Increased volume) x (Gross margin)
Open New Markets	Solutions that allow the company to access a new market that was unreachable.
	Sample Calculation: (Increased volume) x (Gross margin)
Cross Selling	Solutions that enable the selling of one product to facilitate the selling of complimentary product. Also, systems may enable sales teams to sell horizontal and vertical solutions across the company.
	Sample Calculation: (Increased volume) x (Gross margin)
Vendor of Choice	Supporting the competitiveness of the company's business. If a solution helps create greater satisfaction with the company's products, it would follow that the company has greater security in this specific market segment share.
	Sample Calculation: Change in market segment share or price premium realized due to customer preference.

Time-to-Market

Concept: Focused on ensuring and accelerating leadership in the marketplace by making sure products get to market first or ahead of schedule. Any solution that reduces time to market (TTM) is calculated under this business value dial. Time to market is often a critical factor in enterprise competitive success. Product and technology leadership often correlates to a company's market segment share (MSS), and may also afford the firm a pricing premium. IT solutions that enable a lower TTM can provide a clear competitive advantage.

Example: Electronic design collaboration programs can reduce TTM by allowing teams of engineers from raw materials suppliers, component suppliers, and end-product integrators to collaborate on a design in parallel, rather than each having to wait until another group has finished.

As a result, the end product can reach the market faster and capture the first-to-market MSS gains and/or pricing premiums.

Financial Tips: When dealing with this business value dial, a firm must make an estimate of how many points of MSS it can get for each additional week it cuts from TTM. This estimate will preferably be based on prior experiences with similar products in similar markets, but of course it is very difficult to control for all variables in this area. The firm can calculate the resulting MSS value by multiplying the MSS percentage gain by the total available market and multiplying that by the expected gross margin. To increase confidence that improved TTM caused these outcomes, use a multiple variable regression analysis to include other factors, such as pricing differences and product feature richness. This process can get quite complex, but it provides a useful estimate for setting project priorities.

Optimizing Existing Markets

Concept: Solutions focused on increasing or adding revenue or units shipped to current MSS. This business value dial measures what happens when an IT solution allows the company to capture more MSS or average selling price (ASP) within its existing product lines and markets. Such efforts can focus on improved target marketing through electronic customer resource management, demand analysis, and pricing.

Examples: When an organization deploys an IT solution that facilitates a faster, more accurate demand forecast by getting regular and common data feeds from customers and the field sales group, the process limits judgment points and accelerates data collection. The solution provides a fresher more accurate picture of product demand, which in turn feeds into the product build-plan process to ensure that factories are turning out the exact products the market wants. The result is increased MSS because the firm now has products to meet perishable demand, and higher selling prices because it can sell products without discounting.

When a company is able to effectively utilize customer information purchase histories, sales types, delivery channels utilized, geographic region, price points and so forth, data analysis can pinpoint marketing efforts to obtain more sales or sell-up customers to a higher-end product. When carefully analyzed, the data might also reveal that customers of type A are more reachable through channel B and that an untapped market exists for product C.

Financial tips: When taking this approach, it's essential to demonstrate with historical inventory and stock-out data that an improvement in demand forecasting will indeed result in more sales or higher selling prices. Compare historical demand forecast to actual demand variance. Excess product inventory represents an over-build situation, when a firm might want to reduce the price to move the product whereas stock-outs represent an under-build situation. One method of getting a snapshot of real demand is to adjust upward actual sales for the period to account for tracked stock-outs, and adjust sales downward to reflect tracked discounts that were granted.

Opening New Markets

Concept: This business value dial captures the contribution of IT solutions that allow a firm to access a market that was otherwise unreachable or cost-prohibitive to enter. Accessing new market can represent significant value.

Example: This business value dial is helpful where markets are diverse or geographically dispersed, but accessible through the implementation of an IT solution. Consider products that are distributed through established industrial middlemen but sold to the final customer though dealerships. The firm has a real interest in expanding its marketing and technical reach to each of the dealers without having to rely on the distributors, who may not have goals and plans aligned to those of the company. But how does a sales force cost-effectively reach as many as 50,000 dealers spread from Shanghai to Cleveland? Web sites can bridge this gap by providing secure access to technical white papers, marketing information, sales support links, and product specifications. Web sites can also support personalized buying, rebate and marketing offer tracking, and links to authorized dealers. For channel partners, Web sites can provide real-time inventory availability and pricing information. A direct tie-in to down-channel associates can open new markets, resulting in increases in both market segment share (MSS) and average selling price.

Financial Tips: Assessing gains of this nature usually requires an analysis of the current total available market (TAM) and current MSS and pricing conditions, and then assessment of the MSS and pricing incremental gains expected. Each case is unique; no cookbook formula applies. This has historically been an area where operational optimism can lapse into unrealistic euphoria, but valuation estimates can often be kept grounded in reality via close attention to the results from test cases and pilot implementations. The IT finance professional should be aware that deploying tools such as these might also show benefits to be gained in other business value dials. For example, moving customers to Web support may allow the firm to focus its sales force on key accounts, thereby raising employee productivity.

Cross-Selling

Concept: IT Solutions that enable the selling of one product to facilitate the selling of complementary products. Also, systems may enable sales teams to sell horizontal and vertical solutions across the company. This occurs when solutions create cross-referencing complementary products to field sales teams, or even directly to customers. Successful increases in the cross-selling business value dial can result in increased business opportunities and higher average selling prices.

Examples: A sales organization might deploy an IT solution (*e.g.*, a content management system) capable of relating various products according to product compatibility. When a sales representative looks up a midsize server, for example, the content management system lists storage systems and network switches as companion products and identifies more powerful servers as sell-up opportunities. In addition, the system highlights a special-purpose database server as an alternative product from a recent acquisition—something the sales person may not be familiar with. Web sites such as Amazon.com provide an excellent example of cross-selling by offering books related to the customer's choice.

An online system can accept an order and automatically inform the customer that the requested product could be properly maintained with a service agreement, upgraded in performance, or used in conjunction with other products.

Financial tips: As in all of the value dials that touch market segment and selling price, there is no "one" formula for valuation. Each case is unique. Be sure to carefully assess current sales results and the actions of competitors before assuming large gains. Some system implementations may be designed so that clear data is received that essentially proves that cross-selling occurred, but in other cases it can be quite difficult to establish causation in this value dial.

Vendor-of-Choice (VOC)

Concept: Supporting the competitiveness of a company's business, the VOC value dial accounts for the *good will* benefit that occurs when certain IT solutions deliver features that delight customers, but do not necessarily deliver specific, quantifiable business value. It is logical to assume that considerable increases in VOC measures lead to preservation or gains in market segment or average selling price, but these benefits might not necessarily be evident in the data, or might occur on a significantly time-lagged basis. For IT solutions that are inward facing, improved VOC can be linked to other business value dials, such as headcount management, under the assumption that satisfied employees are both more productive and less likely to leave the company.

Examples: An organization can modify its order-management automation to allow direct feeds from its customers' systems. A direct data feed eliminates an entry step for the customers, which in itself is not material enough to gain sales or increase product price, but it does result in increased customer satisfaction.

When a company modifies its Internet site to improve usability, customers can more easily access information, have their questions answered more often, or have an easier time finding and ordering products. This improved user experience increases customer satisfaction, but it might be difficult to make a direct connection to sales levels.

Other system implementations may enable faster order fulfillment or improved performance to delivery date commitments. This may result in a combination of increased product sales or price premiums, captured in other dials, and general improvement in customer satisfaction.

Financial tips: It is not uncommon for VOC benefits to be associated with features rather than the whole solutions. These features are important, but may not be the main reason for deploying an IT solution. This would not be the case when the main reason for deploying the IT solution is to improve the over user experience, VOC is the main value dial in this case. It is also likely that the actual result of increased VOC shows up in other business value dials. For example, improving the workflow of an application may result in few errors during data entry reducing rework by the employee and increasing job satisfaction.

Program managers are often quick to attribute great importance to issues of VOC, but be sure to put the entire picture in perspective, carefully considering the customers, products, markets, and competitive

Ongoing Business Value Assessment at Stratigent

Stratigent is a Web analytics consulting company specializing in providing a variety of strategic services to clients that focus on site optimization. The Web's highly visual presentation of material to thousands of visitors provides an opportunity to run experiments both quickly and efficiently. For retail sites, the business value outcome of common interest is conversion, which means that a visitor makes a purchase.

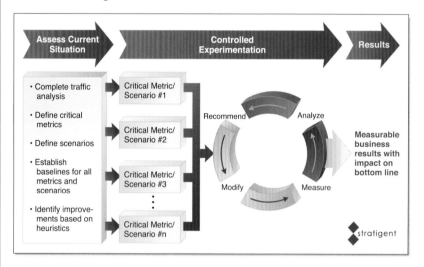

Stratigent's approach is shown in the figure above. After conducting an initial assessment of the site, Stratigent develops a testing plan, and determines which metrics should be used to measure the success of these tests, like conversion rate. Experiments are run by randomly assigning visitors to test cells, with each cell viewing different creative options. When the necessary sample size is reached, typically in a few days, the data is analyzed and the most successful creative option is selected and put into service. Running experiments replaces intuition when making Web site design decisions.

forces. In cases where VOC-type problems are indeed important in differentiating between a company and its competition, a program that makes material changes in these features can generate quantifiable gains. In that case, the company can evaluate the total available market, current market segment and average selling price and then estimate the amount of saved or gained business the features can generate. As with the opening new markets, optimizing existing markets, and cross selling, this value dial requires judgment and analysis that cannot be easily summarized in a static algorithm.

Table 2.4   Business Value Dials Related to Working Capital

BV Dial	Definition	
Days of Inventory (DOI)	Reductions in days of inventory lead to value in finished goods, work in process, or raw material inventories	
	Sample Calculation:	(Value of 1 day) x (Days of inventory removed) x 15% (Weighted average cost of capital)
Days of Receivables or Days of Sales Outstanding (DSO)	Solutions that allow the company to receive payment from customers faster, minimizing time spent waiting for payment.	
	Sample Calculation:	(Dollar value of receivables) x (Days of receivables removed) x 15% (Weighted average cost of capital)

Days of Inventory Reduction

Concept: Reductions in days of inventory (DOI) lead to value in finished goods, work in process, or raw material inventories. Managing working capital involves careful management of inventory levels. An IT solution that lets the firm operate with a lower level of inventory creates value by shifting balances from inventory to cash on the balance sheet.

Examples: IT solutions that impact DOI most often occur in demand forecasting and factory planning. Standard business processes that relay *system of record* field sales information to the factory provide a timely, consistent and accurate demand trigger. By obtaining demand information more quickly, with fewer errors, and interpreting that demand information into a timely build-plan reset, less buffer inventory is required. The net result is a reduction in overall DOI. Programs that reduce lead-times on incoming raw materials or outgoing customer shipments also have a positive impact of DOI.

There are three key considerations in correctly valuing the savings in DOI:

■ Type of inventory—Obtaining greater accuracy for building-to-order requires a primary focus on reducing the inventory of finished goods, though it may have an impact on work in progress and on raw materials. Carefully examine any proposed changes to determine whether the change will reduce DOI across the board, or in just one inventory stage. Built-to-order process calls for partial assembly. Incoming materials programs focus on reducing the inventory of raw materials.

■ Fixed vs. variable costs—The value of a DOI reduction is not necessarily the fully-absorbed cost of units not built. Also consider the issue of fixed vs. variable costs. If an organization has significant capital investments in factories, those assets will continue to depreciate, and that depreciation will be reflected in the cost of the remaining units in inventory. In these cases, the proper way to value the savings is to use variable costs.

■ One-time vs. recurring benefits—In ROI/net present value (NPV) models it is important to decide how to best represent DOI reduction, since reducing DOI is really a one-time event. Once the inventory has been brought down, this new level is used moving forward. Depending on the model and the context of calculations, it may make sense to show this savings as a one-time avoidance of a cash outlay, or as the opportunity value of the event per year by applying the firm's weighted average cost of capital (WACC) to the one-time event.

Days of Receivables or Days of Sales Outstanding Reduction

Concept: Solutions that allow receiving payment from customers faster, minimizing time spent waiting for payment. Days of receivables is very similar to the DOI concept. By collecting accounts receivable (A/R) more quickly, balances can be shifted from A/R to cash.

Examples: IT solutions that help a company receive payment from customers more quickly produce benefits in this business value dial. An example is electronic funds transfer. However, less direct solutions can also have significant impact on this value dial. Frequently when customers exceed their payment terms, it's because they are disputing some element of the invoice—tax calculations, improper pricing, wrong number of units and the like. Many of these errors go back to failures in integrating business processes and systems. If business processes improve accuracy on invoicing, fewer disputes occur and the consequence is faster receivables.

As with DOI, a company can view reducing days of sales outstanding (DSO) as a one-time event leading to a more desirable forward-looking run-rate. Alternatively, a company can interpret it as an annual opportunity savings by applying the firm's WACC. When using the DSO reduction business value dial, it is important to work closely with the credit department to understand the practical limitations of DSO reduction as well as the real causes of the current DSO levels.

Measurement Framework for Business Value

Human Factors Engineering techniques help to define objective collection and quantification of business value data. The team focused on developing a strategy that allowed framing measurement questions across a wide range of settings found within Intel and that would be *technology neutral (i.e.,* not linked to any specific type of IT). Since many IT solutions impact employee productivity, a primary consideration for this framework was a focus on end-users and what they do in terms of IT.

Our measurement framework focused on the three areas which resulted in the formula illustrated in the Figure 2.1 and explained in detail below:

- *Context*—The value as determined by the environment into which the organization will deploy the technology solution.

- *Variables*—The items that the organization has operationally defined for measurement (*e.g.*, business value dials)

- *Timeframe*—The period within which the measurements will occur. For comparison purposes, that period must be long enough for at least two separate measurements (*e.g.*, baseline and post-implementation).

Context

Context can be defined as the environment into which an IT solution is deployed. Context is a key element in defining an overall measurement approach. It determines the ease or difficulty of collecting data to support a business value proposition. For example, saving five minutes for one end-user might have a very different value for a company than it would for a different end-user, depending on how easily a particular end-user can apply the time savings to another job related task.

As another example, an IT organization implementing a new printing solution might find that in one context the most important driver for determining business value is how many sheets per minute it can print, while in another context, the key driver is the speed with which the

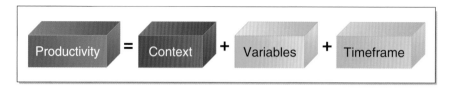

Figure 2.2 Framework for Measuring Productivity

printer comes out of power saving mode. In yet another context, it might be the cost per printed sheet.

Variables and Operational Definitions for Business Value Dials

To measure accurately, variables or business value dials must be defined in terms of the precise techniques (*e.g.,* how and when) that will be used to measure them within an identified context.

The goal is to move from abstract concepts to concrete, measurable variables. Within each context, define variables that are:

■ Reliable—measurements that are consistent over time

■ Valid—measurements that capture the intended concept

Operational Definitions: An Example

If eight people are asked to measure aggression and report their findings, the likelihood that we would see agreement among them is very low, as each person will define and measure aggression subjectively.

The solution is to use *operational definitions*. Give the same eight people the following instructions: "Today you are going to measure aggression. To do this you will go to Washington Elementary School, from 1-2 pm, go the sandbox in the northwest corner, and, using this form, count the number of times one child either strikes or pushes another child."

When the reports are in, there will be some discrepancies, but overall the data will be similar. Operational definitions are necessary to measure business value. Without operational definitions in place, everyone may be measuring, but it is highly unlikely that is measuring exactly the same thing.

To define employee productivity operationally, distill the business value dial to a set of basic measurable indicators of productivity improvements. An IT solution might result in incremental or "evolutionary" changes, as follows:

- Removal of an activity an end user performs
- Reduction in the time it takes to complete an activity
- Reduction or removal of end-user errors either by reducing the number of processes to achieve the same outcome (thereby lowering the probability of an error) or by reducing the cost associated with making an error
- Reduction in time needed to gain proficiency in an activity

Other changes that an IT solution can bring about can be seen as innovative, rather than evolutionary. These are changes that enable the restructuring the nature of the activities to eliminate all or a portion of them. Examples of such innovations include:

- Replacing manual asset handling and required support processes with RFID broadcasted to a recorder
- Moving from conferencing via phone line using an audio bridge plus application sharing and meeting minutes to a fully integrated calendar that calls meeting participants, shares documents for editing, and transcribes the meeting
- Replacing standard password authentication using a data input device with a biometrics reader
- Replacing a set of instructions and improved user interfaces for network configuration and billing while traveling with a solution that enables seamless network hopping with secure identification and automatic billing

Timeframe

To properly determine business value, it is critical to collect baseline data and post-implementation data. Baseline data is information on the business value dials that the IT solution, as described in the operational definition, is expected to impact. For the post-implementation data, the same information is collected again after implementing the IT solution.

The timing of these activities may vary. For example, if the introduction of the IT solution results in the removal of the current system, baseline data must be collected prior to introduction. If two IT solutions are deployed at the same time, it is possible to collect both data sets at the same time. The differences between these data sets provides the basis for identifying business value and is integrated into other business value measures to identify the solution's bottom-line impact. In practice, data is often collected at multiple points in time.

Some metrics or business value dials are easier to quantify than others. For example, while calculating days of inventory is straightforward—the value of the dial can simply be counted—measuring employee productivity takes a bit more work. Still, accurate measurement is the heart of an IT Business Value program, and measuring productivity is both worth doing and can be done. Our methodology for calculating increases in employee productivity is described in detail in Chapter 4.

The Business Value Process

Several groups within Intel have worked to develop a process that over time has proven repeatable. This process has evolved with the help of many different groups including Intel Finance. Based on previous experiences, this process has matured and is now being used as a best known method (BKM).

It is also important to note that not all IT solutions are developed according to the process shown in Figure 2.3. In the real world, it is often IT's customers, not IT, who initiate a project. Moreover, not all steps within the process fall within the responsibility of the ITBV team member who gathers business value data. Also, many projects are seen as urgent, and an initial ROI is not formally developed. View the steps shown in Figure 2.3 as the best possible situation.

Step 1 — Understand the Customer

In order to understand the true value of any IT solution, you must first understand the customer's business. Then, and only then, can you begin to understand how any IT solution will support the success of the customer's business unit.

It is critical to understand the business unit's strategic objectives and how they relate to corporate strategic objectives for IT to be able to support business unit success.

It is important not only to connect with the end-user and customer, but to live and breathe their challenges. Success should be measured based on the IT organization's ability to support and meet the customer's strategic objectives.

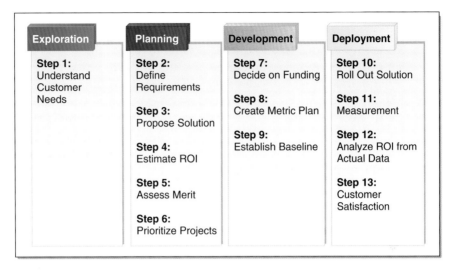

Exploration	Planning	Development	Deployment
Step 1: Understand Customer Needs	**Step 2:** Define Requirements	**Step 7:** Decide on Funding	**Step 10:** Roll Out Solution
	Step 3: Propose Solution	**Step 8:** Create Metric Plan	**Step 11:** Measurement
	Step 4: Estimate ROI	**Step 9:** Establish Baseline	**Step 12:** Analyze ROI from Actual Data
	Step 5: Assess Merit		**Step 13:** Customer Satisfaction
	Step 6: Prioritize Projects		

Figure 2.3 The Business Value Process

Within Intel, we employ user-centered design specialists to make sure we understand the needs of the end users and that these needs are taken into account during the initial stages of projects. This process is called user-centered design or usability engineering.

Step 2 — Define Requirements

It is important to clearly define any problem you are trying to solve in terms of end-user and customer needs. It is critical to make sure the IT solutions being offered satisfy the needs and can meet or beat the customer's expectations.

There are times when the customer may state clearly what they need and may offer ideas or potential solutions. Customers can generally identify needs based on their frustration with cumbersome business processes, bottlenecks in current processes, and their experience with error-prone processes. Defining opportunities can happen at times when the customer is not complaining or concerned, but when with a new technology or creative uses of existing technology, IT can offer a breakthrough system that will offer benefit to the customer. This is when IT can identify an opportunity, get the customer on board with solution development and implement a solution that is of high value to the customer.

Strategic planning solutions occur when there are IT business reasons to offer a solution. For example, when the operating system and office applications are upgraded because a vendor is planning to end of life an existing solution. In these cases, it is incumbent upon IT to understand the impact of such a change on the customer, provide necessary advance communication, training and cooperative planning to enable the customer to embrace the change. Frequently when this type of solution is implemented it will offer the customer added functionality that they should be informed of and trained on, to ensure they take full advantage of the new solution.

Step 3 — Propose Solution

Once a need is identified—that is, an opportunity exists or a strategic planning solution is indicated—the next step is to define the solution that IT will deliver. The solution proposal should include a clear and concise problem statement, a solution description, a set of assumptions and a description of what success would be as defined by the customer and IT. It is at this point that the first high-level pass should be made at identifying the impacted business value dials.

An example of this might be when the customer success measures include process improvements that result in the process being completed in less time with fewer errors and fewer people. IT success measures would be all of the customer success measures and could also include more typical IT-focused measures. These might include IT measures such as integration of new solution with existing solution occurs with no unscheduled downtime.

Step 4 — Estimate ROI

Once a solution that will serve the customer's needs is identified, it is time to assess whether the solution will have a positive ROI.

IT project managers should work with their Finance Analysts to identify all costs and benefits, including the impacted business value dials and potential critical success indicators (CSI) the customer might want to track for the project. By identifying and engaging with designated finance resources early on in the process, it allows the financial resource/analyst to come up to speed on the project early and avoid time delays, but more importantly, financial analysts are an excellent resource when planning what and how to measure the impact of a solution. Financial resources usually bring with them a wealth of knowledge relating to how other projects have been measured, success, and failures. Leveraging this knowledge is essential early on in the planning process in order to avoid common mistakes, pitfalls and ensure the success of the measurement plan. It is also worth noting that there

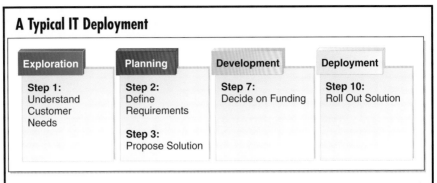

While the business value process unfolds in thirteen steps, typical IT deployment often occurs in just five steps.

Pros: In this scenario, the IT organization is attempting to deliver something that the customer or end user wants or needs. Management makes a decision whether to roll the solution out. It may be a faster process than documenting everything in advance.

Cons: There is no measurement—not even customer satisfaction—so there's no way to determine if the solution satisfied the needs of the users. There is also no ROI estimate, so there's no good way to gauge what, if any, return might have been achieved.

should be tight alignment between the CSIs and the business value dials identified for the project. In many cases, the CSIs and the business value dials will be one and the same.

Step 5 — Assess Merit

When the estimated ROI is complete, it is time to assess what is known. Using a list of questions, the IT PM is better able to decide whether the project has merit and should be presented to management for support.

Here is a sample list of questions:

- What is the business need/opportunity?

- What is the solution?

- How realistic is it that the solution can be implemented in the environment with timing that will meet the customer's needs?

- Is it scalable, flexible?

- What is the return on investment and how long will it take to show a positive return (*e.g.*, payback period)?

- What are the benefits for IT as well as the customer?

- If project managers determine that a project does not merit presenting to management, they have an opportunity to go back and redefine needs (Step 2) or to devise an alternate solution (Step 3); if not, the project stops here.

Step 6 — Prioritize Projects

Because the objective of the ITBV program was to develop and embed a repeatable and uniform business value measurement process, the program focuses on systematically tracking and measuring the business value of IT solutions for which the investment decision has already been made.

Before the decision to invest in a solution is made, IT organizations must decide which proposed solutions have the most value and are the best candidates for investment. The process of prioritizing where limited resources will be spent to pursue new solutions requires a different, but related process. To meet this need, Intel's IT organization collaborated with several business units to develop a prioritization tool that helps identify the relative value of one project compared to another project.

This tool, called the called the Business Value Index (BVI), takes into account 25 different data points for each project and uses a weighting algorithm to prioritize the various initiatives. The BVI methodology helps prioritize IT investments through assessing the potential business value.

A sample BVI graphical result is shown in Figure 2.4. In this example, four projects are plotted on the business value and IT efficiency axes with the size of the bubble indicating the relative financial attractiveness of the investment. The right-most project, which is also the largest bubble, offers the highest value on all three dimensions.

BVI analysis complements the ITBV analysis work that measure a project's ROI against the forecasted ROI. Like the ITBV methodology, the BVI is based on a common language and framework. What differentiates it, however, is that the BVI compares proposed projects in the light of their potential business value.

In particular, the BVI :

- Forecasts the degree of an IT investment's alignment with corporate strategy, its impact on IT efficiency, and its financial merit

- Uses constant, pre-defined business-value criteria to provide a level comparison of multiple investment options

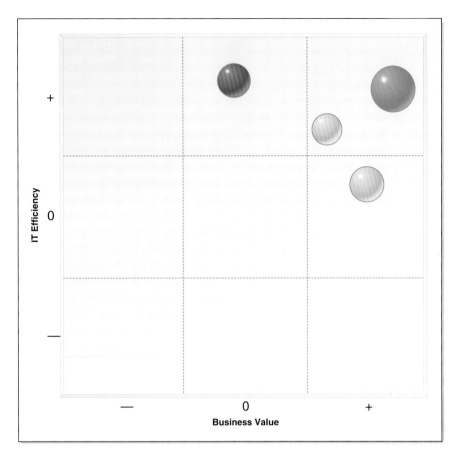

Figure 2.4 Sample Results of a BVI Assessment on Four Projects

■ Provides criteria-weighting that enables "what-if" analysis and rapid adjustment to changing business priorities

■ Displays results in a matrix that enhances comparative analysis of multiple investment opportunities

The BVI also provides factor comparison analysis to reveal the factors that most influence the investment's assessment and to reveal how each investment adds value in different ways.

For a more thorough description of the Business Value Index, please see Curley's *Managing IT for Business Value (2004)*.

Step 7 — Decide on Funding

Once project proposals have been fully documented and prioritized, it is time for IT management to make a decision about which projects will be resourced and which ones will not.

If a no-go decision is given, the IT project manager (IT PM) may decide to return to Define Needs (step 2) or Propose Solution (Step 3) and re-evaluate the plan, looking for alternatives. If a *no-go* decision has been made, there may also be an opportunity to go back to the customer and assess the customer's ability to resource the project. If the solution is showing a high return for the group, the customer may make the decision to resource the project.

Step 8 — Create Metrics Plan

Once the project is resourced, the metrics plan should be developed. This step in the process is designed to ensure a plan for measurement (*i.e.,* metrics plan) for quantifying the business value of a project is documented. This plan should be aligned with a full project plan. It is during this step that the majority of the work will happen in refining the business value dials that have already been identified with respect to how and when they will be measured.

It is important to document the metrics plan to show how and what you measure will directly support the estimated ROI. It is important that the customer be involved in this step to make sure that what you measure has value to the end user or customer, to ensure it is aligned with their CSIs, and to ensure that they will see that IT delivered. The key to business value is that the customer recognizes the value and that IT does not have to spend time convincing the customer of the value.

Step 9 — Establish Baseline

Once the metrics plan has been documented, the next step is to develop a baseline that directly supports the metrics plan. Only by establishing a credible baseline is it possible to measure actual gain or loss realized due to the IT solution. It is important to establish a baseline before the solution is implemented; unfortunately, in the real world, that's not always possible. Under some circumstances it is possible to capture good baseline data after a solution is rolled out.

There are at least two credible ways to do this:

■ For two similar populations, one using the new solution while the other does not, then use the latter group to establish baseline data.

■ In rare cases, groups will already be gathering the needed data before the new solution is deployed, and this historical data can establish a baseline.

Step 10 — Roll Out Solution

This step was not designed to be a project management process or guideline; it is the metrics guideline. In many cases, the IT PM doing the business value work may not be the same IT PM responsible for the solution deployment. This step is called out as a synchronization point in the process. The metrics program continues after the solution is defined and rolled out.

Step 11 — Measurement

Once the solution is rolled out, the next step is to measure the results. Specific metrics were defined (step 8) based on the impacted business value dials. These metrics were then baselined (step 9) and will now be assessed again in the measurement step to ensure accurate comparisons.

By establishing a baseline and measuring results after a project rolls out, the impact that the project had can be assessed. This difference or delta, is the basis for determining the actual business value that has been delivered.

Step 12 — Analyze ROI from Actual Data

At the completion of measurement, the data generated is analyzed and an actual business value is determined. At this point it is important to go back to the ROI/Financial Analysis step (Step 4) and review the ROI that was forecast. The CSIs that the customer established should also be reviewed as part of this process if they did not get directly represented in the metrics plan or the estimated ROI. By going back and comparing forecasted results with actual measured results, it is possible to determine process improvements and it also provides a closed loop to hold individuals accountable for the forecasted ROI.

Step 13 — Customer Satisfaction

It is important to check in with the end-users and customer to see if they believe IT delivered the forecasted business value. Generally, this is in the form of a survey. While this data is not generally used to develop the business value of a project, it is an important step in understanding the customer better and how the solution has impacted them, so it is included here for completeness.

The Importance of Feedback

Feedback loops help tune a project while it is underway and should improve execution of future projects. Feedback is a continuous process that occurs during all steps. However, there are three important aspects with the business value process that should be considered with respect to feedback. First, IT solution owners need to hear what is learned during the business value process. Second, the ITBV team should be prepared to modify their own tools and techniques based on feedback during the evaluation process. Lastly, the ITBV team should store intermediate work products generated during the evaluation for future reuse and reference.

Summary

Measuring business value depends on shared terminology and well-defined variables, that is, business value dials. While some business value dials will be unique to an enterprise or industry, many are common to all businesses. By principle and example, this chapter offers a rich collection of business value dials.

Measurement of business value comprises context, variables, and a timeframe. Context is most commonly the tasks that comprise work for an employee. Variables measure success at business tasks such as time to complete a task or error rate. For business value studies, timeframe refers to measures taken before and after a new solution is deployed. Differences between baseline and post-implementation measures are indicators of business value gained.

The process of measuring business value is tightly integrated with the development and deployment of the IT solution. IT managers and their customers work with the ITBV team to develop appropriate measures and to synchronize the measurement timeframe with the IT project schedule. Feedback throughout the process is essential.

The Finance Perspective

*Mathematics enhances the ability to handle more ambiguous
and qualitative relationships that dominate
day-to-day financial decision making.*
—Alan Greenspan

Three IT initiatives are on the table, each promising future contributions to business value and each with its own price tag. The IT budget is stretched and only one of the initiatives is affordable at this time. Monies spent this year pay back over the years to come, which further complicates the decision making. What financial tools are available to approach this problem in a methodical way?

This chapter introduces key financial concepts and explains the important role that Finance people play in an ITBV study. Finance organizations are often major supporters of ITBV initiatives. An improved capability to assess returns on IT investments is a shared objective for both the IT and Finance organizations. With stronger methodologies for evaluating IT's business value, the Finance organization is better able to understand investment opportunities within the IT domain and to compare investment opportunities across the enterprise.

A keen focus on financial analysis is an important part of making IT run like a business. Business value contributions to the enterprise constitute the IT organizations revenue stream. Well-run businesses understand the relationship between investments and that revenue stream, and that is exactly the goal of an ITBV analysis. An IT organization oriented toward precise measurement of investments and outcomes in dollar terms will necessarily be more disciplined in achieving its goals and objectives.

The importance of documenting credible financial results in an ITBV analysis cannot be overstated. A few IT initiatives have hard, measurable benefits—such as the outright automation of jobs or a dramatic improvements in inventory turnover. Most IT initiatives, however, produce benefits that are commonly described as *soft* and difficult to associate directly with the IT deployment.

The struggle to quantify IT's soft benefits is well recognized. No less an authority than former U.S. Federal Reserve Chairman Alan Greenspan spent a great deal of his last 10 years in office remarking on both the tremendous contributions of IT to economic productivity, and the tremendous difficulty experienced by the economics community in attempting to quantify those contributions.

New Swan, a manufacturing company located in Ludhiana, in the state of Punjab, India, recently completed a financial analysis of business value for a potential IT investment. This chapter presents the methods and results of New Swan's analysis as practical examples of financial concepts and calculations.

IT Makeover at New Swan: Overview

New Swan Autocomp. Pvt. Ltd. is a small company in India's automobile components industry. Founded in 2003, the company plans to grow its business from $3 M in 2005 to a target of $22 M by 2008. However, even at its current size, the young company was struggling to track fundamental business information, such as inventory, employee attendance, and payments.

New Swan participated in Intel's SMB Makeover Program. One goal of the program was to measure business benefits of IT investments. Thus, New Swan is an example of Intel's ITBV process applied in a small-company setting. While the dollar values are smaller, the concepts of business value dials and financial analysis are the same. A detailed account of this makeover can be found at Intel Corporation (2006).

Introduction to Finance Concepts

Historically, the implicit model for IT cost centers has been the *market model*. While there are variations, the fundamental idea is that value of IT services is roughly equal to the price that the IT customer is willing to pay. The simplest variation is fixed allocation—costs are prorated and charged back to segments of the enterprise in proportion to overall usage, headcount, or some other aggregate measure. In a slightly more sophisticated variation of the market model, IT services are metered and sold to customers based on a usage charge— so called, pay per view. To make the market competitive, some organizations encourage IT customers to entertain bids from third-party providers.

The market model transfers the question of business value from the IT organization to the customer and that is its fundamental weakness. While variations in the market model represent reasonable starting points, none satisfactorily answers the challenge of measuring business value delivered. Often the only available stopgap for investment decision making, the market model does nothing to put better data into the mix. The IT customer is the right person to make the decision, to be sure, but without hard data, the decision cannot be well founded. Moreover, without follow-on measures of actual business value delivered, the quality of the decision will never be known. Intuition needs to be supplanted by empirical data, explicit assumptions, and consistent analysis methods.

The market method is primarily useful for setting a minimum *bar* of business value. For an IT organization in general or an IT initiative in particular, minimal success means at least a payback equal to the investment plus the cost of money, that is, the return expected if the enterprise simply banked the cash rather than investing it at all.

Return on Investment

Factoring in the cost of money is fundamental to a second family of financial models. The central mechanism is discounted cash flow and the family of models provides different perspectives on the return on an investment. These models are well established, used in a wide variety of business contexts, an area taught in most introductory finance courses. In fact, the use of discounted cash flow calculations and ROI analysis is necessary for an ITBV study to be credible to business and financial managers.

Return on investment (ROI) analysis is a primary tool for the prioritization of investment of scarce resources. Precisely because resources are scarce, some items not funded will have acceptable ROI values when examined in isolation. When a collection of projects are compared, however, it is ROI analysis that identifies the set of projects that provide the greatest return, that is, the maximum business value. Given the risks and costs of IT investments, ROI analysis is crucial for identifying projects which generate the most value, as well as screening out projects that may actually reduce net business value if deployed.

Thus, the main objective of ROI analysis is to provide financial guidance for decision makers who want to optimize business value returns. These returns can come in several forms, including increased revenue, lower costs, stronger vendor-of-choice scores, improved employee satisfaction. Some types of returns are much easier to measure than others.

A basic ROI analysis for any business initiative, IT or otherwise, is made up of four primary components: benefits, costs, a discount rate, and a time period.

- *Benefits* are typically cash inflows but can also arise from cost avoidance or from a reduction in spending relative to a recognized baseline.

- *Costs* are the cash outflow and come in the form of labor, software, hardware, taxes, or other cost.

- The *discount rate* is the cost of capital for the organization over the time period of the analysis.

- The *time period*, typically three years for an IT investment, sets a boundary for when benefits and costs, including the cost of money, accrue.

All inflows and outflows are expressed in terms of cash, which is in contrast to the language of accrual accounting. For example, a capital investment in a new IT system requires an up-front sum of cash. In the accrual system, the corporate balance sheet recognizes a part of that expense as depreciation over a period of time. For purposes of ROI analysis, especially involving capital expenditures, the focus is on the up-front cash investment and in the possible reduction in taxes in future years resulting from the recognition of depreciation. Depreciation itself is *not* a cash item and is ignored. Translation of accrual data to cash data can become quite complex, and, consequently, ROI analysis generally requires the expertise of financial professionals.

The choice of a discount rate can be a complex decision as well. Many companies use a weighted average cost of capital (WACC) as a standard discount rate. A commonly used rate is 15 percent. However, the value of a WACC varies widely across companies and depends, among other things, on the company's capital structure and on the relative volatility of its stock price. In all cases, the WACC represents the annualized return on investment that a corporate investor would expect. In other words, investments made within a company should have return rates equal to or greater than the WACC or investors would be better served if that cash fuelled a share buyback or a dividend.

Deriving a WACC is not complex mechanically, but does require an understanding of several advanced financial topics. Companies take many different approaches in the selection of a discount rate and some use different discount rates for different business segments or project types. A detailed discussion is beyond the scope of this text. Interested readers will find deeper explanations in financial textbooks, such as *Principles of Corporate Finance* by Brealey and Myers (2002).

IT Makeover at New Swan: Proposed Solution and The Cost of Capital

Intel IT experts and Nuron, a local ISV, proposed that New Swan invest in an ERP system hosted on a server with ten client workstations to better manage inventory, purchasing, sales and distribution, finance, and payroll. The experts also recommended obtaining two laptop computers for senior managers, to improve their ability to monitor business activities while travelling.

The total estimated cost, in US dollars, was $10,341 for deployment in year 1, followed by an ongoing cost of $1,693 in years 2 and 3. Consistent with interest rates for business loans in India, New Swan set its cost of capital at 10 percent.

Approaches to Calculating ROI

ROI can be calculated and reported in several different ways. In most cases, alternative ROI values are simple transformations of each other. Data leading to any correctly computed value can be recomputed as needed. Payback period, discounted cash flow, net present value, internal rate of return, and profitability index are five common ROI metrics. Each provides a different perspective on ROI. All are helpful to decision-makers weighing IT investments and allocating scarce resources.

Payback Period

Payback period is the length of time it will take for cumulative net cash flow (*i.e.*, the benefits) to equal the initial investment. Net cash flow is the total cash inflow minus the costs for the period of that cash inflow.

For IT investment decision-making, payback period is the estimated length of time to when the cumulative net cash flow equals zero from an investment point of view. When examining a single investment, payback period answers the question of how long the company should expect to wait for the break-even point. For differential decisions, a ranking by payback period for a collection of investments reveals those investments that most quickly reach break-even.

In technology sectors, shorter payback periods are often favored due to uncertainty with the constant and rapidly changing nature of the industry. In contrast, public sector investments may demand and support a longer payback period.

This method is simple and easy to calculate, and easy for shareholders and customers to understand. It simply tells us when the investment's benefits overtake its out-of-pocket costs. There are drawbacks to its simplicity, however.

■ Payback period does not take into account cash inflows earned after the payback period. If payback was achieved in six months, then what is the business value contribution of the solution after three years? The cumulative net inflows that accrue after the payback period are business value estimates.

■ Payback period does not take into account the cost of money. Future cash inflows must pay back an initial cash outlay at a later date. In larger corporations, necessary cash is usually allocated from the corporate treasury; in smaller companies, this cash is generated by accepting debt. The cost of money is an important component not captured by the basic payback period metric.

Discounted Cash Flow

Discounted cash flow (DCF) analysis enriches the payback period calculation by including the cost of money and benefits that accrue after payback has been achieved. Once the net cash inflows have been estimated for each year of the project, they are adjusted (*i.e.,* discounted) to reflect the fact that, in real terms, money received at some point in the future does not hold the same value as money received today. Two factors affect the adjustment: the opportunity cost of not having the money to invest today (*i.e.,* discounting) and the risk of not receiving the payment in the future.

The Time Value of Money. Discounting falls under a broader concept, the time value of money (TVM), and discounted cash flow is highly similar in its behavior to compounding, which is another, more familiar TVM calculation. In the case of compounded rate of return, the question becomes, "Is $1,000 today worth $1,000 at a future point in time?" And, if invested without risk, then the answer is certainly "No," because present value (PV) will grow in accordance with the interest rate to a future value (FV) that is greater than $1,000. With an interest rate of 10 percent compounded annually over five years, a PV investment of $1,000 grows to a FV of $1,611, as shown incrementally in Table 3.1.

Table 3.1　Value of $1,000 invested with a 10% annual rate of return

Time	Interest Earned	Total Investment
Year 0	—	$1,000
Year 1	$1,000 x 10% = $100	$1,100
Year 2	$1,100 x 10% = $110	$1,210
Year 3	$1,210 x 10% = $121	$1,331
Year 4	$1,331 x 10% = $133	$1,464
Year 5	$1,464 x 10% = $146	$1,611

With present value of the investment (*PV*), rate of return (*R*), time (*t*) and future value (*FV*), a direct calculation is as follows:

$$FV_t = PV(1+R)^t \qquad\qquad (Eq\ \#1)$$

Using this formula, the year 5 value in Table 3.1 is calculated as follows:

Step 1: $FV_t = \$1,000(1 + 0.10)^5$

Step 2: $FV_t = \$1,000(1.10)^5$

Step 3: $FV_t = \$1,000 * 1.61051$

Step 4: $FV_t = \$1,611$

The process of adjusting the future value of money to reflect its present value is called discounting and discounting is the opposite of compounding. Setting aside risk, receiving $1,611 in five years time is the same as receiving $1,000 today, from a TVM point of view. Mathematically, the formula for calculating PV given a value for FV is the same except that FV is known and PV is the unknown. Reorganizing the equation to solve for PV results in the following:

$$PV = FV_t / (1+R)^t \qquad \text{(Eq \#2)}$$

If the question is, "For a 10 percent rate of return, what is the value today for $1,000 received in five years time? Equation #2 computes the value, as follows:

$$PV = \$1,000 / 1.61051$$

$$PV = \$621$$

Thus, $1,000 received today is not the same as $1,000 received in five years because the money can be invested over that time period. This is the time value of money. With this concept in hand, here are common ways of applying discounting to costs and benefits to inform investment decision making.

Discounting a Cash Flow.   Equation #2 is the key to preparing a discounted cash flow. Consider a project that is expected to deliver a net of $100,000 in benefit over each of three years. Using equation #2, and a 15 percent rate of return, the calculation of DCF is as follows:

Year 1: $DCF = [\$100,000/[(1.15)^1] =$ + $86,957
Year 2: $DCF = [\$100,000/[(1.15)^2] =$ + $75,614
Year 3: $DCF = [\$100,000/[(1.15)^3] =$ + $65,752

$$DCF_{1-3} = + \$228,322$$

This example shows that the cumulative benefit of this investment over three consecutive years is $228,322 when restated in today's present-value terms. Simply summing the benefits and using $300,000 as a measure of cumulative benefit would be an overestimate because the discounting rate is not taken into account.

Net Present Value

Building on the DCF, net present value (*NPV*) is the net difference between the future stream of benefits and costs converted into today's money terms (*i.e.*, present value). The formula is as follows:

$$NPV = I_t + [FV_t / (1 + R)^t] \qquad \text{(Eq \#3)}$$

In Equation #3, I_t refers to an investment in year t, FV_t refers to the future value in year t, and R refers to a discounted rate of return or, on occasion, an expected rate of return obtained from other investments of similar risk. The discounted rate of return usually has a company-defined value. Investments of a similar risk are expected to produce similar returns. Using the same company-defined discount rate for a collection of competing investment opportunities produces NPV values that can be meaningfully compared.

Using NPV analysis, an analyst can calculate whether today's cost of an investment is matched by discounted cash flow benefits in the future. Continuing with the same example, given the present value of future profit streams (*e.g.*, FV=$100,000 a year from Year 1 to year 3), a discount rate is 15 percent, a once-off $180,000 initial investment (*e.g.*, FV_0=($180,000) at Year 0), then NPV calculation is as follows:

$$\text{Year 0: } NPV_0 = (\$180,000)_0 + [\$0/[(1.15)^0] = \quad -\$180,000$$
$$\text{Year 1: } NPV_1 = (\$0)_1 + [\$100,000/[(1.15)^1] = \quad +\$86,957$$
$$\text{Year 2: } NPV_2 = (\$0)_2 + [\$100,000/[(1.15)^2] = \quad +\$75,614$$
$$\text{Year 3: } NPV_3 = (\$0)_3 + [\$100,000/[(1.15)^3] = \quad +\$65,752$$

This example shows that today's investment of $180,000 will generate a cumulative future value of $300K, which is worth $228,322 in today's dollars. The return on investment indicator for this 3-year *NPV* analysis computed as follows:

$$NPV_{0-3} = -\$180,000 + \$86,957 + \$75,614 + \$65,752 = \$48,323$$

Internal Rate of Return

Internal Rate of Return (IRR) is another DCF calculation that indicates the attractiveness of an investment and can be used to rank or compare alternative investments. IRR is a special case of *NPV* and is the discounted rate of return required for the future values of an investment to be equal to the initial investment.

Solving for the rate of return so that overall NPV equals zero is not simple algebra. There are software applications readily available to calculate IRR; otherwise, trial and error is required. The procedure calls for substituting various discount rates into the *NPV* formulas until the result converges on zero.

For the example at hand, a IRR of 30.6 percent yields the following result:

Year 0: $NPV = (180)_0 + [\$0/[(1.30636)^0\,] \qquad = -\$180,000$
Year 1: $NPV = (0)_1 + [\$100,000/[(1.30636)^1\,] = +\$76,549$
Year 2: $NPV = (0)_2 + [\$100,000/[(1.30636)^2\,] = +\$58,596$
Year 3: $NPV = (0)_3 + [\$100,000/[(1.30636)^3] = +\$44,855$

$$NPV_{0\text{-}3} = -\$180,000 + \$76549 + \$58,596 + \$44,855 = \$0$$

IRR analysis complements NPV and provides a different perspective on investment attractiveness. IRR ignores the magnitude of the NPV payoff and thus a small investment could easily have a higher IRR and a lower NPV when compared to a larger investment. IRR analysis can lead IT strategists to select a set of smaller investments with higher yields which together outperform a larger project both in IRR and total NPV.

IT Makeover at New Swan: Return on Investment

Based on detailed analyses of cost reduction and revenue enhancement opportunities driven by the new IT systems, analysts estimated that the total expected benefits would be $45,364 in year 1, $53,773 in year 2, and $51,698 in year 3, Combining expected cost, benefits, and a 10 percent rate of return, the NPV for this project is as follows:

Year 0: $NPV_0 = (\$10,341)_0 + [\$0/[(1.1)^0\,] = \qquad -\$10,341$
Year 1: $NPV_1 = (\$1,693)_1 + [\$45,364/[(1.1)^1\,] = \qquad +\$39,547$
Year 2: $NPV_2 = (\$1,693)_2 + [\$53,773/[(1.1)^2\,] = \qquad +\$42,748$
Year 3: $NPV_3 = (\$1,693)_3 + [\$51,698/[(1.1)^3\,] = \qquad +\$37,148$

$$NPV_{0\text{-}3} = -\$10,341 + \$39,547 + \$42,748 + \$37,148 = \$109,102$$

This calculation is simplified for clarity. It assumes no benefit in year 0, and does not discount expenses in years 1 - 3.

Profitability Index

The profitability index (PI) computes a familiar ratio based on the cost of the investment and the net present value of the benefits that accrue over time. By using NPV values, the PI takes the time value of money and the cost of future investments into account.

In the simple example, PI is represented mathematically as:

$$PI = NPV_{1-3} / I_0 \qquad\qquad (Eq \#4)$$

Using data from our previous examples, we know that the NPV_{1-3} following an initial investment of $180,000 total $228,323, and so the value of PI is as follows:

$$PI = \$228,323 / \$180,000$$
$$PI = 1.27$$

PI taken on its own reveals little other than to indicate that this investment returns more than its cost when future cash flow is discounted. Like IRR, PI is a useful tool in ranking investments. Where investment funds are unlimited, any PI with a value greater than 1 should be invested in. Where investment funds are limited, only the highest PIs should be invested in.

Unfortunately, the profitability index method carries some risk of being manipulated by savvy managers. Breaking up an initial investment into smaller, time-phased components often results in projects earning a higher PI ranking. This is a reminder that financial analysis and decision-making methodology must be accompanied by managerial judgment and insight into the substance behind the numbers.

The Broader Issue of Risk

Risk can wreak havoc with ROI estimates and actual outcomes. Consider the consequences of a modest cost and schedule overrun. When an IT deployment is three months late and one third over budget, then the ROI calculations change dramatically. Keeping to the same example, such an overrun would affect the project NPV as follows:

Year 0: $NPV = (\$180,000) + [\$0/(1.15)^0] = \quad -\$180,000$
Year 1: $NPV = (\$60,000) + [\$75,000/(1.15)^1] = \quad +\$5,217$
Year 2: $NPV = (\$0) + [\$100,000/(1.15)^2] = \quad +\$75,614$
Year 3: $NPV = (\$0) + [\$100,000/(1.15)^3] = \quad +\$65,752$

$$NPV_{0-3} = -\$33,417$$

With delay and cost overrun, the NPV for the project turns negative, indicating that the investment did not produce business value. This result underscores the important interplay between ITBV analysis and the IT organization's capability to field solutions reliably and predictably.

Other ROI Approaches

Real-options analysis merges ideas from options trading with traditional discounting and cost/benefit analysis allows for soft or indirect benefits that cannot be restated in dollar terms. While the DCF family provides the foundation, real-options analysis and cost/benefit analysis are useful extensions when building an understanding of ROI for an IT solution.

Real-Options Analysis

When future cash flows are uncertain, an incremental real-options approach can be helpful. Real-options analysis has been applied to capital investments where there is high volatility or uncertainty surrounding future cash flows. An option is the right, but not the obligation, to make an investment. An option gains value when volatility allows for the possibility of a large return on investment in the future, that is, a significant upside opportunity. And, the option approach is useful when the opportunity is on the horizon.

In a nutshell, a small initial capital investment enables the IT strategists to keep alternatives within reach without a full-scale commitment to an enterprise-wide deployment. A detailed explanation of real options is beyond the scope of this book. Interested readers should look to Dixit and Pindyck (1994) as a useful reference about how to apply real options analysis to capital investments.

Cost/Benefit Analysis

Cost/benefit analysis allows for claims of soft benefits that are more subjective. For example, a reduction in reputational risk is a soft benefit associated with an investment in IT system security. Such a benefit is difficult or impossible to define with a precise operational definition in a traditional discounted cash flow analysis. The empirical precision of DCF becomes a burden when interpreting indirect costs and benefits. Widening the scope is important in such situations.

Qualitatively identified costs and benefits can still be converted into dollar terms based on an expert's subjective judgment. Assumptions and estimates can be supported by analogies within the enterprise or from the industry at large. Accomplishments and disasters documented in IT publications ought not be ignored.

Innovative IT solutions are particularly sensitive to the risk that cost and benefit may not turn out as expected. As a result, ITBV analysts are more cautious when deploying novel solutions. Pilot studies and other hedges against risk are important in these situations.

Each metric has its own strengths and weaknesses and using any one metric may fail to provide a complete picture of the potential value from your investment. Curley (2004) recommends using a combination of metrics (*e.g.*, NPV, IRR, PI and Payback Period) on each investment to avoid one-dimensional analysis.

Explicitly stated assumptions are pivotal to an accurate analysis. Sensitivity analysis can model how changes in underlying assumptions affect estimated returns. Modelling assumptions that reflect optimistic, pessimistic, and more-than-likely outcomes is a best practice. When key assumptions are identified, further analysis can be conducted to increase the level of understanding and confidence before arriving at a final investment decision.

IT Makeover at New Swan: Cost/Benefit Analysis

In addition to dollar estimates of business value, analysts measured a number of other benefits. Senior managers reported improved ability to manage business operations, for example, which enabled better and quicker decisions and reduced operational risk for the company. Inventory level was reduced from 30 days to 19 days due to improved control systems. Senior managers were able to remain in touch with operations, which improved day-to-day management while allowing for more vigorous sales activities. Two new customers were acquired leading to an additional $2.2M in revenue for New Swan.

The Finance Perspective

The role of finance in most companies is often poorly understood. Finance often appears to be in the role of saying "no," putting the brakes on spending, and avoiding waste. Even finance professionals can lapse into understanding this to be the essence of their jobs, especially in the context of day-to-day budget management. However, the true role of Finance is to act as an agent of the shareholders and to provide a quantitatively driven voice that guides shareholder money to the investment areas of highest return. Simply saying "no" is inadequate. Successful performance entails saying "No dollars here, because the higher ROI is over there."

The IT Paradox

In the ebb and flow of business, especially in large enterprises, IT planners and ITBV analysts have noted a difficult trend, which is summarized in Figure 3.1. Intel's Doug Busch first noted the relationship between IT budgets and a firm's business cycle. In times of growth, IT budgets rise along with the company's revenue and demand increases for sufficient IT capacity to enable growth. When the rate of growth is zero, the company focuses on internal efficiencies to improve margins. While the IT budget shrinks, demand increases for systems that reduce cost and improve operational efficiencies. The IT organization attempts to throttle down variable costs, while accepting fixed costs in areas such as network infrastructure. Finally, and most ironically, when growth turns negative and the IT budget shrinks further, the company turns to IT for more help in cost avoidance. Both fixed and variable costs must be reduced across the entire enterprise.

The IT paradox, that demand for IT services goes *up* during bad times, can be a powerful *double whammy*. Its effect can be mitigated by implementing a service chargeback system that links the IT budget directly to customer demand. But even the most exquisitely designed chargeback framework will do no more than provide cost relief for currently-defined services. What remains missing is a systematic process to determine the potential value of new IT services and projects. This is exactly the purpose on an ITBV program.

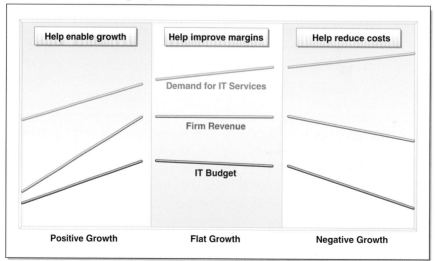

Figure 3.1 The IT Paradox

Critical Finance Decisions

When launching an ITBV program, the project manager relies heavily upon the finance department in several critical decisions. Made incorrectly or with insufficient finance expertise involved, these decisions will undermine the integrity of the program and reduce support within the organization.

Discounted Cash Flow

The first critical decision is use of discounted cash flow as the core of the program. While IT programs often generate many *soft* returns, the intent with any ITBV program must be force out the softness. By insisting that all BV measurement be reduced to cash flow impact, Finance creates a strong incentive for gathering robust data and quantifying it. This is critical for program credibility and central to developing a sound ITBV methodology.

ROI Time Horizon

Choice of the ROI time horizon is the second critical decision for Finance. For IT investments, a 3 year period is a good default time horizon. While many IT investments have returns extending significantly beyond 3 years, it is difficult to forecast those returns with precision. The mutability of business processes, organizations, and of business itself contributes to this uncertainty. And, as new technologies emerge, existing systems require significant new investment 4 to 5 years after initial deployment (*e.g.*, RFID and inventory management systems). Maintenance costs begin to rise as functionality is upgraded and security systems are strengthened. It is often difficult to accurately predict the cost of these mid-life investments. A 3-year horizon is a good starting point for most IT organizations given these offsetting factors.

An enterprise doing business in a stable industry might be well justified in choosing a longer horizon, while a startup might even consider employing a 1 or 2 year horizon. Finance may set different horizons for different types of investments. However, the multiple-horizon approach will need a solid rationale since excessive complexity can undermine credibility and may also create opportunities to manipulate the system.

Business Value Dials

The third critical decision is agreement on a set of *business value dials*. As discussed in Chapter 2, business value dials can range from direct impact on revenue, to reduction of inventory, to reduction in operational headcount, and finally to improvements in employee productivity. In establishing business value dials, Finance and the ITBV team must identify the most important business value indicators and certify that the indicators can be measured accurately and affordably.

More broadly, Finance takes the lead in defining what is meant by business value. The ITBV team, which includes the customer, helps by explaining the solution's requirements. In a on-line retail enterprise, for example, customers are likely to value high availability for the company's storefront during critical holiday shopping periods, reliable and secure payment systems, and an efficient coupling of storefront systems to inventory and fulfillment systems. These requirements help to identify the right business value dials.

Forecast and Actual Measurements

IT Makeover at New Swan: Business Value Dials

New Swan chose a small number of business value dials, including traditional measures of operational efficiency: days of receivables, days of payables, and days of inventory. Other dials included risk avoidance, direct income, and hardware/software cost avoidance.

Actual measures of days of inventory taken before and after the solution was deployed revealed that inventory levels had dropped from 30 days to 19 days, which was a significant improvement. Automated management of receivable and payables improved cash flow management for the company.

The finance organization also takes the lead in designing standard methods for both forecast and actual ROI analysis—a *dual measurement* approach. In the overall scheme of trying to manage IT for greater business value, it is not enough to rely entirely on forecast ROIs. Finance and the ITBV team prepare forecast ROIs to inform investment decisions and actual ROIs to confirm the forecast and measure actual business value contributions. The dual measurement approach has far reaching impacts. IT initiatives are not credited with business value contributions until systems are in production and actual benefits are measured. The ITBV team will divide its time between modelling and forecasting the potential effects of proposed solutions and the measuring the actual effects of deployed solutions.

ROI forecasting remains critically important as a way to prioritize investment opportunities. And, in a less obvious way, the early focus on

ROI sets operational goals and expectations that, to borrow from Vince Lombardi, "Actual business value isn't everything, it's the only thing."

When operational managers become aware that receiving funding depends on a strong forecast ROI, they also need to understand that programs will be held accountable for delivering on that forecast in order to be considered successful. These two incentives counterbalance each other and improve the credibility of forecast data.

Rules for Counting

There are three key finance issues related to the choice of ITBV projects: what to count, what not to count, and how to avoid double counting. Each of these issues brings Finance to the foreground in the ITBV process.

What to Count

The ITBV process is forward-looking. Finance can help the ITBV team to focus on new IT programs that are likely to bring new business value to the company. While it is tempting to consider the entire IT portfolio as within the scope of ITBV analysis, there are good reasons to reduce scope. In a nutshell, measuring a change in business value is more useful and more practical than attempting to measure ongoing value. The corporate message system is certainly valuable, and probably indispensable. But without baseline data, attempts to establish its business value contribution will be difficult or impossible. Keep in mind as well that there are many pitfalls for an IT organization that trumpets the impact of past accomplishments.

What Not To Count

Finance and the ITBV team must come to agreement on projects that are categorically set aside. To remain closer to IT customers and end users, consider setting aside the study of systems and projects entirely contained within the IT organization. Re-engineering an application to reduce network and support costs is an example of an internal IT project. While in the end the company will benefit from this reduction in IT costs, an ITBV analysis of projects with a direct benefit to business wins out over projects that reduce IT support costs.

This decision has consequences within the IT organization. For IT managers who are customer-facing, ITBV analysis fits well with their goals and objectives. However, IT managers responsible for infrastructure and ongoing systems will likely be disconcerted to hear that their projects will not be counted toward business value goals.

In the long run, of course, reductions in IT costs do contribute to the ITBV goal, which is to increase the cost recovery ratio. Since cost recovery is the ratio of value delivered to total cost, Any reduction of costs would help improve this metric's value.

$$Cost\ Recovery\ = \frac{IT\ Business\ Value\ Delivered}{Total\ IT\ costs}$$

Avoid Double Counting

An important principle for financial accountants is maintaining strict independence among categories when sorting through and placing dollars in the chart of accounts. When all credits and debits are counted exactly once, then aggregates and summaries are in synchrony, and the balance sheet balances. This same principle applies to multiple measures of business value, but in a slightly different way. In order to compute overall business value as the sum of contributions from multiple IT initiatives, these initiatives must be independent from one another.

One consequence of avoiding double counting is that not all business value contributions will be documented, or at least not documented in isolation. For the foreseeable future, ITBV measures of business value contributions represent partial views of the overall benefits of IT. By excluding IT initiatives that roll out a mixed bag of new capabilities that overlap with previous or ongoing ITBV studies, some values will be overlooked, to be sure.

Setting Initial Financial Goals

The long term success metric for an ITBV effort is to prove that the IT function is, at a minimum, paying for itself and that new projects are expected to deliver a return on investment that includes the cost of capital and discounted cash flows. Aiming for a Net Present Value of $0 may sound underwhelming, but to financial analysts, getting one's money's worth is a good thing. The goal is well formulated, easily articulated, and provides a threshold that in many cases can be exceeded.

Other objectives to keep in mind when working with Finance to set initial financial goals include the following:

■ Set financial goals that help to change the mind set of the IT organization. Articulate that goals are intended to direct management and employee attention to projects with the highest expected business value.

- Use financial goals to bring IT planning in line with other organizations in the enterprise. Proposals with forecasted and actual ROI are typically required for line-of-business managers. Financial goals help to show alignment of IT and business unit priorities.

- Standardize financial goals in ROI terms with a consistent methodology for valuing IT investments. Standardization is particularly important for global companies where business value analyses will be conducted in several geographical regions.

With all these factors in mind, financial goal-setting requires balance to ensure solid progress towards each objective. It is unrealistic to expect that an ITBV program can be immediately mature enough to analyze and demonstrate a full payback of IT spending. Establish a modest goal that is equal to 10 - 20 percent of the overall IT budget. While the initial financial goal is important to the ITBV program, the core objective in the first year should be to establish the program, develop the measurement methodology, and begin the IT culture shift as IT begins to operate like a business.

The number and types of programs supported by the IT organization also affects goal setting. IT organizations that deploy a few large projects accounting for most of the perceived business value should consider establishing a cap for each program's contribution to the IT organization's business value goal. This is to ensure that the entire IT organization becomes business-value oriented. If one or two programs deliver all the value needed to meet the overall goal, the business value message will not permeate the entire IT organization. There is no magic ratio here. Finance and the ITBV team consider the issue and then decide on the best approach.

In some companies, ITBV performance can be linked to an internal incentive system. When success leads directly to employees' bonuses, there will be a dramatic boost in attention and sense of urgency.

Balance is the key. An outrageous goal in the early stages of an ITBV program can lead to catastrophic results. It is easy to underestimate the difficulty of institutionalizing a new measurement culture. Missing a preposterously large goal is far worse than exceeding a more reasonable one. Credibility vanishes and the ITBV team is demoralized. Work with Finance to set a goal large enough to require considerable effort, but realistic enough that, with solid work, it can be achieved.

BV ROI Spreadsheet

An ROI spreadsheet streamlines the ITBV process. The spreadsheet provides a template enabling ITBV and IT staff to gather their own business value data. The tool increases the effective reach of the Finance organization. ROI spreadsheets need not be fancy and complex. A good template serves as a checklist to ensure that key information is collected. In fact, a relatively simple template will be more useful to financially unsophisticated users. A standard ROI spreadsheet will bring commonality to the financial analysis process.

Spreadsheet templates run the risk of becoming black boxes. Almost every IT opportunity is different and may require different financial analysis techniques and parameters. A generic template may not include key inputs that were not present in any past assessment. Intelligent design trade-off decisions will need to be made in this area. For example, a relatively generic template might best be used only as an initial screening tool for projects. Additional templates are available that provide more detailed and situation-specific support for projects which meet screening criteria.

An ROI template will reflect choices made about business value dials. If an organization chooses and defines days of inventory as a key business value dial, then users of the ROI template will need to understand its operational definition (*i.e.*, what to count) and the template designer will need to understand how the indicator dial's value is to be converted into dollars. Also, parameters that remain fixed across projects can be managed centrally by the template owner. For example, standard burden rates for employees can be updated regularly and published as a part of the ROI spreadsheet.

Typical ROI Spreadsheet

- *Introduction*: Contains brief instructions for the BV ROI template. The Introduction includes the purpose and rationale for providing a tool and framework to gather and calculate business value, target audiences, roles & responsibilities, key contacts, and the finance ROI standards.

- *Instructions*: Explains how to use the BV ROI template. Subsections provide detailed instruction to corresponding worksheet names. Instructions contains all the information necessary to complete the worksheet along with explanations of what can be changed and default values used in all calculations.

- *Cost Assumptions*: Enters all cost assumptions for the IT project throughout the life cycle. Cost Assumptions will include items such as:
  - The total cost associated with employees of the organization responsible for the work described in the line item.
  - Hardware costs associated with procuring, installing, making fit for use the described equipment.
  - Software costs associated with procuring, installing, making fit for use the described software. This may include internal development cost.

  The type of cost is also identified, for example, capital cost vs. a current period expense.

- *Business Value Dials*: Shows all current business value dials. Expected benefits will come from one or more of the defined value dials.

- *Benefit Assumptions:* Enters all benefits assumptions for the program/project throughout the life cycle. This section follows a similar format to the Cost Assumptions.

- *Benefits Summary:* Lists all the benefits to be realized from the IT project and requests a calendar date when benefits are expected. Benefits Summary is linked to the business value dials and additional information is gathered on each benefit.

- *NPV Engine:* Collects the remaining project information that is required and calculates the final business value ROI.

ROI Spreadsheet and Intel's SMB IT Makeover Program

The small and medium size Business (SMB) IT Makeover program is designed specifically for small and medium sized business in emerging markets. The program aims to help SMBs understand how to gain business benefits by investing in IT. Experts from Intel IT work with technology solution suppliers to understand the current and future business needs of a SMB and to help design an appropriate IT solution which creates value for the business.

The IT@Intel program also works with the SMBs to help measure the business benefits created by the IT investment using a model specifically developed for SMBs. This model is based on the ITBV ROI spreadsheet, but this approach was seen as too complex for small business and needed to be simplified. The spreadsheet was modified to capture business benefits within the proven Intel framework, but in the language of smaller businesses.

Tool Modification

In four incremental steps, the ROI Spreadsheet was simplified and tailored to the generic needs of small and midsize businesses. Those steps are as follows:

- Step 1 – Reduce overall complexity.

  SMBs do not have professional financial analysts, trained project managers, and human factors engineers to support the measurement of business value. The ROI spreadsheet was simplified so that small business users could confidently guide themselves through the evaluation process. For example, to make the tool easier to use a question and answer format was added to guide data entry.

- Step 2 – Simplify the business value dials.

  The business value dials were revised to make them easier for smaller businesses to understand. For example, the several business value dials for revenue covered in Chapter 2 were reduced to a single dial.

- Step 3 – Alter the business value dial calculations.

  Intel-specific assumptions were removed. For example, many of the calculations use specific data for employee overhead, discount rate, etc. This fixed information was removed and the ability to set these values was added.

- Step 4 – Add flexibility.

  To support use internationally, the ROI spreadsheet needed the flexibility to view business benefits in dual currencies—the domestic currency as well as conversion to US dollars. This feature makes it convenient for SMBs to share results with international associates.

Summary

Financial metrics provide a foundation for ITBV studies and ITBV programs. When weighing investment alternatives, ROI metrics provide different perspectives on expected results and provide forecasts of costs and benefits over time. Financial metrics are used throughout business enterprises, but are new to IT organizations. When IT was construed as a cost to be spread across the enterprise as overhead, then these metrics did not apply. When IT is viewed as a business providing benefits in excess of cost, then these metrics become crucial.

Financial analysis for large corporations is a complex task, to be sure. For smaller companies such as New Swan, however, simplified analyses provide significant insight into the business value of an IT investment. With modest training and with the help of an ROI spreadsheet, SMB managers, line-of-business managers, and IT managers can perform basic ROI calculations. Even if these calculations are used merely for screening opportunities, the experience of identifying costs and benefits and calculating ROI helps to cultivate a business value orientation throughout the enterprise.

Chapter 4

Measuring Employee Productivity

An approximate answer to the right question is worth a great deal
more than a precise answer to the wrong question.
—John Tukey

A new rapid-response tool is available to help employees request and receive information during meetings. Support staff using this tool are 20 percent more likely to locate information when it is needed during executive meetings. Will there be an improvement in productivity that impacts the bottom line? Moreover, is the impact significant enough to justify deploying the tool throughout your company's global operations or would selective deployment be a better strategy?

This chapter provides a methodology for addressing these questions. To understand productivity opportunities, it's necessary to observe the behavior of employees performing tasks, listen to their feedback as they use the solution in their daily activities, and survey their attitudes about new IT solutions. To estimate productivity gains, it's necessary to develop productivity measures, conduct experiments, and use statistical methods to make sense of the numbers. These are the two key ideas I use to transform soft indicators of productivity into hard numbers that gauge the business value of IT solutions. Productivity measures and experiments augment business value dials and the financial calculations.

To bring these measurements and experiments to life, I shall illustrate concepts with examples from a productivity study we conducted at Intel in 2003 to measure the business value benefits of Intel® Centrino® mobile technology. I mentioned some of the conclusions of this study in the Introduction—a week's work done in two hours and eight minutes less time. How did we come up with that estimate? Follow the sidebars and you will find out.

Wireless Mobile Technology Study: Overview

Intel IT conducted a study in 2003 to explore the business value contribution of an investment in wireless mobile technology. More than 100 employees were upgraded to wireless notebook computers. Employee productivity was one of the primary focuses of the study because this IT investment was aimed at improving employees' personal and network computing resources. Effects of Wireless Mobile Technology on Employee Productivity (Intel, 2003) is available at the Intel Web site.

Understanding how to measure employee productivity in a reliable and repeatable manner across various IT solutions is an essential skill. The project life cycle comprises four general phases, as summarized in Figure 4.1. We build a plan in the exploratory phase, and then we methodically prepare for the observations and experiments. Data collection is the execution of the most appropriate measurement techniques. Finally, in the data analysis and reporting phase, we make sense of the numbers and pull together a report for the stakeholders and decision-makers.

There are numerous variations of the design and development process; however, all have in common the concept of moving from general system descriptions to specific implementations of those descriptions.

Phase 1: Exploration

Employee productivity studies begin with an exploration phase. The goal at the end of this first phase is a metrics plan (see Appendix C for a template) describing how, when, and where you will collect employee productivity data. Key elements of the productivity assessment plan are as follows:

■ The design of pilot studies, which are needed in some cases.

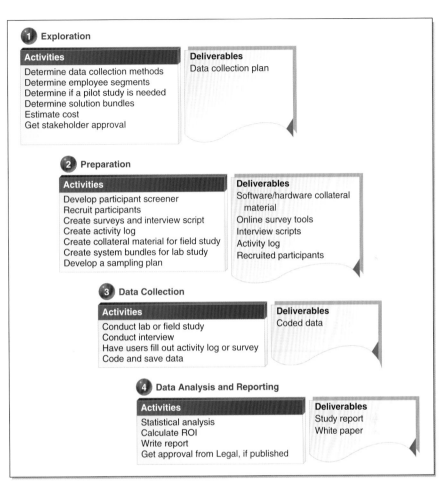

Figure 4.1 Phases of the Data Collection Process

- The design of the observations, measures, and experiments that make up data collection

- The description of the groups or segments of employees to be included in the study

- An estimate of the cost and time line of the study

- Approvals from all parties with an interest in the outcome

This work should be done in conjunction with identifying and defining business values dials and financial metrics.

Data Collection Methods

When conducting employee productivity evaluations, collect data using one or more of six data collection methods listed in Table 4.1. Quantitative methods are those that give us insight into the quality of the user's experience and an understanding of what affects productivity. Quantitative methods measure performance, usually under different conditions.

■ Interviews and surveys are good exploratory methods used to better understand usage models and work environments. The qualitative information from these two methods provides useful input to experimental lab studies which measure quantitative performance differences. Also, these two methods can be used with lab studies to obtain qualitative feedback from participants on the performance differences.

■ Activity logs generated through self reports provide rich data on frequency of use, task duration, and the method used to complete tasks. Activity logs generated automatically by computer systems can also provide data on task duration and task frequency. Also, this data is relatively easy to collect, analyze, and report.

■ Field study and experimental lab studies, while costly to conduct, are good for obtaining detailed information on how well tasks are completed, the frequency with which they occur, and the time required to complete them.

Note that field studies, lab studies, and activity logs produce the data that can be extrapolated to estimate company-wide impacts and weighted with dollars to transform productivity gain into business value.

The real skill lies in selecting which combination of methods to use, based on the advantages and disadvantages outlined in Table 4.1. When encountering little-known (*i.e.*, innovative) IT solutions or when developing new employee productivity measures, it is best to use qualitative methods early in the study to better understand the tasks. Qualitative findings often influence the development of quantitative measures later in the study. When quantitative methods are well understood, use qualitative methods such as open-ended interviewing to explore out-of-the-box possibilities and proceed directly to the quantitative experiment.

It is important to include at least one quantitative method as a part of every productivity study. Without quantitative measures, the study will only deliver soft results (*e.g.*, employees are pleased with the new IT solution). Direct observation and measurement of task duration is

Table 4.1   Six Data Collection Methods

Method	Description	Best Usage	Advantages	Disadvantages
Interview	Employees answer semi-structured questions posed by interviewer.	Identifying employee tasks and methods	Excellent for collecting feedback on the employee's likes and dislikes.	Rarely provides performance data. Subject to reporting bias, which can result in over- or under-estimation.
Survey	Employees answer a series of structured questions.	Identifying employee tasks and methods	Easy to administer with a large number of employees.	Is subject to reporting bias, which can result in over- or under-estimation. Often overused due to ease of administration.
User Activity Log	Employees answer a series of questions on the tasks that they performed.	Quantifying employee tasks and methods	Easy to administer to a large population on a regular basis.	Can interfere with the work process. Is subject to reporting bias, which can result in over- or under-estimation.
Server Activity Log	The network or application server monitors user activities.	Quantifying task frequency and duration	Easy to obtain and query the data.	Adequate server infrastructure required to obtain data logs. Context in which an event occurs and the goal of the user unknown.
Field Study	Employees are observed performing a series of tasks in their work environment.	Identifying and quantifying task frequency and duration	Provides quantitative performance data on tasks difficult to simulate in the lab.	No control over the task and environment variables. Confounding variables can make the data less valid.
Lab Study	Employees perform a series of tasks in a controlled lab environment.	Quantifying task frequency, duration, error rate	Best measures of task performance and control of task and environment variables.	Can only measure tasks that can be reproduced in the lab. Requires time to prepare collateral materials. Introduces the artificial nature of a lab setting.

preferred over people's subjective estimates of time savings. Quantitative measures are key to the validity of the conclusions that the productivity study reports.

Conducting a Pilot Study

To properly design a valid productivity study, it is crucial to identify the important variables. These variables include the types of employees to

---

Wireless Mobile Technology Study: Data Collection Methods

This study consisted of two distinct phases. In the first phase we worked with a small set of employees to better understand how the solution impacted their work and behavior. The qualitative data collected in the first phase was used to refine the data collection techniques used in the second phase.

The second phase included all six data collection methods. We observed usage of the mobile systems by employees at work. We surveyed participants before and after they received a new notebook computer to elicit their sense of satisfaction. We interviewed participants to better understand how mobile access changed the way they worked. We used self-report and automated activity logs to track time and frequency of key activities, such as the location of the participant when doing work. Finally, we designed a performance test to be conducted in our laboratory to provide classic employee performance data to the study. One task was to connect to the network, locate a file, and copy documents from that file to the notebook.

Initially we ran a pilot study and discovered that our survey was too complex and had to be rewritten, underscoring the importance of pilot testing. In hindsight the team decided that more data was collected than we needed to address the basic question: degree of productivity gain.

---

be included in the study, the types of tasks to be performed, employee usage scenarios to be investigated, and environmental factors that may cloud the findings if not properly controlled. In some cases, it is a good idea to investigate these variables in a pilot study.

Be sure to conduct a pilot study if the IT solutions or user scenarios (*i.e.*, usage models) are new, or if little is known about employee behavior. The pilot study will reveal employee profiles, appropriate and inappropriate tasks, and usage models. Findings from the pilot study feed into the overall study plan and will influence the design a lab experiment, determine which employees to recruit, identify appropriate work environments for simulation, and influence the formulation of interview and survey questions.

Keep in mind, though, that when adequate information from other sources is available, a pilot study may not be needed. Typically, other sources include previous user evaluations, employee segmentation data, and job or work analyses.

Using Segmentation to Drive Targeted IT Solutions

At Intel, our IT Market Intelligence professionals apply a consumer marketing technique called *customer segmentation* to better understand how to deliver the right solutions for each Intel IT user segment.

Segmentation is important because it:

- Allows our IT organization to identify, target, and offer the right solutions based on understanding users' needs, attitudes, and behavior.

- Enables IT to avert under- or over-serving segments.

- Enables us to communicate this understanding consistently to everyone across our IT organization in ways that they can easily understand and act upon. We can focus and deliver truly integrated solutions.

- Enables IT product managers to understand target markets, segment-specific usage models, demand, training, and marketing messages, and identifies potential early adopters for pilot studies.

The consumer marketing methodologies we employ provide attitudinal and behavioral data about technology usage. This provides insight about technology adoption and market size that are not available through job role segmentation alone. Understanding users' behaviors and needs, by attitudes as well as by job roles, offers a more complete picture of the user and provides usable data for our customers. Our goal is to become a strategic partner and an IT consultant to our business units. We treat the business units within Intel in much the same way Intel's product groups treat their external customers.

Determining Employee Segments

In most cases, productivity studies segment the population to better understand the business value results and to increase the validity of the study. Employee groups should be based on the target market for the IT solution, using deployment plans or other employee job profile data. A study of a new remote access service, for example, may not need to include administrative employees. Similarly, when studying the productivity benefits of a business intelligence initiative, the study may focus on the strategic marketing staff who are its primary users.

It is critical that studies avoid choosing employees out of convenience or because management decides which groups should be included. To obtain valid results, the employee segments included must represent the final target users for the IT solution. For example, it would not be valid to use administrative assistants when evaluating an application for field sales engineers.

Experimental Design

During the exploration phase, it is essential to decide on key experimental design factors. Complete coverage of proper experimental design and analysis is beyond the scope of this book. For thorough coverage, *Experimental and Quasi-Experimental Designs* by Shadish, Cook and Campbell (2001) is a solid reference.

The purpose of experimental design is to ensure that the study is carried out in a manner that controls as many of the variables that might impact the outcome as possible, given the constraints of working within a production IT setting. Confounding variables will compromise the experiment. For example, if we tested a new engineering design tool in Israel with senior engineers and in Germany with newly-hired engineers, how would we interpret the results? Confounding variables, in this case location and employee segment, make it impossible to determine the actual cause of any observed impact of the IT solution. In a perfect world, studies would be conducted in a completely controlled setting to increase confidence that the results observed are indeed a result of the IT solution.

The following are examples of common experimental design factors:

- *Independent variables.* Typically the baseline IT solution and the new IT solution comprise the independent variable. Measures of productivity are obtained under each condition and compared. Segments of employees is a second example of an independent variable.

- *Dependent variables.* In productivity studies, the dependent variables are performance measures such as task completion times and task completion rates. For surveys, the subjective measures such as user satisfaction ratings are dependent variables.

- *"Within group" design.* The same set of participants are used in a within-group design for both pre-implementation and post-implementation measurement. Using the same people helps minimize data variability arising from individual differences inherent in the participant sample.

■ *"Between groups" design.* Between-groups designs compare productivity measures for two sets of users performing the same task with different IT resources. A between-groups design usually requires more users than a within-group design, but more easily avoids the confounding effect that is introduced when the same person is used for testing both products.

■ *Counterbalancing.* In a counterbalanced within-group design that investigates two IT solutions, the order of presentation varies. To compare two project planning tools, half the participants will start with tool A and then work with tool B while the remaining participants start with tool B and then work with tool A. Counterbalancing controls the confounding effect that can arise when exposure to one IT solution might impact performance on the subsequent IT solution.

■ *Random assignment.* In a between-groups design that investigates productivity for two or more IT solutions, participants should be randomly assigned to the groups. The testing groups could be using pre-implementation (*i.e.*, baseline) and post-implementation IT solutions. Random assignment means that each participant has an equal chance of being assigned to any of the IT solutions under study.

Collaborating with Third Parties

I encourage caution when conducting productivity studies in conjunction with third parties. Most IT solutions aimed at improved employee productivity depend on hardware or software from third-party vendors. For example, at Intel we use standard operating systems, office productivity solutions, and we deploy wireless and wire-line networks with equipment obtained from third-party providers. In many cases we evaluate productivity entirely independently from these suppliers and we often report findings without revealing third-party supplier identity.

The problem we've experienced is added complexity when reporting findings with named collaborators. If a final report and productivity results are to be released publicly with vendor names, then verify that the vendors want to be included by name and be sure to gain approvals from the vendors early to avoid delays.

Wireless Mobile Technology Study: Experimental Design

User satisfaction surveys were obtained before and after the new notebook was given to participants, which is a within-group design. Levels of satisfaction with different features (*e.g.*, battery life, portability) were the dependent variables.

A within-group design was used to compare usage patterns in the first two weeks of the experiment with the last two weeks of the experiment. At the end of the experiment, employees spent less time online in their cubicles and more time online elsewhere.

A within-groups design was also used to compare task performance on the new notebook with task performance on an older configuration. Order of platform testing was counterbalanced to control for learning effects. We randomly assigned the order of the test systems so that just as many participants started testing with the new system as started it with the old system. Completion time, error rate, and satisfaction with performance for common job tasks were the dependent variables.

Deliverable: Updated Metrics Plan

Once the stakeholders have agreed to the evaluation goals and objectives, we create or update a metrics plan with detailed information on the data collection methods that will be used.

The creation of a metrics plan is the focus of Chapter 5. In a nutshell, the metrics plan comprises an outline of evaluation tasks, dependencies, durations, start and end dates, resources required, and any associated cost estimates. Once the plan is complete, we conduct review meetings with all stakeholders and revise, as needed, based on their input. Finally, we close the loop with a formal sign-off by the stakeholders.

Phase 2: Preparation

During the preparation phase, investigators develop all required collateral materials, define and standardize hardware and software, and review all documents that participants will use during the evaluation. For some studies, interviewer scripts are required. Other studies require the development of online survey tools or activity logs. Finally, investigators need to develop a list of study participants.

Defining System Bundles

In our studies, *system bundles* comprise both hardware and software components. This is because an investment in IT is often a hardware/ software upgrade. Comparing productivity using the current system bundle with productivity when using the upgrade is often the core of the study. In these situations, representative combinations of hardware and software are used for comparison. In other situations where the IT investment is in new software applications, it is important to keep the hardware the same for the comparison.

Selection of the new IT solution bundle is determined by two things: the roadmap your IT organization has for the IT solution deployment and the schedule that determine when IT solutions are being upgraded or introduced. Productivity studies must thus be planned with help from IT project managers to determine the configuration of the bundles we are comparing.

Wireless Mobile Technology Study: System Bundles

The bundle of new technology consisted of a notebook using Intel® Centrino® mobile technology and equipped with the most recent versions of the operating system and office productivity applications. This is the experimental bundle we issued to participants for use in their daily work. It is also one of the two bundles used in laboratory experiments. The contrasting bundle used for baseline productivity measures in the study was a notebook using an Intel® Pentium® II processor with legacy operating system and office applications.

For example, if the investment decision is whether to replace systems using the Intel® Pentium® 4 processor and running legacy office productivity applications with new systems using the Intel® Pentium® 4 processor with Hyper-Threading Technology and the latest office productivity applications, then these processors and associated software would constitute the two system bundles for the evaluation. As far as possible, the bundles should not differ in any other capability, such as network bandwidth.

Preparing Surveys, Scripts, and Activity Logs

We use our understanding of IT solutions and usage models to develop questions for interview scripts, surveys, and activity logs. As described in detail in Appendix B, developing tasks and scenarios for lab studies involves gathering task information from several sources and building a list of tasks the participants typically perform as part of their work.

It is a good idea to have questionnaires reviewed by a qualified professional to determine if the items capture the study's objectives. A technical writer should verify the clarity of the language. Once this is done, I recommend giving the questionnaire to a sample of test employees for feedback. It is very common to revise questionnaires based on employee feedback.

When the questionnaire is ready, convert it to a Web-based tool and administer it online. There are many third-party tools available that enable Web-based surveying and don't require software development. These tools ordinarily integrate an end-user interface used to complete the survey with a back-end database to store and analyze the results.

Wireless Mobile Technology Study: Surveys, Activity Logs, Server Logs

We were keenly interested in how employees would use the mobility capabilities. This interest led us to ask employees to indicate location in the activity log. We also asked employees to log the category of work undertaken: *e.g.*, email, file handling, document preparation.

Our surveys focused on satisfaction with the new notebook when compared to the prior notebook. Structured scales examined satisfaction with specific features such as battery life and wireless network operations. Open-ended questions asked about changes in work patterns and impact on productivity.

Our server-based logs of connection to public hotspots showed us that the largest usage was in post-work hours and employees were most often in coffee shops. We were able to calculate average connection times and amounts of data transferred. However, we could not know what tasks the employees were engaged in.

Open-ended questions helped us better understand the data. Employees reported that they were able to use small bits of time to check mail or review a document, time that would have been lost without the wireless capability. From a productivity perspective, our employees had reclaimed formerly wasted time.

Preparing for Lab Studies

Lab studies are complex because they require a great deal of preparatory work. They're often time- and cost-intensive, partly because they usually require large numbers of employee participants and human factors engineers. However, because the laboratory offers a highly controlled environment, lab evaluations do produce more accurate and reliable measurements of employee performance.

Standard preparation for laboratory studies at Intel include the following major steps:

1. Obtain test machines, load standard software builds, create a testing network, and generate email and other user accounts as needed.

   Our primary objective is to standardize the IT environment. In doing so, we take control over all the relevant variables and work hard to avoid confounding them. For example, when measuring the performance of a system bundle over time, we needed to take into account the fact that buffers fill, mail files grow, and thus performance decreases over the life of the experiment. To control this variable, we synchronized all bundles with the same system software at the beginning of each laboratory test. In every way we could, we made the test environment standardized for all participants.

2. Create the test tasks that users will perform.

   Daily work calls on users to perform many more tasks than can be reasonably tested. We create a sample of typical tasks that we believe will provide a broad measure of user performance. The sample should include tasks in proportion to the estimated frequency with which the task is performed in daily work. We build a sample of task that represent a cross-section of task types without duplicating activities. We also consider the capabilities of the bundles in task selection. Namely, all bundles must be able to perform the task. And the task must be executable in the lab.

3. Create familiarization activities and videos, supporting files and documents, and a bootable imaging DVD with the experiment's standard system images.

   I encourage you not to underestimate the need for a complete set of experimental materials. The participants in the study will need to understand what they are being asked to do. They will ordinarily not be familiar with the new IT solution and will need support to navigate successfully. Adequate preparation and piloting of materials is time well spent.

See Appendix C for more information on creating materials for a lab study.

Administering the Evaluation

Plans to measure productivity need a communications component for locating and working with participants. It is a good idea to make sure that the messages that are sent out to employees have been reviewed by your internal communications group. Many organizations have policies and standards for mass emailings and for requesting support from employees. Make sure to be familiar with these policies and follow them as part of your communications plan. Experiments can run into problems when the policies that are in place to communicate with employees are not followed.

Selecting Participants

The first step in selecting participants for a productivity assessment is to define the targeted participant population. Participants are not randomly chosen from the entire enterprise. IT solutions are deployed to targeted end-users or are replacing existing IT solutions. Thus, the available population of end-users is determined using these considerations. For example, it would not make sense to request participation from employees who work on the factory floor for an evaluation of an IT solution targeted for field sales staff.

Once the targeted population is defined, a random sample is formed from that population. This could be accomplished by sending e-mail to randomly selected employees within the population and asking them to complete a Web-based screening survey. A screening survey may be used to further refine the selection based on additional criteria. These criteria might include types and frequency of software applications used, place of work, and types and frequency of network connections.

Our screening surveys also describe the nature and scope of the study, the activities and time commitments of the participants, and our expectations. We give a deadline for responses and make clear that participation is voluntary. Finally, we include a contact name and phone number for additional information. See Appendix C for an example.

We use responses to the screening survey to certify that employees are members of the target population. The screening survey also helps to identify employees who are able to participate. We can analyze these volunteers by type of job, type of computer technology used, availability during the study timeframe, and current use of or interest in the IT solution being evaluated.

It is generally a good idea to use a stratified random sampling plan when conducting employee productivity experiments. A stratified plan divides the employees into groups based on predetermined criteria and samples randomly within those groups. The goal is to ensure that the sample of employees accurately represents the population as a whole. For example, if 80 percent of the users of a proposed IT investment are members of the sales force, then 80 percent of the sample should be drawn from the sales organization.

The common threat to stratified sampling is availability. While it may be easier to use only administrative staff to evaluate a solution that will be used by many non-administrative employees, the results will not be generalizable and the productivity estimates that lead to the business value of the IT investment may be significantly in error.

Wireless Mobile Technology Study: Sampling Plan

For this study, a random sample of 1,800 employees was drawn from the 6000 employees slated for notebook upgrades. Of these 1,800, 652 responded to our online screening survey. Using the survey results, a stratified sample was generated by randomly selecting among targeted employee groups: sales and marketing, managers, technical support personnel, design engineers and programmers, and office and business support staff. Each group in the sample was proportionally represented, based on the total number of employees in these segments.

The sampling was also affected by location. Practically speaking, we needed to choose participants working at sites with wireless infrastructure in place. Our assumption of a 10 percent attrition rate was roughly correct; 94 of the original 106 participants completed baseline and post-evaluation surveys.

When random sampling begins and an employee decides not to participate, then select another employee at random within the stratum. Anticipate roughly an 8-10 percent attrition rate during the study. Oversubscribing your experiment by 10 percent will address this issue.

As part of the overall process, send major communications to a small set of test employees first. This allows you to test any survey tools, data storage, and data analysis plan. It will also verify that the message is understandable, that the survey is complete and answerable, and that employees know how to respond. It is best to send these mass e-mails in a way that prevents an explosion of email should a recipient "reply all" when responding.

In evaluations spanning weeks or months, in which the same participants are measured repeatedly at different times to collect time-series data, manage and track all interactions with the participants. This includes tracking communications, weekly employee participation, termination of participation, and anyone who doesn't complete required data collection tasks. Also, keep track of which participants have completed parts of the overall evaluation, such as interviews, lab studies, and activity logs. As needed, send e-mail reminders to prompt participants for various data.

Phase 3: Data Collection

Once participants have been recruited and data collection tools and collateral materials are prepared and tested, data collection begins. In this section, I will provide greater detail about collecting information with interviews, surveys, activity logs, field studies, and laboratory studies.

Conducting Interviews

Human factors engineers conduct interviews to determine what helps or hinders participants in accomplishing tasks. Interviews can help to identify which business processes to measure in order to establish a link between productivity and other financial variables. Interviews can also be used in pilot studies to identify tasks, to investigate and understand usage scenarios, to identify participant interaction models, and to characterize work habits.

A typical interview should last approximately 30 to 60 minutes and can be conducted in person or over the phone. Use trained interviewers and ensure that a standardized script is followed, but encourage exploratory questions when appropriate. See Appendix C for a sample script.

When studying productivity, our interviewers typically conduct a semi-structured interview covering key topics outlined in a script. Those topics include the types of tasks the participant performs, work locations, ask frequency and duration, likes and dislikes about the IT solution, and suggestions for improvement.

We record the interview sessions using either an audio or video recorder, and then create a digital transcript of the interview. When interview sessions document baseline and post-implementation conditions, we summarize key themes, identify differences in the way the tasks are performed, develop use-cases or step-by-step procedures for both conditions, and perform a content analysis on the information obtained to identify potential qualitative differences. For more information on content analysis, look to *The Content Analysis Guidebook* by Neuendorf (2002).

Conducting Surveys

Surveys can be useful in early phases of a productivity study, especially when trying to identify the tasks the study should measure. By asking questions about how employees do their jobs, problem areas they have, and possible solutions, possible areas to measure emerge. Surveys can also be a useful tool for recruiting people for other activities, such as a field study, an activity log, or a lab study and are an easy way to collect demographic data. Designing surveys, like designing experiments, is a discipline in its own right and full coverage is beyond the scope of this book. See *The Survey Research Handbook* by Alreck and Settle (2004) for a more complete discussion of this topic.

A survey can also be helpful in identifying measurement tasks if the technical solution has already been provided to a segment of the survey population. One approach that is useful is to follow up survey responses with interviews to further explore and understand participants' answers.

Be cautious, however, when using subjective data gleaned from surveys to estimate business value. Research has shown that self-reported data on time savings is typically unreliable. People have difficulty making accurate estimates when they have to aggregate several factors (Wickens and Hollands 1999) and judgment biases may lead to additional inaccuracies (Yates, 1990). Self-reported data on time savings can only serve as a rough indicator for prioritizing which tasks to measure. Assume that participants are equally unreliable across all the areas for which they provided estimates of time saved.

Structure surveys in logical sections to help your participants organize their thinking. Gather background questions for participant profiles together in one place, for example. Group together task frequencies, task durations and locations. User satisfaction scales go well together.

Multiple-choice or open-ended questions asking for feedback on the IT solution are one final commonly occurring group.

Surveys can also provide information on how often a task is done in a particular time period. We have found that participants can generally recall this kind of information more accurately than time-savings information. However, an activity log is preferable to a survey for this information, because empirical data is typically collected while the employee is performing tasks.

Using Activity Logs

An automatic activity log is a time-stamped list of events obtained automatically by logging events on a server or on the employees computer. A manual activity log is the list of events an end user manually records showing how many times tasks are done during a specific time period, such as a week or a day. The recording takes place at or near the time when the task is actually done. Activity logs work well for collecting information on task frequency. They are preferable to surveys because there is less reliance on a participant's memory.

Be aware that task frequency information often varies widely and therefore requires a large sample size to measure it accurately. For example, in a 2003 study on instant message usage, participants reported task frequencies from as low as 0 to over 300 messages per week. In that case, we needed a sample size of over 300 employees to ensure accurate data.

If you need to have participants time themselves performing a small number of tasks, use activity logs to collect task completion time. However, in many cases, we have found that participants do not time themselves and simply guess. For this reason, in most cases it is a good idea to collect task times using lab studies or field studies. Depending on the situation, activity logs may need to be administered twice, once in the pre-implementation and again in post-implementation to determine how many users are using the new IT solution and how often they are using it.

As noted, there are two main types of logs to track participant activity: a self-report activity log that participants complete each day or week, and server-generated activity logs.

Self-Reported Activity Logs

Self-reported activity logs are questionnaires that participants complete. They contain clearly identified start and stop points to record particular behavior. They can measure the types of applications used, tasks performed, number of times the tasks were performed, average task completion time, difficulties in completing the tasks, and system errors. An example of an activity log can be seen on page 251 in Appendix C.

When using this approach we typically ask participants to record task information just after performing the tasks, at the end of the day, or at the end of the week. While having participants enter task information immediately after performing the task increases the accuracy, doing so has the potential to interfere with the work processes. If information is recorded at the end of the day or week, the data is not as accurate, but the participant's work process is less likely to be impaired. Because activity logs contain usage data for each period and rely less on a respondent's memory for this information after extended periods of time have passed, they generally provide more accurate information than interviews and surveys.

Server-Generated Activity Logs

Server-generated activity logs come from network servers or other applications that track application usage data such as frequency of application usage, duration of connectivity, type and volume of files uploaded and downloaded, and location of network connectivity. This data is generally easy to collect and it does not interfere with the normal activities of participants.

One disadvantage of automated logging is the lack of context that might explain an event. For example, it is possible to collect data on the number of times, duration, and time of connection when employees are using a wireless LAN. However, knowing that the employee logged in for a 15 minute session provides no information as to what tasks were completed and what business objectives the employee was trying to accomplish. To some extent, this lack of context can be corrected by using self-reported activity logs that coincide with the server based activity logs or by interviewing participants.

Conducting Field Studies

Observational field studies are useful for collecting task completion times and frequency while participants are actually performing tasks in their work environments. Field studies are appropriate for the following situations:

- Studying tasks for which independent variables can't be controlled in any systematic way or those whose natural environment cannot easily be replicated in the laboratory. A field study is likely to be required to study IT impact in a factory environment, for example.

■ Exploring tasks that are difficult to simulate in the lab, especially tasks that have very little structure or high variability. These tasks typically can be completed correctly in a variety of different ways. Field studies may be the best method for measuring performance on this type of task.

With a lab study, the materials provided may not be representative of the tasks performed in the real world. That, in turn, could result in invalid time measurements. Field studies address this problem because people are in their natural environment performing tasks as they normally do. However, the task still needs enough structure so that we can define a start and end condition for measurement. The need for operational definitions prevails, even in field studies.

As discussed, field studies can also be used during the exploratory phase of a productivity study to better understand what tasks to measure. In this case, the field study is more like an interview. However, because observation occurs in a participant's working environment, he or she is better able to remember a given task and provide more valid data. Investigators are able to understand the task better because they can see how it is actually performed.

When preparing for a field study, it is a good idea to use a checklist of tasks to observe and questions to ask. As always, conduct a preliminary interview to determine which tasks to observe. I have found, on occasion, that a participant does not even perform a task of interest to me as part of his or her job.

Not all locations are fully assessable. If the location is restricted, prior permission might be required in order to collect data in the field. In addition, equipment and documents such as videocassette recorders, micro-cassette recorders, stopwatches, and observer packets may be required; special permission is sometimes needed to bring these items into a restricted area. Ensure these potential issues are investigated prior to going to the field to collect data.

It is always best to take pre-implementation measurements before the IT solution under study is deployed. When asked to take measurements in a situation where the IT solution has already been rolled out, it is possible to ask participants to simulate how they performed tasks prior to the deployment of new technology. This provides a baseline measurement that could be compared to the post-implementation measurement.

However, make sure that the simulated task is measured across a number of individuals and in a manner designed to *underestimate* the average time to complete the task from the baseline period. Since you don't have the true baseline condition under which the original task was done, be careful not to collect data in a manner that will result in overestimating the impact of the new IT solution. Without proper baseline data, it is important to be conservative in these estimates.

Field studies can sometimes be useful for understanding the impact of an increase in productivity on the overall business process. For example, our activity logs of instant message usage showed that with this new communications tool, users were able to get 20 percent more questions answered in meetings. It is important to understand the impact of getting those additional questions answered. A field study that includes attending meetings, in combination with interviews that help you understand the business process better, may help determine the impact of the time savings.

Conducting a Laboratory Study

In order to determine if there's a link between the IT solution and participant performance, it might be essential to collect data in the laboratory. The goal is to ensure that the only variable (*i.e.*, the independent variable) impacting participant performance is the solution, and that other variables are controlled. Methods such as field study may allow confounding variables to affect performance. Data collection in the lab occurs in a controlled environment where users simulate work environment tasks as closely as possible. In the following sections, we review the necessary steps to conduct a lab study.

The informed reader will notice that my description of laboratory studies of employee productivity are similar to standard usability studies. The intent of these two types of study is not the same and there are important differences. The goal when measuring employee productivity is to collect performance data as employees complete test tasks in a controlled experimental environment. Obtaining performance data is one goal of a usability tests, but these tests also seek to understand the nature of issues users encounter when completing the tasks. For that reason, employee productivity experiments do not use all aspects of a standard usability test, such as think-aloud protocol. Interested readers should see Dumas and Redish (1999) for guidance on usability testing and coverage of standard methods.

In addition, because user performance is our primary objective, the level of control over the bundle of hardware and software is greater. For example, we rebuild the system after each test and reset all associated accounts to ensure that the system is identical for each participant and that no information has been altered, moved, or lost when the performance of the next participant is measured.

Lab Test Dry Run

Before beginning data collection in the lab, conduct a dry run to avoid unexpected surprises and to make sure that the sessions are completed within the allotted time. The dry run is conducted using the real test monitors, a small sample of study participants, all the collateral material developed for the test, and it is run in the laboratory. We usually schedule the dry run on Thursday or Friday, so that we can resolve issues over the weekend and have the experiment ready to proceed the following Monday.

Test Session Protocol

During the test session, monitors should follow a standard test protocol. This protocol typically includes welcoming participants to the evaluation, administering a skill assessment when required, conducting familiarization tasks on each system bundle. The employees then work through the test material independently and without interruption. Monitors then complete any post-task or post-test surveys. Monitors end the session by debriefing the employees if necessary and thanking them for their help.

We ask our participants to complete the task at a normal work pace. I want to underscore that monitors should not interfere with the employees' performance. The intent of these studies is not to collect participants' qualitative feedback on the system bundles being tested. To repeat, the primary purpose of the laboratory study is to collect employee performance data in a controlled setting. We are not attempting to determine the usability of the system bundle being tested nor to understand the employees attitudes about the system bundle.

Standard usability labs are equipped with video and audio recording systems, including overhead cameras in the test rooms. This equipment is used to record task completion activities of the participant. Before recording any participants, don't forget to inform them that the session is confidential and explain the policy that your IT organization follows when using recorded content. For some organizations, obtaining a signed

Usability Testing

A usability test is a study aimed at identifying usability issues with an application by observing a representative sample of end-users performing a set of tasks. The application may be a working prototype or a product that has already been launched. Usability testing aims to identify usability defects by finding out, if users complete a task successfully, how fast they do each task, where they stumble, what problems they have, where they get confused, and what their level of satisfaction is with the application.

Usability testing can also have different objectives based on when it is conducted in the development process. *Explorative testing* gathers input from participants in the early stages of application development to understand the target end users and to decide the appropriate direction for the application's look and feel, navigation, and functionality. *Assessment testing* occurs when the application is close to deployment to get feedback on usability issues and to fix them. Evaluation testing is done to validate an application subsequent to deployment.

A typical user sample is around 8 to 12 participants in each test. If the user base has different user segments, representatives of all these segments need to be included in the study. If the users have a range of computer experience, try to include participants ranging from less experienced to more experienced users.

Usability testing is an iterative process that involves testing the application and using the results to modify the application to better meet users' needs. Usability testing can be conducted in a fully fitted laboratory with two or three connected rooms and audio-visual equipment, at the users' workspace with or without portable recording equipment, or remotely with the user in a different location. Remote usability testing still requires that the test monitor be able to observe what the user is doing, listen to the user thinking aloud, and interact with the user by computer or telephone during the session.

During a typical usability test, the test monitor watches users working through tasks with the application and gathers feedback. The test monitor manages the test, gathers all notes, and consolidates and analyzes the information. The result of usability testing is a prioritized set of usability issues along with design recommendations for improving the application.

consent form is required after the privacy and confidentiality policies have been reviewed.

Plan for lab test session to take less than 2.5 hours. In each session, participants can typically complete around 7 to 10 tasks on each of two system bundles. We run 1 person at a time, 1 person per session, and conduct 3-4 sessions per day, depending on how long it actually takes to run the session.

Participants normally take around 60 minutes to complete all tasks on one system bundle. Each situation will vary, but we suggest you attempt to schedule one session in the morning and one in the afternoon. The time between the sessions will be needed to reset systems and all associated network accounts. A good estimate is around 45 to 60 minutes, depending on the strategy used to rebuild the system.

Task Performance Protocol

Before beginning a task, ask participants to read the scenario and task aloud. Give them enough time to understand the task and scenario and to ask questions of the test monitor. If a participant is not able to perform a task for some reason or is stuck due to lack of familiarity with a task, that participant is allowed to terminate participation by stating this to the test monitor. While completion time is the most common measure, other metrics are given in the section on Employee Performance Measurement on page 253 in Appendix C.

Because the goal is to identify how quickly the participant is able to complete the task, any queries from participants after starting the task should be restricted to clarifying what the task is and should not be an explanation of how to complete the task.

Many test plans include a familiarization task. Participants complete the familiarization tasks either by themselves or with the help from the test monitor. We find it convenient to package the familiarization material as a video file. After the video has completed playing, the participant is given one last opportunity to ask any clarifying questions.

Task Completion

There are two easy methods to track a task's start and stop points: a timer application or a stopwatch. A timer application allows the participant to start the timer before beginning a task. When the task is complete, the participant stops the timer. The monitor writes down the task completion time and resets the timer.

Use a traditional stopwatch approach for tasks that require the system to be shutdown or in other cases that prevent the use of a timing application. In those cases, ask participants to say aloud to the test monitor when they're ready to start the task, and then state when they've completed it. The test monitor starts and stops the stopwatch appropriately, then records the task completion time in the test monitor packet.

When the starting point, stopping point, and passing criteria are clearly identified, the test monitor can usually determine if the task was completed successfully using a normal sequence of steps. The "normal" path is the one most participants are expected to follow. Test monitors should have a list these steps in the test monitor information packet. If there is more than one way to complete a task, list the alternative paths in the test monitor packet.

The passing criterion for successful task completion should be based on the correct outcome of a task, not whether the participant used a particular sequence to complete the task. As long as participants reach the defined acceptable outcome, we consider the task to have been successfully completed.

Participants are not given a time limit to complete the task. However, if participants get lost, are taking an excessive amount of time to complete the task, and don't want to quit, the test monitor might suggest that the participant drop the task and move on. The test monitor then records that task as a failure.

Post-task and Post-test Survey

At the end of each task, we ask participants four basic questions:

- How often they do similar tasks during their typical workday or week.
- How much time they spend doing similar tasks during a typical workday or week.
- How unsatisfied or satisfied they were with the ease of use of the task?
- How responsive they felt the system bundle was.

Knowing the frequency and duration of the task when it occurs during normal work helps us to calculate overall time savings.

For measures of satisfaction and responsiveness, we use a 7-point Likert-type scale.

Overall, I am satisfied with the amount of time it took to complete this task (Please circle a number that best describes your feelings toward this task).

Unsatisfied						Satisfied
1	2	3	4	5	6	7

This type of scale provides responses to multiple statements that can be coded and compared to one another in later data analyses. A typical Likert scale uses anchor points like: strongly agree, agree, neutral, disagree, and strongly disagree.

After completing all tasks on a system bundle, we ask participants to complete a set of survey questions developed by Digital Equipment Corporation (Brooke, 1996). The System Usability Scale (SUS) survey provides a subjective score of a system bundle's overall effectiveness, efficiency, and user satisfaction. SUS scores range from 0 to 100, where a score of 100 indicates a highly usable system bundle.

After all tasks are completed on both system bundles, we thank participants for their time and send them on their way. We generally don't compensate employees who participate in our studies.

Phase 4: Data Analysis and ROI Generation

The goal at the end of this fourth and final phase is to understand the conclusions supported by the studies and to create a report or white paper. In this section, we discuss the analysis of employee productivity data and how it is used as part of the overall plan in calculating the business value for an IT solution. I will also briefly review the contents of a typical productivity report and the steps needed for publication.

Compiling Qualitative Data

Interviews, surveys, and activity logs provide a wealth of information on usage models and participant behavior. Analyzing this data will help you to understand positive and negative comments from your participants, to identify any new behaviors that might have emerged during the evaluation, and to get this information back to the right IT professionals so it can be addressed.

Wireless Mobile Technology Study: Data Collection Highlights

This study used nearly all the data collection techniques and each provided different insights into the business value benefits of the mobile bundle. Here are a few highlights of methods and their unique findings:

- Field observations early in the study and interviews late in the study helped us to understand the concept of time slicing and time shifting. It should be noted that the team had not expected these behaviors; they emerged from routine data analysis during the evaluation and resulted in modifications to the data collection tools during the final stages of the evaluation.

- Location entries on self-reported activity logs showed the widening variety of places where employees were working, particularly including work done at home.

- We used the SUS to measure user perception of ease of use for both systems. This survey indicated a sharp upturn in employee satisfaction with the new notebook's wireless capability.

- A laboratory test comprising seven tasks provided employee performance measures taken under controlled conditions.

- We also discovered some limited problems related to the deployment of the technology, and these issues were passed along to the team responsible for deployment.

For example, when we evaluated the deployment of Intel Centrino mobile technology notebooks, we uncovered new behavior that we had we had not anticipated.

- Employees began "slicing" time. Wireless mobile computing allowed employees to make productive use of formerly wasted slices of time between larger tasks.

- "Time shifting" became commonplace. Wireless mobility allowed workers to redistribute their working time around professional and personal obligations.

Analyzing Performance Data

The activity log, field studies, and lab studies provide task completion data. Data obtained from these studies is coded and compiled. To evaluate the differences between conditions, perform statistical tests such as a t-test or an analysis of variance (ANOVA), using standard statistical software packages.

- t-test: A t-test compares the difference between averages for two sets of observations and indicates when the difference is not likely to result from chance.

- ANOVA: An analysis of variance, which is based on the same assumptions as the t-test, compares the averages for two or more sample groups to determine if the group averages are significantly different from one another.

The result of a t-test or an analysis of variance is the probability that the observed differences occurred by chance. Differences that are not likely to occur by chance are the ones to trust. Statistical analysts typically consider two thresholds to determine whether the pattern of results is due to chance: probability of chance is less than or equal to 5 percent (results are significant), and probability of chance is less than or equal to 1 percent (results are very significant.)

Performing statistical tests is not necessarily required in order to draw conclusions about employee productivity. Rather, the statistical analysis allows us to better understand how confident we are in the difference. A significant difference, however, is not required to achieve a significant impact on business value. As long as the data have been collected objectively, you should be confident about the results.

Calculating Employee Productivity

Analyzing the task performance data from the pre-implementation and post-implementation obtained from activity logs, field studies, and lab studies provides the task completion time difference for each task. Task frequency data is obtained from participant response to surveys administered as part of the lab study, field study, or activity log. The average timesaving for each task and for each time period is calculated by multiplying the average time difference and the average task frequency for that task. Average timesavings for all tasks by summing up the averages for each of the tasks.

Most IT solutions result in productivity improvements, with tasks being completed faster when compared to the old IT solution. Watch for

Wireless Mobile Technology Study: Summarizing Results

Once the data was collected and analyzed, the results were summarized and presented in both an internal report and made available to the public.

Participants completed the commonly performed office tasks an average of 37 percent faster using the new system. Migrating saved employees approximately 5 percent of a typical 40-hour work week, or about 100 hours per employee, per year.

There were changes in the end-user behavior. These included a greater sense of control over work locations, the use of wireless steadily increased during the evaluation, and the combination of improved battery life and form factor resulted in the notebook becoming a constant companion.

positive or negative results in the example that follows to ensure correct interpretation of these calculations. Table 4.2 shows how to determine timed saved or lost for each task measured using the average task completion time and average task frequency per week. The process is explained in the following steps:

1. Calculate the average task completion time for the baseline (T_A) and post-implementation (T_B) using the data from activity logs, field studies, or lab studies for each task measured in the evaluation.

2. Calculate the difference between the average baseline and average post-implementation times for each task measured ($T_A - T_B$).

3. Calculate the average task frequency per week (F) from participant responses to surveys administered as part of the lab study, field study, or activity log for each task.

4. Calculate the time saved (lost) for each task per week by multiplying the difference from Step 2 by the frequency from Step 3 to get the timed saved (lost) for each task: $(T_A - T_B)$ x F

5. To determine the total time (T_{All}) saved (lost) across all the tasks per week, add up the result for all tasks in the table.

Table 4.2   Calculating data on time savings

Task	Average task completion time (T_A)	Average task completion time (T_B)	Difference (T_A-T_B)	Frequency per week (F)	Time difference (T_A-T_B) x F
Task 1	T_{1A}	T_{1B}	$(T_{1A} - T_{1B})$	F_1	$(T_{1A} - T_{1B}) * F_1$
Task 2	T_{2A}	T_{2B}	$(T_{2A} - T_{2B})$	F_2	$(T_{2A} - T_{2B}) * F_2$
...					
Task M	T_{MA}	T_{MB}	$(T_{MA} - T_{MB})$	F_M	$(T_{MA} - T_{MB}) * F_M$
			Total time saved (T_{All}) is sum of times saved for all tasks		T_{All}

To calculate the total time saved for the company, use the following equation:

Employee Productivity Benefit = $Y * N * W * T_{All}$, where

Y = Number of work weeks in a year, typically 49

N = Total number of employees in a company targeted for the IT solution

W = Average wage or burden rate for an employee, in dollars per hour

T_{All} = Total time saved (or lost) per week across all tasks measured.

If employees come from different geographical regions with different burden rates, calculate the average burden rate by weighting the employees in each region to compensate.

Because the ITBV team partners with members of finance they will help ensure that the employee productivity data is accounted for in the overall business value of the IT solution. For example, if you conducted the employee productivity evaluation in a manufacturing environment, you will also want to determine the impact of employee productivity on the productivity of the manufacturing system. To do this, you might look at changes in unit throughput time, scrap reduction, increased production per unit time, and so forth.

Presenting the Data

Once the qualitative and quantitative data are compiled, we generate a document, typically an internal evaluation report or a white paper. We present an analysis of the data and we include both participants' successes and failures to stress our objectivity. The initial draft of the document is sent to different interested parties from various business units for comment. If the document is to be published externally, we send it to appropriate organizations for approval. Because compliance reviews take time, the project needs to plan for this in the overall timeline. To help reduce delays on critical projects, we communicate with key teams (*e.g.*, the Intel legal team) before beginning the study. That helps set expectations about when the white paper is due and what it will contain.

Summary

We have conducted numerous employee productivity studies at Intel in a wide range of work settings. We have successfully used data from our studies to measure the business value of proposed IT solutions. Our evaluations are also used to justify investments in IT solutions. Our sales and marketing group has used productivity data in presentations to customers.

Because our studies are used in such diverse and visible ways, we have been extremely careful to ensure that the studies have been designed with objectivity, the data collected systematically, the data analyzed using appropriate statistical procedures, and findings presented without bias. Measuring employee productivity continues to be a useful way for Intel to quantify business value and calculate the return on investment of new products and processes.

Chapter **5**

Measuring the Impacts of IT

A problem well defined is a problem half-solved.
—Albert Einstein

It is time to bring the business value measurement components together into a complete study. A business value study contains an integrated set of business value dials, financial metrics, and productivity measures. The study plan, which we call a metrics plan, identifies these variables along with the segments of employees to be sampled. The metrics plan contains a calendar with milestones that lead to a final determination of business value.

While IT business value studies share some common qualities, each study is unique. In this chapter, I will illustrate the concepts with a study conducted at Intel in 2004 to evaluate the impact of migrating from dial-up networking to broadband networking (Lichtman and Mondolo, 2005). To strengthen the discussion, I have included two additional study synopses in Appendix B. Readers are encouraged to compare and contrast these three examples.

Migrating to Broadband: Project Description

In 2004, Intel was providing employees with a virtual private network (VPN) for use in conjunction with broadband remote network access. However, many employees continued to use dial-up networking (DUN). This study set out to investigate why DUN usage persisted and what business value might be obtained if employees using DUN migrated to broadband networking in conjunction VPN.

In my experience, the metrics plan is a living document. Early drafts focus on scope, names of business value dials, and the nature of the IT solution while often lacking details such as the precise operational definitions for the business value dials. The emphasis in this chapter is on how the metrics plan takes shape and how it integrates the techniques discussed in previous chapters. I also want to identify and wrestle with the challenges we have faced over the years. While we are methodical when investigating IT and business value, ours is not a perfect science. We shall begin, however, with the metrics plan.

Developing a Metrics Plan

The first step in conducting a business value study is the development of a metrics plan. The metrics plan should cover the basic information required to ensure objective data collection during the entire evaluation process of an IT solution.

We use the same outline for all metrics plans, but the information in that outline varies in complexity. The complexity of plan can be driven by:

- The business value dials being measured.
- The type of information that was available for these dials.
- The complexity of the IT solution.
- The complexity of underlying business processes.

It is important to understand that a metrics plan will integrate the various aspects of evaluating an IT solution and evolve over the life of the study. For example, the metrics plan may be very general early on in an evaluation, with refinements occurring over time as information is learned, as shown in Figure 5.1. Especially with new technologies, it is not always clear exactly what to measure. The first draft of the metrics plan may simply identify that observations of end users and pilot testing are needed in order to clarify what to measure. It is not uncommon to refine metrics plans as part of the evaluation process based on results from IT solution proof of concepts or pilots.

The refinement that occurs within the metrics plan is a direct outcome of getting a better understanding of the IT solution and the impact on the business value that it delivers. Consistent with the ideas of managing IT to maximize business value, you want to develop early estimates of the business value dials and how they would be measured, and then use this information as supporting data for the success of proof of concepts or pilots and feed it back into the decision process.

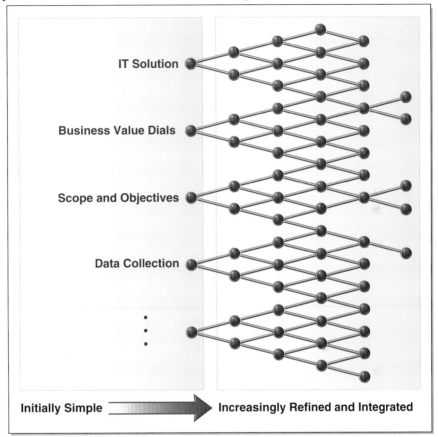

Figure 5.1 Refining the Metrics Plan

Description of the IT Solution

An early section of a metrics plan should include specific details of the IT solution. All relevant information should be spelled out. This information is typically available in documents associated with the IT solution. Examples of what might be spelled out are as follows:

■ Is this IT solution part of a larger program?

■ How is this solution related to the roll-out of similar IT solutions?

■ What is the primary driver behind deploying the IT solution?

■ What is the scope of the IT solution? Is the solution to be used in a single department or across the entire enterprise?

This section should contain enough information to allow comparisons to existing metrics plans for completed studies. There are two reasons for making this description rich and complete:

1. We want to assess independent contributions to overall business value so that we can safely add these contributions together without counting the same contribution twice.

2. We also want to capitalize on studies examining the impact of similar technologies to avoid duplication of work required in documenting the metrics plan.

Migrating to Broadband: Collecting Data in a Phased Approach

The remote connectivity team had a roadmap for IT services they managed and provided to Intel employees; part of this strategy was to determine the cost effectiveness of the services provided. In the early stages of the investigation existing data was reviewed to determine DUN usage vs. broadband in conjunction with VPN, and if a value opportunity existed. The next phase was a proof of concept that refined financial assumptions from the initial investigation, collected additional data, and developed supporting business processes. The final phase was solution roll-out and data collection to verify the outcome against the forecasted ROI.

Identifying and Defining Business Value Dials

Getting the business value dials identified that the IT solution will impact and figuring out how to make the link from IT solution to business value dials is critical. When working to identify the business value dials that will be impacted by the IT solution, the study designers should prepare an inventory of all information and data available for the IT solution.

One of the first steps is to gather and review any information on the IT solution's ROI that has already been completed, either by finance or the IT project manager. However, keep in mind that not all projects will come with fully developed ROIs. Also, keep in mind that this ROI is considered preliminary, with the final ROI being developed after rigorous business value measurements.

In preparing the inventory, we review current information, looking for various items that could help determine how accurate the ROI information is for the project. The initial review starts with some basic questions:

- What is the source and age of the data?
- How was the data collected and stored in the system of record?
- Who owns the data and who was responsible for data quality?
- What controls were applied when collecting the data and how often is it updated?
- What business decisions have been made that depend on the data?

We found that asking about business decisions based on the data to be most illuminating. If no one can answer this question, or if the data in question is only one component of the decision making, then more data and more work will be required. The key idea here is to make sure that any information feeding a business value ROI is reliable and valid.

Migrating to Broadband: Identifying Business Value Dials

There were two key business value dials in this study, the cost of DUN resources and the value of increased productivity for employees who migrated to the broadband system.

Cost avoidance: Reduce the number of DUN users who connect for long periods of time and decrease DUN consumption (dial-up time spent connected to the network).

Employee Productivity: Minimize the time spent uploading and downloading from the network by using faster broadband data transfer rates and reduce the number of disconnections during network sessions.

It is important to understand that business value dials can interact. For example, employee satisfaction can interact with employee productivity, either positively or negatively. In addition, a single business value dial can generate more than one operational definition, as Figure 5.2 illustrates. To operationally define employee productivity, each measured task must be defined and the data from all tasks aggregated into a single metric. Also, since operational definitions include how and when business value dials are to be measured, it is not uncommon for this process to uncover legacy data. A comprehensive metrics plan has all this information identified.

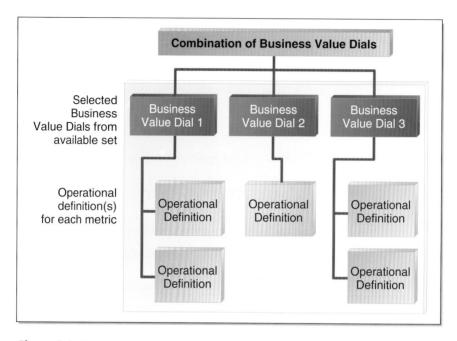

Figure 5.2 Business Value: A Combination of Factors

Business value dials are used in combination and it is important to consider the development of a set of metrics. Design the combination of business value dials and operation definitions to cover the main areas of value delivery. A key idea behind developing a comprehensive plan is to ensure that the best combination of relevant metrics is identified and defined for measurement. An excellent and highly readable discussion on developing families of metrics can be found in Harbour (1997).

How many business dials?

In the course of doing the work to decide which business value dials to measure, be aware that there are often many more items to measure than can be measured. In deciding what to measure, consider which business value dials will capture the greatest return for the effort expended in the measurement process. We found that around two to four business value dials typically captured the majority of value for an IT solutions and that identifying additional dials quickly reached a point of diminishing returns.

Once the study architect has reviewed the available data and made a first pass at selecting appropriate business value dials, it is time to review them with the stakeholders—representatives of the customer, finance, and the business value assessment team. Agreement is needed that the business value dials identified are accurate and will capture the business value impact of the IT solution.

When the business dials have been identified, then operational definitions can be constructed, tested, and reviewed by the stakeholders. The metrics plan should include these operational definitions along with notes about where and when these measures will be taken.

Migrating to Broadband: Study Scope

The team began by assuming that not every employee would be a good candidate for migration from DUN. For example, broadband options are limited in some regions and travel might necessitate DUN usage. The study was done internationally across all major regions; this included cost data in the forecast ROI. The solution was more than just IT and required business process changes and employee education; this work was also included in the scope of the study. For example, the IT organization shifted DUN billing from a fixed cost to a pay-per-view model.

Study Scope and Objectives

Metrics plans should clearly define the scope of the business value evaluation to avoid confusion and miscommunication with key stakeholders. For example, the IT solution might be deployed internationally, but the evaluation will only focus on a single geographical region. Part of setting the scope and objectives included addressing the following items:

■ Major areas the study will address and, equally importantly, areas that the study will not address.

■ Which business processes that are either impacted by or supported by the IT solution will and will not be included as part of the study.

■ Locations where the study will be conducted along with a discussion of the technical or resource constraints that were considered when choosing locations.

■ Hardware and software (*i.e.*, the system bundle) that will be included in the evaluation, and agreements or partnerships with third-party providers, if any. Product features selected for testing should be tied directly to customer requirements.

■ Expectations held by Finance, Customer, IT, and the study's appraisal team. These expectations should align with the choice of business value dials.

■ All uses of the data when the study is complete. For example, will the data inform a particular IT deployment? Will the data also be published externally?

Locating a measure that the IT system impacts directly is often the main factor in determining the best metric. In a chain of events, impacting one variable may also impact others, but the first variable is often the easiest to measure. For example, with software applications, productivity (*i.e.*, improved time to perform a task) is often the easiest variable to measure because it is the first one directly impacted by the application. In other cases, the availability of data for a particular variable may guide the decision to measure it. For example, if data on factory output is automatically recorded, that variable might be a good candidate for measurement.

Data Collection Techniques

Data collection techniques constitute another section in the metrics plan. In the early versions of the metrics plan, the data collection methods might not be fully understood. This is generally acceptable in the early stages of developing the metrics plan or when the evaluation itself is for an IT solution that is a proof of concept or pilot. However, as new information is learned, I encourage you to update and refine the data collection descriptions in the metrics plan.

Use existing data whenever possible. We found that there are typically a number of systems in place to track indicators related to or that are affected by IT solutions. For example, days of inventory or the time it takes to perform routine maintenance on a piece of equipment can usually be obtained in a system of record. Be sure to evaluate the quality of the data used in a system of record.

The link between data and the IT solution must be clearly stated in the metrics plan. The link must be explicitly called out so that the connection between the IT solution and changes in the system of record data can be established. If the IT solution cannot be explicitly linked to the data, it is possible that the IT solution might have an impact, but that the impact won't be reflected in the system of record. While this might seem obvious, we found that it is often overlooked. Access to data does not guarantee access to the right data.

Include in the metrics plan the name of the individual or group that owns the data and include the information they provide about the validity and reliability of the data. The data owner needs to be responsible and be accountable for the data being provided as part of the evaluation.

Migrating to Broadband: Data Collection Techniques

The study used two major data collection techniques to determine the business value, server based activity logs and field studies. The IT department upgraded the DUN system to make it easier to collect data; including items like modem speed, total data uploaded, total data downloaded, and total connection time.

The server data was used to calculate thresholds for different regions to identify the "tipping point" for migration. For example, in Asia, the average cost of broadband was $34/month and the average cost of DUN was $0.07/minute. Simple division shows that DUN users who are online for more than 468 minutes/month should move to the broadband system simply to lower the cost of connectivity.

A field study was done to develop estimates of the impact to employees that result from getting disconnected. This part of the study measured the number of weekly disconnections (session terminations) for three different types of connections used by employees when working from home to determine average recovery time and frequency of occurrence.

Employee Productivity and the Metrics Plan

When employee productivity evaluation is part of the metrics plan, then include and explain the purpose of each data collection technique. Early drafts of the metrics plan may indicate that on-the-job observations are to be conducted first and that an experiment is planned with employees performing typical tasks. Later versions of the metrics plan should contain detailed descriptions of tasks to be measured based on initial data gathering efforts. For more information on measuring employee productivity see Chapter 4.

Measurement Timeline

Every metrics plan needs a project schedule and timeline. In addition to understanding that both baseline and post-implementation data is

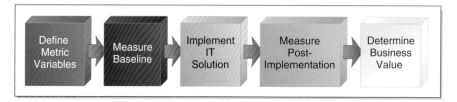

Figure 5.3 The Measurement Process

required, document the timeline of when this data will be collected using the selected techniques. Figure 5.3 shows the basic sequence of events for the measurement process.

It is important that the baseline and post-implementation data collection requirements be clearly outlined with dates, locations, expectations, and any requirements for the key stakeholders. We found that the timing of these activities can vary from situation to situation. For example, if the introduction of the new IT solution results in the removal of the current system, baseline measures must be captured prior to introduction. If, however, the two systems are deployed at the same time, it is possible to collect both data sets at the same time. In both cases, the differences between these data sets, when integrated with other data, provide the basis for identifying the IT solution's overall business value. The same basic sequences of steps can be used to evaluate pilot tests, proof of concept experiments, as well as, enterprise-wide deployments.

Baseline Measurement

A critical step in measuring the business value of an IT solution is to capture a current performance baseline. Baseline data establishes a benchmark for current performance that is used to establish the difference between baseline performance and post-implementation performance. As noted, multiple techniques such as analyzing system-of-record data, performance metrics, surveys, and semi-structured interviews can all be used to collect baseline data.

It is important to take baseline measurements under conditions that match as closely as possible the conditions under which the post-solution measurements will be taken, regardless of the IT solution or business value dials being quantified. When measuring individual workers, the working environment of the people being measured is a factor in selecting the right approach. For example, when assessing the impact of a new design tool on the engineering design process, be sure to take both the baseline and the post-solution measurements from the same phase in the product development process. Similarly, any experiments in the retail industry would need to control for seasonality, which is a powerful variable in that industry and many other industries as well.

Ideally, conduct baseline measurements before doing post-implementation measurements. In some instances, however, the IT solution might already be implemented; with the previous system removed it might be difficult or impossible to directly measure the baseline condition. In these cases, one of the following five options can potentially overcome this problem:

- Take the baseline measurement on another group that is still using the older, legacy system and whose job tasks closely match those of the post-implementation group.

- Ask participants in the post-implementation condition to simulate how they performed tasks previously and measure the simulated behavior.

- Construct an experiment that recreates the baseline condition, and then measure how individuals complete tasks in that situation.

- Obtain data from databases or other repositories that can be used to determine or approximate the baseline condition.

- Ask people in the post-implementation group to estimate the time it took to do the tasks. This option is the least desirable method because of inherent limitations with self-reported data.

If you can't use any of these approaches, it might be that you simply can't obtain baseline data. In these cases it is very hard, if not impossible, to make solid statements about the business value of an IT solution.

Migrating to Broadband: Baseline and Post-Implementation Data

The study used a system upgrade to track data before and after implementation. Since the IT department upgraded the DUN system it was easier to collect and document usage data. The upgraded nodes allowed for direct comparisons on the same data from the baseline and post-implementation. In this case, the conditions between the baseline and post-implementation are identical in all regards, except for the IT solution.

When measuring baselines, it is important to test the assumption of a 100 percent end-user adoption rate in performing tasks supported by the new IT solution. For example, we calculated an average frequency of occurrence for new tasks, and in combination with the size of the total population, calculated time saved. We found that some evaluations are more complex and that using this approach can result in overestimating the business value of the IT solution.

It follows that any new method for accomplishing tasks will not achieve a 100 percent adoption rate in most cases, even if the new method is more efficient than the old method. Therefore, the task method adoption rate needs to be taken into account so as to not overestimate the benefit. I suggest factoring in end-user adoption rates for IT solutions as a standard part of your metrics plan.

Multiple Baseline Conditions

We discovered that, in some situations, people use a variety of methods to perform a particular task. This is often the case for tasks that involve long sequences of activities to accomplish a goal, resulting in the potential for multiple baseline conditions. I recommend using one of the following processes to address multiple baseline conditions:

1. Identify the different methods that people use to accomplish each task and determine whether individuals stick to one method or use more than one method to perform a task.

2. Measure how long it takes to perform the task with each of the methods.

3. If individuals stick to one method, then calculate the percentage of people who utilize each of the task's methods.

4. If individuals use more than one method, then calculate the percentage of the time each person spends with each method.

However you plan to acquire baseline data, include a description in the metrics plan.

Post-implementation Measurements

After implementing the IT solution, the post-implementation measurements for the same business value dials are taken. The baseline and post-implementation data sets are then compared to determine the differences. As much as possible, conditions for the post-implementation measurements should match those of the baseline. Our goal is to defend the assumption that the new IT solution is the independent variable responsible for changes in value for the business dials.

To illustrate this concept, let's say we are comparing the impact of an IT solution on the time it takes to perform a preventive maintenance

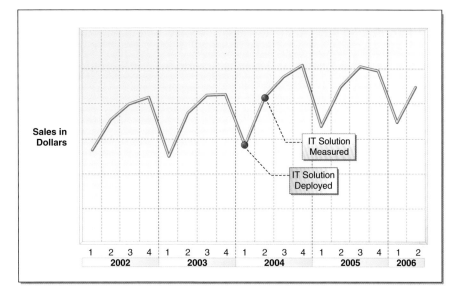

Figure 5.4 Sales Cycles and Business Value Measurement

procedure on a piece of equipment in a factory. We must measure the same procedure on the same piece of equipment, at the same phase in the manufacturing process, with the same type of factory worker. If we're comparing cycle time in a bottleneck area of the manufacturing process, we want to take our baseline and post-solution measurements from the same phase of the manufacturing process to provide a useful comparison.

Similarly, when looking at software engineering or hardware engineering design groups, it's important to take baseline and post-implementation measurements from the same phase of the development process. To understand the impact of a new design tool that speeds up the design review process, we must take baseline and post-solution measurements from the same stages that are impacted by the IT solution.

Consider the following example to help explain the idea behind this concept. The retail industry operates under a highly cyclical sales cycle. Depending on when an IT solution is deployed in this context and what business value dials are impacted; a positive or negative result could be shown based solely on the timing of the data collection (See Figure 5.4). These concerns cannot be overstated. See the discussion of confounding variables on page 86 for a principled discussion in the context of experimental design.

Aligning Measurement with IT Rollout

It is also critical to ensure measurement activities remain tightly aligned with the IT solution rollout. The timeline for measurement activities is determined based on a number of considerations.

■ When is the IT solution first available for pilot testing and when will it be deployed more widely? From this a timeline for collecting the baseline data can be determined.

■ How difficult will it be for employees to learn to use the new IT solution and how long will it take before their performance stabilizes? The answer to this question may require a pilot study.

■ Are there any business conditions that would limit when data can be collected? For example, it is difficult or impossible to collect data from Finance when they are trying to close the books to report corporate earnings.

Timeline Dependencies

In the process of developing the study's timeline, dependencies will emerge and should be flagged for careful review. Typical risks include the timely rollout of the IT solution, access to end-users, and business driven considerations.

For example, in one of our studies, a voice over IP (VoIP) project in a manufacturing area, we were unable to gather data because the phones did not work as planned. And then we discovered that some people were using their own cell phones for the same tasks that would have been impacted using the VoIP phones. Even if the VoIP phones had worked as planned, we would not have been able to assess the VoIP impact because the evaluation was confounded by the other phones.

In another example, we had to depend upon an intermediate group to gain access to the population of employees we needed to measure to establish a performance baseline. This intermediate group did not provide the team with a sufficient number of names and were slow in getting the names they did provide. As a result, the majority of the employees had already installed the post-implementation software application, disqualifying them from participating in the baseline data gathering activities.

Evaluation Locations

The metrics plan should include a list of locations where data will be collected and the reasons for choosing those locations. Common reasons include limits set by the IT deployment plan, availability of support for the IT solution, availability of end users, location of the data collection team, and location of the target end-users.

When conducting productivity studies, the type of data collection will affect location. For laboratory studies, the location of labs will play a significant role in the overall evaluation plan. Field studies, in contrast, take the observer to the workplace and should allow for wider sampling at more locations.

Documenting the Study Design

The metrics plan should also document the key elements of your study design. Here is a checklist of topics to be addressed.

- *Experimental design*: For productivity experiments, identify the independent and dependent variables and discuss whether the experiment is a within-groups or between-groups design. Our most common design is a within-groups comparison of baseline and post-implementation performance.

- *Employee segmentation*: Identify the criteria used to categorize and target participants in the study. Show how segments align with the business value dials and the target population for deployment of the IT solution.

- *Employee sampling plans*: Explain how sampling will assure that the results are broad based, representative, and thus generalizable to the population at large. A stratified random sampling plan is best when measuring productivity impacts on employees.

- *Data sampling plans:* Indicate whether all available data will be analyzed or whether using a subset is planned. When existing data is available but expensive to obtain or analyze, it is best to randomly select a sample of that data.

- *Mitigation of extraneous events:* Include procedures for avoiding unusual or extraneous events during baseline and post-implementation measurement periods. Plan and be aware of other projects that may impact employee performance and confound the research.

- *Participant recruitment*: Describe the recruitment process and allocate time to develop recruiting materials such as Web-based screening tools.

- *Identification of all user activities*: From the user's point of view, identify all the activities expected. Activities might include filling out surveys, performing tasks in the laboratory, or simply conducting one's daily work while IT usage is monitored or the employee is observed. For additional information on how to conduct a task analysis see *User and Task Analysis for Interface Design* by Hactos and Redish (1998).

- *Identification of user tasks:* Provide operational definitions of the tasks that users will perform. Identify which data collection methods will be used to measure performance on these tasks.

- *Prioritization of user tasks:* Sort tasks by their frequency of use and identify the most important tasks to measure. Consider the speed as well as error rates and include an evaluation of the cost of an error. A prioritized list of tasks included in the metrics plan will help to decide which tasks should be measured and which should not.

- *Categorization of tasks:* Analyze the degree of structure for tasks. Highly structured tasks are relatively easy to measure because they often have low variability. In contrast, a less-structured tasks are often highly variable, difficult to represent as procedures, and difficult to measure. Both categories should be included if at all possible.

This portion of the metrics plan contains the core of the measurement process. It cannot be written in a single draft, but must evolve as more information is gathered. Moreover, some of these items, such as descriptions of sampling plans and recruitment procedures, improve as they are reviewed and incorporated in subsequent metrics plans.

Required Team Members

Most evaluations will require skills that are outside the ITBV team. It is important to list all the required resources in order to make the metrics plan successful. This section should list all the team members and skills needed to support the evaluation, the role they will play during the evaluation, and what level of support is expected.

Migrating to Broadband: Financial Analysis of DUN Investment

The financial analysis carries forward actual data collected for Year 1 to Years 2 and 3 to estimate the business value over three years. Using the Year 1 reduction data provides a conservative scenario for the 3-year NPV since it assumes no additional reduction in DUN usage. Note that the NPV is not tax adjusted.

The employee productivity benefit—time saved due to faster data transfer and fewer disconnections, less the new time spent connected via broadband—is shown in the total time saved and with a 50% adjustment applied. After taking all project and support costs into account, the business value for this IT solution is $14.3 million.

Financial Analysis of DUN Investment

Benefits	Year 1	Year 2	Year 3
Cost Avoidance			
Americas: Users removed from DUN	913	913	913
Americas: Cost Savings/User/Year	$ 216	$ 216	$ 216
Europe: Users removed from DUN	590	590	590
Europe: Cost Savings/User/Year	$ 348	$ 348	$ 348
Asia: Users removed from DUN	1,018	1,018	1,018
Asia: Cost Savings/User/Year	$ 360	$ 360	$ 360
Financial Benefit (cost avoidance)	$ 769,008	$ 769,008	$ 769,008
Employee Productivity			
Annual Productivity Benefit	$10,092,624	$10,092,624	$10,092,624
Annual Productivity Benefit X 0.5	$ 5,046,312	$ 5,046,312	$ 5,046,312
Total Benefit	$ 5,815,320	$ 5,815,320	$ 5,815,320
Project Costs			
Installation Costs (total)	$ (289,082)	$ -	$ -
Project Management Cost	$ (519,150)	$ (519,150)	$ (519,150)
Total Cost by Year	$ (808,232)	$ (519,150)	$ (519,150)
Business Value			
Net Business Value	$ 5,007,088	$ 5,296,170	$ 5,296,170
Present Value (discount rate of 15%)	$ 5,007,088	$ 4,773,176	$ 4,491,524
3 yr. Net Present Value	$14,271,788		

Table 5.1   Typical ITBV Project Schedule

Evaluation Activity	Start Date	End Date
Develop test plan	WW30	WW32
Select user segments for testing	WW31	WW31
Conduct planning/goals meeting with stakeholders	WW31	WW31
Develop test tasks	WW31	WW32
Develop task scenarios for lab testing	WW31	WW32
Develop collateral materials for test scenarios	WW32	WW32
Develop questionnaires	WW32	WW32
Develop integration strategy with HW/SW	WW32	WW32
Complete experimental design and validate	WW32	WW32
Complete sampling plan and recruitment process	WW32	WW33
Secure HW/SW	WW32	WW32
Develop measurement criteria	WW32	WW32
Schedule participants	WW31	WW32
Prepare test materials	WW32	WW32
Set up the lab for testing	WW32	WW33
Pilot test	WW32	WW32
Conduct the evaluation	WW33	WW33
Organize, summarize and analyze data	WW33	WW34
Prepare Report	WW34	WW34

Review Data and Determine ROI

It is important to clearly outline in a metrics plan the work required to complete the ROI within the metrics plan. This will help ensure that this critical step is not overlooked and it keeps everyone cognizant that the final result of data collection is determining the business value of the IT solution.

Exceptions Should be Noted

No two evaluations are identical and you should list any aspect of an evaluation that is unusual, noting any exceptions to how you would normally conduct the evaluations, and any other aspect of the evaluation that the team feels should be captured for reference. For example, if the evaluation is being done within a very short timeframe, and it impacts the scope of the evaluation, it should be captured in the plan and the impact or potential impact on the evaluation documented.

Generate a Detailed Project Schedule

In addition to a timeline and details regarding the study design, the metrics plan should include a detailed schedule. Table 5.1 offers an example of a business value study that began on work week 30 and ended four weeks later. Notice how all of the tasks are running in parallel to some degree. This is a sure signal that careful planning and monitoring is required.

Metrics Plan Challenges

For the remainder of this chapter, I want to step back from the details of the metrics plan and the business value study to reflect on larger issues. In describing the elements of a metrics plan, I was detailed and prescriptive. Metrics plan challenges is a more theoretical discussion aimed at helping readers embed the metrics plan in a larger context.

Business Process vs. Employee Task

Employee productivity can fundamentally be measured at two levels, process improvements and task improvements, as shown in Figure 5.5. When looked at this way, process improvements are at the macro level and task improvements are at the micro level. Business process improvements show productivity improvements at the organizational level and employee productivity improvements show improvement at the employee or task level.

Many situations require that measurement start at the employee or task level with data that is then aggregated to the process or workgroup level. While the task and employee are not necessarily equal, we typically measure employees accomplishing a task using an IT solution. You can't measure a task without measuring an employee. However, a process can be measured, can cut across multiple individual workers, and can be quantified without measuring individual employees.

For example, it would be possible to measure the impact of an IT solution on an order fulfillment process without necessarily measuring the individual workers involved in the process. In this example, there is still a reduction in either the time it takes an employee to complete a task, tasks have been automated, or task have been removed to get the improvement. This example assumes that a process level metric is available for the time to fulfill an order. When this is not available, you would need to measure the individual tasks that make up the process and then aggregate this data to determine the improvement in the order fulfillment process.

For other situations it might not be possible to measure the process as outlined above. For example, when measuring the effects of a new team software solution that facilitates meeting management, there is no process timeline like the one for the time it takes to complete the order fulfillment process. Meetings may have "steps," but the odds are that not all steps are required. It is this type of situation that fits the framework in

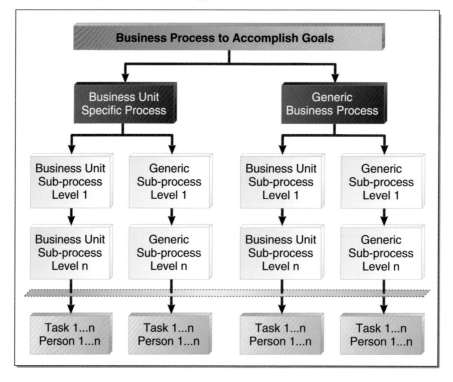

Figure 5.5 Disaggregating Business-Level Processes into Employee Tasks

Figure 5.5. To measure process improvements in meeting management, the best location for the measurement activity is going to be at the individual or task level. The final measurement of the process and any associated improvements will be the combination of the individual measurements and any system processing time (*e.g.*, data handling, routing, approvals).

At the core of this approach is the idea that IT solutions impact individual workers and it is those impacts that are most measurable. However, the real business value of the solution might best be captured by showing the impact on the process that is improved by the IT solution, not by showing it at the individual or task level. Many eBusiness applications that automate transactions and data handling fall into this category.

Cumulative Benefit Calculation in a Multi-Year Program: Program vs. Project

Not all IT solutions are single-deployment models. In fact, many IT initiatives are multi-year programs that roll out as a series of projects, as shown in Figure 5.6. In order to measure these programs properly, a model is needed that accounts for multiple deployments over time and ensures that the right baseline is used when determining the impact.

Productivity improvements can be viewed along a continuum: as a single implementation in time or as multiple deployments as part of a solution. If the solution spans multiple products or projects, the productivity improvement for the solution is the cumulative impact of all the implementations.

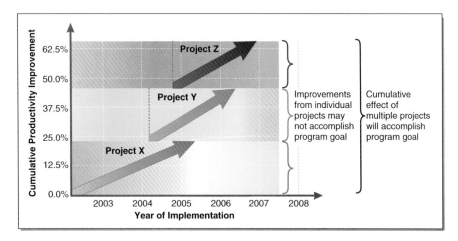

Figure 5.6 Productivity Improvement over a Multi-year Program

Table 5.2 Equations for Cumulative Productivity Measurement

The productivity change (P_{0-1}) due to Project X comparing IT Solution 1 and IT Solution 0 can be given as: $\quad P_{0-1} = (T_0 - T_1)/T_0$ $\hspace{3cm}$ (Equation 1)   where T_1 is the average task completion time for all the tasks using IT Solution 1 and T_0 is the average task completion time for all the tasks using IT Solution 0.
Equation 1 implies that: $\quad T_1/T_0 = 1 - P_{0-1}$ $\hspace{3cm}$ (Equation 2)
Similarly, the productivity change (P_{1-2}) due to Project Y comparing IT Solution 2 and IT Solution 1 can be given as: $\quad P_{1-2} = (T_1 - T_2)/T_1$ $\hspace{3cm}$ (Equation 3) $\quad T_2/T_1 = 1 - P_{1-2}$ $\hspace{3cm}$ (Equation 4)   where T_2 is the average task completion time for all the tasks using IT Solution 2 and T_1 is the average task completion time for all the tasks using IT Solution 1.
The productivity change (P_{2-3}) due to Project Z comparing IT Solution 3 and IT Solution 2 can be given as: $\quad P_{2-3} = (T_2 - T_3)/T_2$ $\hspace{3cm}$ (Equation 5) $\quad T_3/T_2 = 1 - P_{2-3}$ $\hspace{3cm}$ (Equation 6)   where T_3 is the average task completion time for all the tasks using IT Solution 3 and T_2 is the average task completion time for all the tasks using IT Solution 2.
The productivity improvement for the overall program can be measured as: $\quad P_{0-3} = (T_0 - T_3)/T_0$ $\hspace{3cm}$ (Equation 7) $\qquad = 1 - (T_3/T_0)$ $\qquad = 1 - [(T_1/T_0) \times (T_2/T_1) \times (T_3/T_2)]$ $\qquad = 1 - [(1 - P_{0-1}) \times (1 - P_{1-2}) \times (1 - P_{2-3})]$ $\hspace{1cm}$ (Equation 8)

For example, assume that an IT Program consists of three projects in succession involving three IT solutions. Consider the following:

■ The baseline for Project X with Solution 1 is Solution 0 (*i.e.*, the baseline or current state).

■ The baseline for Project Y with Solution 2 is Solution 1.

■ The baseline for Project Z with Solution 3 is Solution 2.

The assumption is that the Project X, Project Y and Project Z occur in series, but not in parallel. Given this, there could be three productivity measurement activities:

1. Comparing Solution 1 with Solution 0.

2. Comparing Solution 2 with Solution 1.

3. Comparing Solution 3 with Solution 2 at the end of Project X, Project Y, and Project Z, respectively.

The productivity gain for Project X, moving from Solution 0 to Solution 1 is labeled as P_{0-1}. The productivity gain for Project Y, moving from Solution 1 to Solution 2 is labeled as: P_{1-2}, and the productivity gain for Project Z, moving from Solution 2 to Solution 3 is labeled as P_{2-3}. The equations for calculating productivity gains are shown in Table 5.2.

Table 5.3   Hypothetical Example of Cumulative Gain for an IT Program

Project	Pre (Time in Minutes)	Post (Time in Minutes)	Improvement (In Percentage)
X	1000 (T_0)	800 (T_1)	20% (P_{0-1})
Y	800 (T_1)	720 (T_2)	10% (P_{1-2})
Z	720 (T_2)	540 (T_3)	25% (P_{2-3})
Overall	1000 (T_0)	540 (T_3)	46% (P_{0-3})

If the productivity changes due to Project X, Project Y, and Project Z are gains of 20 percent, 10 percent and 25 percent respectively, as shown in Table 5.3, then $P_{0-1} = 0.20$, $P_{1-2} = 0.10$ and $P_{2-3} = 0.25$. Using equation 8 from Table 5.2 leads to the following:

$$P_{0-3} = 1 - [(1 - P_{0-1}) \times (1 - P_{1-2}) \times (1 - P_{2-3})]$$

$$= 1 - (0.80 \times 0.90 \times 0.75)$$

$$= 0.46 \text{ or } 46\%$$

This same formula can be used even if there is a productivity loss. For example, as shown in Table 5.4, what would be the overall productivity change for a series of projects in an IT program is made up of Project X, Project Y and Project Z with a gain of 20 percent, a loss of 10 percent and a gain of 25 percent, respectively?

determine the best approach to value an IT solution that impacts employee productivity.

How to calculate the value of employee productivity

Whenever possible, connect IT-enhanced employee productivity to other business value dials that have a more direct link to the enterprise bottom line. Some of these measures include:

- Reduction in cycle time
- Headcount reductions
- Increase in output

Increases in employee productivity can also affect quality measures that have an impact on the company's bottom line. For example, decreasing the number of employees who are overwhelmed with tasks will likely result in their making fewer mistakes, which might result in a reduction in the amount of scrap or material that requires rework.

Time savings

In our experience, people typically overestimated time savings. In one case, self-reported estimates from a survey were more than double the measured time savings. In another instance, self-reported survey data was approximately four times the measured benefit.

Unfortunately, many IT project managers are unaware of these limitations and use survey data to make unrealistic employee productivity claims. On occasion, this shortcoming has led upper management to quickly dismiss the credibility of employee productivity data.

Bottom-line increases rely on a basic formula:

$$Profit = Revenue - Expenses$$

To have any impact on the bottom line, IT solutions must affect either revenue or expenses. As IT solutions enable decreases in labor and capital, value can be derived from the value of the labor and capital saved. Alternatively, as IT solutions tools help generate more revenue with the same amounts of capital and labor, the value of the tools is the increased revenue and corresponding profits.

We often use the valuation strategy discussed in Chapter 4, *i.e.*, multiplying time savings by the employee burden rate, a rate that reflects all the increased costs incurred if one more employee is hired: salary, benefits, training, and travel expense.

In the ITBV program, we apply a discount factor to compensate for what I call a general employee productivity metric (*e.g.*, when employee productivity cannot be reliably linked to other tangible business value dials). Valuing general or corporate-wide productivity gains as employee-time saved multiplied by the average burden rate can overestimate the short-term value of the gains, as this approach doesn't fully capture the use and context of the time savings. For example, if IT saves every non-task-oriented employee 15 minutes per day, what is that worth? How do we properly value 15 minutes? Is it worker-, task-, or tool-specific? How do we isolate other variables?

Let's consider introducing an IT solution that reduces the design cycle by 10 percent. This can be quantified in a number of ways. The first is to simply value it using the general employee productivity method discussed above. While this number will show benefit and is a direct measure of the change, it is also the least interesting. Can the time saved be linked to faster time to market? If so, how will this be done? Perhaps it can't be linked to time to market because another bottleneck exists in the overall process. Is the time reinvested in the design? If the time saved as a result of the improvements is used to refine the design or conduct additional testing, it might show up in a quality indicator. Is it possible to link the improvement to fewer engineering change orders (ECO) after product shipment? ECOs are costly, and reducing them will have a direct impact on the bottom-line. This example highlights the concept of direct and indirect measurement. Direct measurement is observing and quantifying the immediate metric of interest: employee productivity. The indirect measurement is determining how that time manifests itself in other metrics.

Context-specific considerations

One approach to valuing employee productivity solutions is to look separately at solutions targeted at three general types of workers: structured-task workers, specific-knowledge workers, and the corporate-wide population.

Structured-task workers

Valuing productivity improvements for employees in task-oriented or structured positions is, in concept, quite simple. In fact, the industrial engineering discipline has been developing and refining techniques in

Where Does the Time Go?

When a new process is put into place and studies indicate that employees can do an hour's work in 45 minutes, then where does the 15 minutes of "free time" go? Ian Campbell, CEO of Nucleus Research, believes that knowledge workers are less likely to convert that time into additional work when compared to employees with more highly structured jobs. Conversion efficiency is the percentage of time applied to additional work.

Type of Worker	Conversion Efficiency
Assembly line workers	95-100%
Call center support	90-95%
Administrative and support help	70-80%
Engineering (technical)	75%
Engineering (non-technical)	65-75%
General staff within a group (marketing, PR, accounting)	60%

Use this table to establish discounting factors for applications that save time for different kinds of workers.

this space for over 100 years; admittedly not all of this time has been focused on what we have been calling IT solutions. In situations with highly structured work, such as a call center or assembly line, we can measure changes in worker output that result from IT solutions. For example, it's easy to measure the number of calls per hour, the number of orders processed, or the number of products assembled. Because of the structured nature of their jobs, we know the effects of providing task workers with more time. This productivity improvement can be translated to reduced time to complete tasks, directly into headcount reductions, or in the completion of additional tasks.

For example, the ITBV program valued an automated diagnostic tool that allowed factory workers to quickly identify production line problems. There were two effects on labor costs—fewer people were needed to diagnose assembly-line problems and worker idle time was reduced. In addition, the tool reduced the number of defective products we had to scrap. We valued that tool by the sum of the cost savings from reduced labor and scrap.

Specific knowledge workers

It is generally easier to value IT solutions for non-task-oriented workers than for enterprise-wide released tools. Knowing how additional time can be used before implementing an IT solution makes it easy to link its value to the bottom-line. This is the case when deploying an IT solution to a team or specific type of worker, when the IT solution is for a specific type of project, and when the value of the project is known.

For example, the ITBV team studied design teams who were using a new database containing detailed specifications of many previous products. When comparing this team to design teams who were not using the repository, two significant effects emerged: decreased labor weeks and a potentially increased market segment. The repository teams developed product designs using fewer engineering person-weeks. This result, in turn, allowed products to get to market more quickly and led to larger revenue streams. The business value for this project was the cost of saved labor plus the increased product income.

Corporate-wide population

Putting a value on corporate-wide employee productivity solutions is more difficult than assessing value gained for specific groups. Examples of corporate-wide productivity solutions are collaboration software, wireless LANs, and remote access. The bottom-line impact of knowledge worker productivity is inherently long term and indirect. It is more difficult to link people's labor (*i.e.*, time) to specific output (*i.e.*, work) in the short run.

The most straightforward way to value non-structured general employee productivity is to measure the time savings and then multiply that by the average burden rate for the employees using the IT solution. However, depending on the size of the impacted user segment, this approach can yield numbers that are unrealistically large when valuing enterprise-wide solutions. This is one of the reasons the ITBV program discounts corporate-wide productivity gains by 50 percent.

For instance, Intel provides most employees with remote access and notebook computers so they can take their computers home and to both onsite and offsite meetings. Employees also have access to wireless LANs. This mobility increases worker effectiveness, productivity, and the ability to work outside the office. As with corporate-wide collaboration tools, we value these productivity gains by measuring the increased time available for working multiplied by the labor burden rate, and discount it by 50 percent.

Looking ahead, corporate-wide productivity tools are likely to result in the need for fewer office workers to complete the same amount of work. These tools are also needed to keep labor expenses on a par with the competition. Thus, in the long term, the true value of incremental corporate productivity improvements significantly outweighs burden rates.

Additional considerations

Continuous and non-continuous timesaving. One reason for using a discount factor when valuing general employee productivity gains is to account for non-continuous time savings. Although we have not had an opportunity to collect data to support this idea, we suspect that productivity tools that save office workers a larger block of time are more valuable than those that save several smaller time segments, even though those smaller segments may add up to the same total block of time. In fact, there is a growing body of research on the detrimental effects of interruptions in the work place that is consistent with this line of thinking. See, for instance, Mark, Gonzalez, & Harris (2005).

For example, consider a productivity solution saving employees a 1-hour block once a week as opposed to a different solution saving employees 30 seconds, 120 times per week. The smaller segments of time freed up by the latter are more likely to be used up by non-essential activities that do not lead directly to bottom-line increases. Conversely, larger continuous time segments are more likely to be used in a productive manner that benefits the company. Therefore, when valuing productivity savings, it would make sense to discount smaller time segments more heavily.

Materiality is context-specific

The business value of employee productivity is specific to the context (*e.g.*, manufacturing, help desk, information worker), the type of employee, and the job. Figure 5.7 suggests that small gains in some contexts, such as manufacturing, may be valuable, but that the same gain in another context, such as for an information worker, either is not as valuable or is less easy to determine.

In task-oriented job functions, small gains may have large impacts, but for information workers, it's difficult to know what the smallest gain required is before it becomes meaningful. Within the manufacturing context, the value of gains in employee productivity, as measured through classic time and motion studies, will eventually level off as you

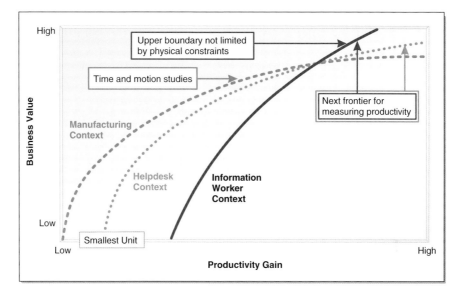

Figure 5.7 Context and Time

reach the physical limits of the manufacturing equipment. To get to the next big jump a breakthrough is needed in the manufacturing process.

With the information worker, however, there is no such constraint on the upper limit of the value that can be generated from the productivity gain. For example, freeing a sufficient amount of time for a design engineer might well contribute to the development of an innovative new product that may otherwise not have happened.

Context is a key consideration when measuring employee productivity. Saving a block of time for an employee in one context can have a very different value for one company than it would for a different company, depending on the employee's pay scale and how easily a particular employee could use the time to accomplish another task. Knowing how to accurately measure these various scenarios is the next frontier in measuring and determining the real business value of employee productivity gains.

Feature improvements vs. new solutions

When evaluating incremental improvements, discounting productivity time savings is also warranted. Often the extent of productivity gains depends on whether the IT solution is a new one that replaces a legacy system or an improved version of a current solution. For example, substantial productivity gains would be expected from replacing a fax-based order-entry system with one that's Web-based. On the other hand, minor enhancements to a Web-based order system may not show significant gains.

New versions of applications already in use often contain several small changes that add marginally to productivity. It may take a series of version changes before overall productivity improvement becomes impressive. For example, if a company is moving from an earlier office productivity package to the most current integrated office application suite, the gain in productivity is more perceptible than a move from the current version to a new version with minor updates of the same software. It's important to note, however, that if a company stops making incremental improvements in productivity tools, it will lose the smaller productivity gains and find the eventual necessary major upgrade more difficult to implement and to require increased training costs.

Productivity gains and the bottom line

Even in cases where a clear link between productivity solutions and financial metrics cannot be established, IT solutions may still have value. If an IT solution only addresses a small sample of workers at one point in a process, determining its full impact may be difficult, especially if the solution does not address bottlenecks in the process. However, additional implementations of the IT solution may result in new process improvements that can be linked to financial variables.

It is often not possible to immediately realize the full benefit of an implementation, as it may take time for people to learn how to use the technology effectively. There might be unanticipated new uses and new users for the technology that will yield greater value over time. As shown in Figure 5.8, to realize the full value of an IT solution, the IT ecosystem that the solution is deployed into must be part of the overall deployment model for an IT organization.

Where did the value go?

On occasion, an IT project produces little or no measurable financial benefits. Productivity benefits don't always translate into financial benefits, as financial valuations are made at an organizational level, while productivity improvements are made at the process level. Many variables come into play between the process and organizational levels, and in some cases, other variables can mask the benefits of productivity gains. If the IT solution was aimed at non-strategic processes, productivity

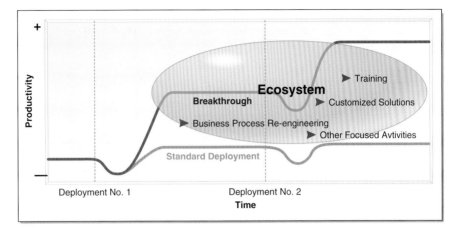

Figure 5.8 Managing the IT Ecosystem

gains might exist but not generate a significant financial benefit. In other cases, the IT solution may only partially support the work processes.

It is also the case that employee productivity can suffer if the IT solution doesn't match end-user needs. Employing a user-centered design approach that documents end-user activities impacted by the IT solution for the entire process can identify problems that are preventing productivity gains or financial benefits. Correcting these problems can trigger those benefits. Simply deploying a new solution will not guarantee productivity increases. For a solution to increase productivity it must support employee tasks, and those tasks in turn must support the business objectives. The fit between the task and technology is a key determinant to employee productivity (Goodhue and Thomson, 1995).

Companies often make decisions or investments that don't have an immediate impact on the bottom-line but are instead designed to increase output capacity for the future, when greater demand is expected. For instance, they make continued investments in building new manufacturing facilities even when demand is low so as to be ready for future upturns in demand. IT improvements that enable greater output capacity from each worker can be a similar strategy. For example, increasing the productivity of manufacturing workers during a non-constrained period may not have a financial impact until a later date when factories are operating at maximum capacity in a constrained environment.

Table 5.7 Structured Work and Structured Tasks

		Structure of the Tasks		
		Low	Med	High
Structure of the Work Setting	High	Though the work environment is highly structured, the task delivery does not follow a certain routine. (*e.g.*, customer call escalation)	The workplace is automated, but the task is not as routinized. (*e.g.*, call center jobs)	The user follows a precise routine in a work environment in which tasks are paced and automated by external systems. (*e.g.*, packaging of mother boards and circuits)
	Med	The nature of the job, its scope and impact, which determine the work environment, constantly change. There are some certain sets of processes and best-known methods to follow providing some task structure. (*e.g.*, middle managers)	Shifts in the market and the company affect the job demands. These knowledge workers make their work semi-deterministic. (*e.g.*, support organizations such as HR, Finance, Legal)	These workers participate in teams with projects ranging from months to a couple of years giving them a medium range of visibility and control over work. However they follow a high degree of standard engineering procedures to accomplish their goals. (*e.g.*, engineering computing and design)
	Low	Crisis management of sporadic issues for which there is no known solution or cause. Crises happen infrequently, but sometimes takes days to quell. (*e.g.*, executives and long-range planners)	Office administration is another job where the worker is pulled in different directions, but still follows determined steps to accomplish the goals. (*e.g.*, marketing administration)	These workers follow a standard routine to resolve issues, through they may not have any control as to when and how the problems arise. (*e.g.*, maintainers of chip manufacturing, test and assembly machines)

Finally, while the data collection tools covered so far allow for an objective approach to the quantification of employee productivity, there are still many issues. For example, we can't always make the connection between employee productivity and various financial aspects that might be modeled as part of the overall benefit to a company.

Some types of employee work are easier to measure than others. In some cases, it can be difficult to make a link between employee productivity and direct financial impacts.

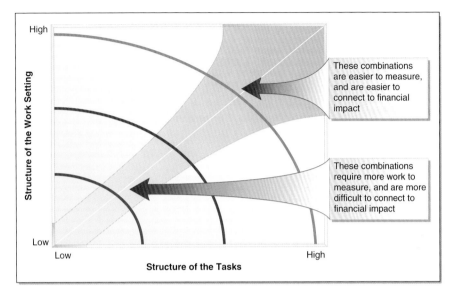

Figure 5.9 Employee Productivity Framework

Specifically, as Figure 5.9 shows, it's easier to measure and compare the highly structured work settings and tasks typically found in manufacturing environment than the often unstructured settings and tasks typically found among knowledge workers.

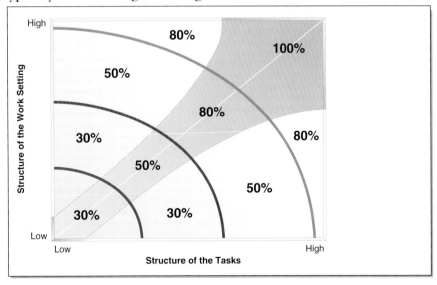

Figure 5.10 Suggested Employee Productivity Valuation

Figure 5.10 shows one approach Intel is exploring—that it might be possible to develop a systematic method by which the structure of the work and the structure of the work setting can be combined to determine the most appropriate discount factor. To do so would require a solid definition of the two concepts so that the framework could be used across a wide range of settings.

The examples in Table 5.7 represent one possible approach to defining the concepts from Figure 5.10 into a working model that could be used to categorize various types of jobs. This is similar to the approach suggested by Nucleus (See "Where Does the Time Go?" on page 138.).

Summary

A sound metrics plan is the backbone of an IT Business Value study. It is a living document that is augmented as new information is obtained. The metrics plan becomes a contract between the ITBV team and the stakeholders who oversee the project. While plans vary, we have identified the major sections in the plan and provided examples of the issues that should be discussed and agreed upon.

No magic formula exists for measuring business value. At Intel, we have established a framework for placing a value on employee time savings. By considering the context, defining which variables to measure, and insisting on baseline as well as post-implementation measures, we have established a credible process for gathering data. When we work with our Finance partners to establish the actual value to the corporation of these time savings, our consistently applied and robust data-gathering techniques provide strong evidence to support the value that we claim.

It is our intent, by sharing this information, to help our IT associates in the industry as they face the daunting task of placing value on the work performed by IT shops around the world on a daily basis.

Chapter 6

Launching a Business Value Program

Efficiency is doing things right; effectiveness is doing the right things.
—Peter F. Drucker

To inform an IT investment decision, a standalone business value study can provide important insights. However, to optimize the use of the IT budget calls for an ongoing program that systematically investigates IT and business value. This chapter outlines the essential building blocks of an effective business value program, advises how to assemble the necessary team, and offers suggestions for running the newly-launched program. The important ideas fall into three large domains, as follows:

- Business value and IT governance: Integrating the business value program with the IT organization and the overall management of the company.

- Building the ITBV team: Identifying the skill sets required to plan and execute ITBV projects on an ongoing basis.

- Tools and operating processes: Developing a methodology that is trusted, standardized, and efficient. This includes closing on standard business value dials and a definition of business value.

As I explore these domains, I shall include specific examples from Intel's Business Value program. Effective business value programs have essential components in common, including strong, clearly-defined management support, Finance department buy-in, and a dedicated business value team.

Over time, a program can develop an extensible, technology-independent framework with a standard methodology for measuring the business value of information technology. The ITBV team can develop processes and procedures to build a portfolio of business value studies that document the value delivered by information technology solutions. The effect of executing these activities the same way over time is that a firm-level metric of IT-enabled productivity develops over time. As more IT solutions are measured and stored in the portfolio of business value, the more the total IT contribution to the business is captured.

Business Value Programs and IT Governance

Strong senior management support is essential for an effective IT business value program. This support should come from the CIO on down. Without continual management support and accountability the program cannot succeed.

Accountability depends on clearly defined goals for the ITBV program. Corporate management must confirm the criteria that measure success and agree to factor the results of ITBV analysis into their strategic decision-making process. At the onset, many IT solutions are typically considered overhead costs that should be reduced or minimized. The ITBV team sets out to measure not only IT costs, but also tangible measures of business value attributable to IT investments.

Directives from Management

Typically, senior management sets forth the key governance principles upon which the ITBV program will be established. Here are four basic principles:

- All documented results must be certified by representatives from both IT finance and Customer finance.

- Results can come from direct cost savings, indirect cost savings, direct revenue, or indirect revenue. However these results have to be *customer facing*, that is, results that benefit the customer who made the investment. Results that improve internal IT productivity, for example, are not counted toward the goal.

- All projects must deploy new or incrementally improved IT solutions. The ITBV team will perform baseline measurements and post-measurements to calculate the actual impact of the IT solution.

- Business value contributions should only be counted once. Be sure that project contributions are clearly independent of one another.

Building an ITBV program often involves breaking new ground. If the team is not clear about what senior management expects to get out of the program, it can waste time chasing unproductive themes that do not turn out to align with what management actually wants. Undirected activity will result in slow progress, and eventually upper management will withdraw their support.

Setting Initial Goals and Objectives

Once senior management has outlined basic expectations, the next challenge is to create a statement of goals and objectives for the program. This statement provides purpose and focus and clearly defines the management support required. It also helps guide the day-to-day actions of the project team during the creation and operational phases of the program. Expect the statement of goals and objectives to be refined as senior management and the project team gain experience.

ITBV at Intel: Initial Goals and Objectives

After much iteration, the ITBV committee settled on the following:

IT Business Value Goals: Intel's IT to be an industry leader and influential in setting business value metrics standards. Intel to maintain its position as an industry leader and influence in setting business value metrics standard.

IT Business Value Objectives: Develop and embed throughout IT and Intel credible and repeatable business value measurement processes for IT products and services.

Forming the ITBV Project Team

I recommend launching an ITBV program in two steps. The first step is to create a startup team composed of with well-respected individuals within IT. Senior managers with experience in IT strategy, employee productivity, operational effectiveness, and finance are good candidates. Include individuals with a background in measurement and analysis of human behavior (*e.g.*, human factors engineers, industrial engineers, ethnographers). Ensure that at least some of these team members can continue when the startup team is disbanded, to ensure continuity as the program is started. The startup team needs to build the basic infrastructure for the program, establish an oversight committee, and form a dedicated ITBV program team to take over the project.

Here are the major tasks that the startup team must complete.

Create the Program Infrastructure

The startup team should define basic processes for getting the program up and running and begin to generate the high-level processes that will be needed to run the IT Business Value program. These definitions should include how the program will report results, how to determine which project to track as the program comes on line, and so on.

Establish a Program Oversight Committee

To secure ongoing support, determine who from the initial senior management team that is supporting the creation of the program will be on the management review committee (MRC) that will oversee the project by reviewing program goals and the status of the work. This initial group may not be the ongoing MRC. The ongoing MRC membership is best determined when the dedicated program team is assembled. However, the program oversight process needs to happen early to ensure ongoing support and to provide a forum for resolving issues related to getting the program up and running.

Verify Expectations

Although management expectations were initially defined, project goals and objectives outlined, and a skeleton MRC formed, it is prudent for the startup team to revisit and verify all key assumptions with senior management before forming the dedicated team. Senior management can pass day-to-day control over to the MRC when executives are confident that the program is launching as intended. We found that senior management changed their stance on issues from time to time as they gained more experience with business value measurement issues.

Form a Program Team

The startup team should then seed a dedicated program team with core representation from the startup team and having the same basic skill sets. This team will move into action when the startup team finishes and be responsible for carrying out the final implementation and day-to-day operation of the program.

It is important that the dedicated program team include members who worked on the startup team. This will enable a smooth transition to the operational model, provide a history of how the program evolved, and reduce rework as new members are brought onto the team. It is also important that the members who were on the startup team receive and incorporate feedback from the new team members.

The Dedicated Program Team

Once the basic framework for the program has been outlined by the startup team and approved by key stakeholders, the ITBV Program has to be staffed and the remaining process details completed so the program can begin to operate. Our dedicated team for this task consisted of representation from three groups: IT Finance, Human Factors Engineering, and IT project management.

The skeleton MRC that was set up during the startup phase was then filled out with additional representation. This expanded MRC was to approve the program's operational processes, the reporting structure, and the rules that govern the work. The MRC also would act as the final approval body for programs that would be counted toward the goal set by senior management.

Roles and Responsibilities

The dedicated program team should be headed by the *ITBV Program Manager* who oversees all projects, solves problems escalating from project teams, speaks for the ITBV program, communicates with the management chain, and manages MRC meetings. Larger ITBV programs might include an *ITBV Research Manager* to oversee measurement projects, ensuring that the measurement plans are scientifically sound and can stand up to rigorous analysis by the MRC. A Research Manager is the likely candidate to participate in industry forums or work with universities interested in studying the measurement of business value.

The research manager can also support the publication of reports and white papers that give further credibility to the work of the entire program team.

In our experience, we found that six roles needed to be filled with members of a dedicated program team to successfully complete each ITBV study. These roles are shown in Table 6.1 and described subsequently.

Table 6.1   Six Key Roles for Teams Conducting Business Value Studies

Customer	IT Project Manager (IT PM)	Business Value Project Manager (BV PM)
Human Factors Engineer (HFE)	IT Finance	Customer Finance

Customer.   The customer who intends to purchase the product, service, or solution will need to work with the IT organization to define the business value anticipated as a result of implementation. The BV PM consults with the customer and the IT PM to help define the appropriate variables and set goals. Also, to the extent that the customer has baseline data from reporting systems or other projects, the customer will need to make that information available to the team, review the results, and give feedback on the analysis process. Customers also participate in planning baseline and post-implementation measurement activities. Maintaining a good relationship with the customer is of central importance to the ITBV program team.

IT Project Manager.   The IT PM functions as the intermediary between the customer and the ITBV team. In particular, the IT PM is responsible for:

- Working with the customer to see that long-term product strategy and life cycle information is thoroughly delivered or obtained and that it is fully qualified, understood, and clearly communicated to the program team.

- Working with IT Finance to define the preliminary ROI estimate.

- Certifying that the ITBV team understands the technical aspects of the solution, along with the timeline and any potential challenges. In addition, the IT PM is responsible for describing all IT projects included in the IT solution that will be rolled out simultaneously or within a short period of time.

Communication skills are crucial for the person filling the IT PM role. If communication with the team breaks down, failure will ensue.

Business Value Project Manager. The BV PM has to pull it all together. The BV PM assists the IT PM with planning, setting strategies, and integrating project activities through the exploration, planning, development, and deployment phases of the program life cycle. The BV PM also works with customer and end-user groups to identify potential benefits and coordinates with the HFE team as it prepares its work, makes certain that design, development, data quality principles, testing, and deployment of solutions are in accordance with business needs. The BV PM ensures that IT Finance has all the data needed to develop the solution's financial results. Finally, the BV PM works with the customer and with IT Finance to validate the outcomes and monitor the actual results over time.

Human Factors Engineer. The HFE is responsible for collecting, calculating, and ultimately demonstrating the impact of what have been traditionally seen as soft—or intangible—benefits. The HFE supplies the objectivity needed to clearly define productivity improvements that IT delivers and to make those improvements tangible to the customer, the business units, and Finance group.

In addition to this work, the HFE provides overall guidance on the data collection methods. Most HFEs have a background in experimental design and analysis, which will prove to be invaluable in the development of an overall measurement approach and in defining the metrics plan for each IT solution studied.

IT Finance and Customer Finance. Finance manages the nuts and bolts of validating the financial assumptions and makes the final financial calculations of value delivered. Representatives from Finance keep IT PMs and the ITBV project focused on the value of pure cash. The typical ROI models—depreciation, net present value, and traditional finance methods—become allies in strengthening the true value of IT. Finance validates and revalidates the metrics and measures that the ITBV team uses, as well as all calculations that result in dollar claims.

To maintain objectivity, it is best for IT PMs to work with the business unit Finance teams for additional analysis of the final numbers and come to agreement on the value delivered.

In larger enterprises, both the IT organization and the customer's organization will have separate financial personnel. In this case, IT Finance would be responsible for:

- Reviewing all metrics plans with an eye toward the rules and guidelines of the ITBV Program.

- Ensuring that the business value metrics defined and methodology meets the financial requirements, are financially sound, and meet the intent of the ITBV Program.

- Working with the IT PM to develop traditional ROI estimates.

- Educating the ITBV Program team on strategies and assumptions made when developing traditional ROI estimates.

Customer Finance would be responsible for:

- Reviewing all metrics plans with an eye toward the business and ensuring that what was being measured will yield a measurement of true business value.

- Working with IT finance to approve the business value ROI (BV ROI).

At this point, the basic groundwork is in place. Expectations have been set by senior management, objectives for the program are documented, and the team is formed. It is now time to shift effort to the next major task: defining the operational processes for the program. As you make this transition, be sure to consider ITBV assessment processes already in place when deciding which operational processes to develop and how they should be integrated into the existing processes.

Developing Operational Processes

So far this chapter has concentrated on the essential elements for building an ITBV program: gaining support for the concept and assembling teams with the appropriate skill sets and business orientation.

This section focuses on how to get the program off the ground and running. This is the nuts and bolts of how the program can operate once the groundwork has been established.

The Business Value Program flow diagram shown in Figure 6.1 serves as a high-level roadmap of Intel's operational processes, standard tools, and templates, and identifies the key decisions that the ITBV team must make. The first set of decisions in the upper half of Figure 6.1 ask whether a study should be launched at all. In the lower half of the diagram, tools such as the ITBV ROI spreadsheet are brought into play. The flow chart ends with a monthly update of findings posted to a dashboard for the general manager of the IT organization.

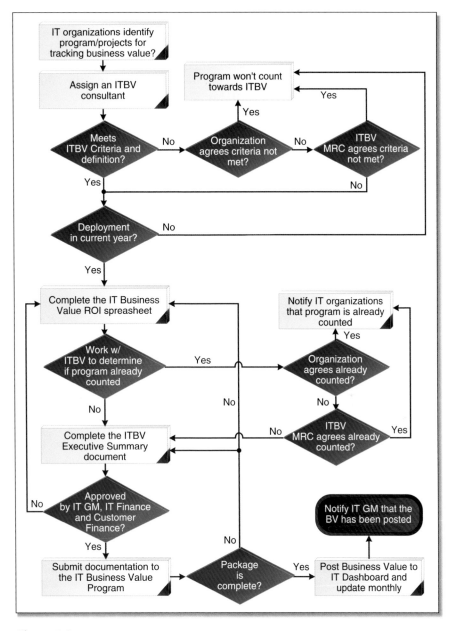

Figure 6.1 Business Value Program Flow Diagram

Of course, when launching a new program, preparing such a flow chart is not the first step. The methods and tools identified in this flow diagram were built and improved over a four-year period. Working with Finance to hammer out strong financial metrics and defining robust business value dials is the first task.

Working with Finance

The importance of cooperation and support from Finance is difficult to over-emphasize. Consistent formulas and assumptions are needed to make the comparisons and compute business value gains. In many cases, pre-existing ROI analyses may need to be reworked. A strong and consistent set of financial measures is necessary, and they must be established early in the life of the ITBV program.

Furthermore, in the context of measurement, it is vital that the associated Finance group take ownership of assessing the materiality (*i.e.,* the financial significance) of projects and certifying the final BV ROI estimate. With the help of Finance, the ITBV program can aim for high impact projects early on. Prioritizing business value study opportunities by the expected financial impact will help avoid situations in which the costs of measuring the benefits are greater than the benefits themselves. By focusing on high-impact programs, the IT organization will begin to assign resources where they will have the largest bottom-line impact.

Developing a Standard Business Value ROI template (BV ROI)

It is essential to establish a common set of tools before beginning the measurement process. Don't be surprised to find a mix of different ROI estimates, value propositions, and benefit summaries when reviewing existing ROI analyses. Bringing consistency and common validation procedures is the first challenge for the ITBV program team.

In some cases, the ITBV program cannot leverage pre-existing ROI and benefit measures due to inconsistencies. In our experience, many projects had solid requirements and useful implementation plans, but insufficient detail on what the business value expectations were and how they were to be measured. The project owners had spent time on developing and deploying IT solutions and then went on to measure operational health. The Finance group helped the project owner account for spending and staying on budget, but did not emphasize measuring what the original ROI estimate intended to deliver, either before or after.

Business value dials are an important component of a BV ROI template. As discussed in detail in Chapter 2 (see "Business Value Dials" on page 20), business value dials tap into well-defined operating measures that are transformed into dollars and fed into the ROI calculations.

To build a successful program, you'll need to work closely with your Finance group to develop a BV ROI template (*i.e.*, a spreadsheet or other forms-based calculator) that includes the business value dials. Moreover you will need to create supporting calculations for each business value dial, as well as guidelines for filling out the standard template. We strongly recommend that you first define the business value dials before starting work on a spreadsheet tool.

The before-and-after data provides a closed-loop process the help verify the accuracy of the original forecasts that were used for justifying the project. For example, if an IT solution planned to deliver a 2 percent scrap reduction for a given factory, and the business value metrics showed an actual reduction that was smaller or even zero, this experience should be applied to similar projects in the future. Or, consider office productivity investment decisions. The BV ROI template encourages re-examining assumptions and estimated values against the actual data.

For us, the BV ROI template became a standard tool for the Finance organization and helped emphasize the importance of business value measurement for each IT solution. Chapter 3 provides a detailed look at ROI and other financial metrics.

Defining Standard Processes

Three key processes describe much of the work of an ITBV team.

- An *Initial Screening Process* that qualifies appropriate projects for inclusion in the ITBV program.

- An *ITBV Analysis Process* that studies qualified projects by analyzing business problems and using business value dials to measure results.

- A *Consulting Process* that focuses on the projects that did not qualify for inclusion but are worthy of some systematic examination.

These processes lead to a final review that makes recommendations for the timely execution of the IT system launch and gives suggestions for publicizing the program and its benefits.

Initial Project Screening Process

The first step is identifying the projects for inclusion in your program. Note that not all IT products and services require business value metrics. For example, assessing the value of using a telephone vs. mailing a letter will provide little insight into potential IT improvement, even though telephony is an important part of many IT shops.

As a starting point, it is best to develop a small set of decision rules that are consistent with the intent and definition of business value for your program and use these rules as an entry gate to the remaining processes that the team develops and implements. At the outset, focus on identifying and prioritizing projects with the high anticipated business value. Schedule these projects first, and then work down the value chain.

Table 6.2   Qualifying a Candidate IT Solution

1. Is this a new IT-designed solution intended to meet specific customer needs? If so, describe. • *Explanation*: New solutions designed by IT that solve existing customer problems or improve productivity are likely to qualify for the ITBV Program.
2. Did the customer fully define the problem or opportunity and the solution before engaging with IT? If not, what value-add was IT to this project? • *Explanation*: If a customer comes to IT with a fully defined solution to their problem and has simply selected IT as the supplier, the solution will likely not qualify for the program. However, if the customer has come to IT with a solution and IT adds value by enhancing the solution, designing it differently than the customer had specified to create a better design, it would likely qualify for the ITBV program.
3. Is this an existing IT solution? If so, how does the new customer differ from the existing customer? How will the new customer benefit? • *Explanation*: If the solution already exists in the environment, the only way this might qualify for the program is if the solution is for a totally new customer. For example, an organization responsible for reuse of surplus capital equipment could count new business value if the process and supporting tools are deployed to a business unit that is not currently engaged in this activity.
4. Is this a replacement of or an upgrade to an existing IT solution? If so, describe the incremental benefit the customer will realize. • *Explanation*: If an existing IT solution is being replaced, it must offer additional functionality or productivity to the end user in order to count for the program. Solutions that are replaced and have no beneficial effect on the end users or that are simply business as usual, do not qualify for the ITBV program.
5. Is the target of this solution internal to IT? If not, be sure at least one of the questions above has a full description. • *Explanation*: Projects that reduce IT costs to the customer or benefit IT and not the customer do not qualify for the program; they may be worthwhile projects, but they don't meet the spirit of the program.

Over the first six months of our program, we developed five key screening questions, as shown in Table 6.2. To accomplish the initial project screening, we linked our BV PMs with each IT department and had the project managers meet with their peers in these organizations to understand the internal customer, their top projects planned for the year, and the expected results from those projects.

Based on how your IT group is set up, you might consider a similar approach or at least one in which your team partners with Finance, the solution portfolio managers in the IT organization, the governance board (*i.e.*, your equivalent of our MRC), and the IT planning group.

The decision points in the screening process are shown in the flow chart in Figure 6.2. One goal of this screening process is to develop a pipeline of qualified projects on which to base eventual decisions about prioritization and allocation of project funding. The better the information about the business value of a solution, the better the decisions can be on which to fund in any given year.

Is the Project Funded?

During the first months of the program, it a good idea to focus only on projects that have already been funded or approved for funding. Developing a prioritized list of projects that are funded and ready to be measured through the program should be your primary job in the early stages of the program because you need to show progress and results in order to keep the program moving forward.

If the project has not been funded, the team should offer limited support—mostly to help the IT PM define business value metrics and to share strategies for successfully defining the business value of an IT solution.

To aid in tracking projects and their status, our team entered projects into our IT BV database (see "Business Value Data Dictionary" on page 260 of Appendix C for a template with detailed field-level descriptions of this database). We used this database to develop forecasts and track the status of our activities. We also used this database to re-engage with projects that we didn't have the resources to consider during the initial months of the program. As time allowed, we brought these projects into the measurement process. Over time we engaged with more projects that were at various stages in the funding and development life cycle. Thus, the database acted as a portfolio of business value across the projects being tracked and measured.

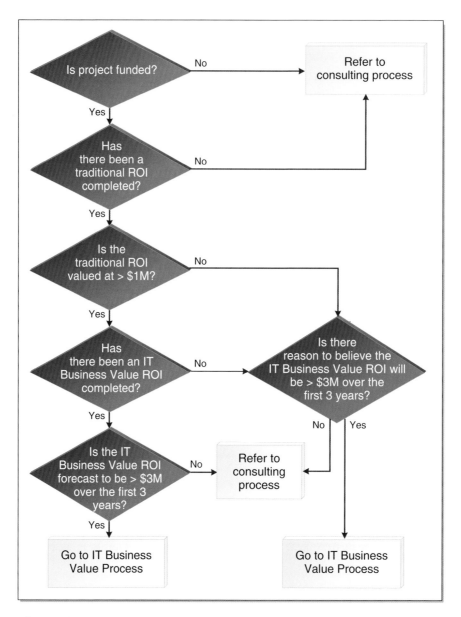

Figure 6.2 Screening Process Overview

Inevitably, some projects will fall outside of the processes you build to manage the program. For projects that you cannot or will not track as part of your ITBV program, we suggest offering consulting services and a Web site that shares the tools and templates your team develops.

Has a traditional ROI been completed?

For projects that are already funded, some type of traditional ROI document has probably been developed by the project manager or by Finance. If an ROI document is available, make sure that the project owner provides it to the BV PM. If no ROI document is available, it may be best to refer it to the consulting services process, especially in the early days of an ITBV program.

A missing ROI is not necessarily an indication that the project lacks business value. There are many reasons that projects do not have a formally documented ROI. If your initial review indicates that the project has potential and satisfies the rules of your program, add it to projects under investigation, knowing that an ROI will have to be developed.

Does the standard ROI forecast a material value?

Each ITBV organization will need to determine a minimum or threshold value, and I would expect wide variances, depending on the nature of the enterprise and the cost and sophistication of the business value study.

We decided that if a standard ROI was available, and if the forecasted NPV over a three-year period was in excess of $1M, we would do additional investigation. This $1M threshold was not engraved in granite in our program; it was negotiable and was just used as a guideline to control the number of projects entering the screening process in the program's early stages.

Has an IT Business Value ROI been estimated?

Traditional ROI forecasts for new or upgraded IT products and services attempt to identify incremental IT costs and benefits. Many of these ROIs also attempt to measure IT customer cost savings and quantify productivity benefits by employing a method of average burden rates to forecasted time savings.

As your program moves from startup mode to becoming operational, you will start to see more programs using the IT Business Value ROI template developed by the team. Your team will have to decide what level of ITBV ROI you will actively engage with instead of just tracking progress. If an ITBV ROI had been completed, did the forecast value meet or exceed the minimum requirement? The minimum requirement we used was a $3M NPV over the first three years of the IT Solution.

Intel's Business Value Index (BVI)

The BVI is a composite index of factors that impact the value of an IT investment. It looks at three factors when evaluating IT investments: corporate impact on Intel's business (IT business value), impact to IT efficiency, and the investment's financial attractiveness.

These three factors are based upon a predetermined set of defining criteria: customer need, business and technical risks, strategic fit, revenue potential, level of investment required, and the innovation and learning that an investment generates. The criteria for each factor are weighted based on the ongoing business strategy and business environment. (See Figure 2.4 on page 51.)

A crucial aspect of the BVI is its ability to reveal the intangible benefits and strategic value of a potential investment. In addition, a series of decision points track the changes in a project's relative value over a period of time.

For tracking and reporting, we required that a project had to be deployed in the year it was counted. If it satisfied the minimum requirement, it entered our tracking process. If it did not meet the minimum, it could be referred to the Consulting Services Process. We set the $3M minimum as a way to control the volume of projects entering the ITBV program for tracking.

It is important to keep in mind that a new program can be quickly overrun with projects if every potential IT solution is accepted for tracking and measurement. As noted, the threshold value must be set based on the specifics for your IT organization. Using a lower value makes sense for smaller IT organizations or organizations with established ITBV programs that can handle the increased measurement and tracking load.

Is there potential for IT Business Value in excess of a threshold?

Not all projects will hit the minimum numbers defined by your program. For example, we decided that if the Traditional ROI was less than $1M, we would assess whether there is reason to believe the IT Business Value ROI can meet or exceed the minimum requirement of $3M. If the project had the potential of meeting the $3M minimum requirement, it was entered into the IT Business Value Process. If there was no potential, then the program went into the Consulting Services process.

Notice that this overall approach is aimed at gaining momentum and studying IT investments likely to contribute a significantly large business value. The approach changes as the program matures for two reasons. First, with optimized processes, tools, and reference databases, your team will lower the cost of business value studies and thus the threshold for ROI. Second, you will have exhausted the supply of investments aimed at large business value contributions. The end result for an established program should be a streamed lined version of this process, as only BV ROI's will be entering.

IT Business Value Analysis Process

Once a project has been screened and accepted into your program, the next step is to work with the IT PMs and IT's customers to fully comprehend the business problem and proposed solutions. The major steps are shown in Figure 6.3.

This step is crucial to shifting the focus from a techno-centric analysis to a user-centric analysis. This is the fundamental shift required to maximize the business value of IT. Too often, solution providers miss the real business value of IT solutions because of their habit of looking at looking at solutions from viewpoint of what technology is available. Firms need to be asking not what solution is available, but what solution will add value to their business.

A key step in the business value analysis process is the development of critical success indicators (CSIs). CSIs should link directly to the success of the customer. When this occurs, the business value dials will become embedded in the CSIs. Solutions deliver measurable IT business value by impacting CSIs that are measures of customer success. Linking IT's CSIs to customer success helps to forge strong alliances.

The data collected in this process is used to build a forecast BV ROI model. The core of our approach is using a NPV discounted cash-flow (DCF) analysis (see "Discounting a Cash Flow" on page 62) to measure an IT solution's impact to the corporation and its shareholders. Once this forecast is completed, the BV PM and the IT PM need to get buy-in from the IT customer. This step is important. Results of the Business Value Analysis set expectations for all the stakeholders.

We learned over the years that our ITBV team members sometimes discover additional or different benefits when establishing a baseline. These new benefits emerge with an improved understanding of the business problem and the customer's needs.

When engaging the customer, the human factors engineer might find that the baseline provides valuable data for making a decision between competing solutions, or that the IT project will not provide the expected

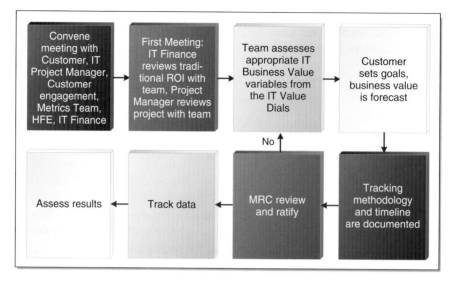

Figure 6.3 The IT Business Value Analysis Process

benefits.   At either of these points, the customer can change the direction of the proposed program prior to substantial investment of dollars and people.

First Checkpoint: Team Validation of an ITBV Project Opportunity

Once an IT solution has passed the screening process, it is assigned to a BV PM. I recommend that the manager convene a meeting that include key stakeholders. These stakeholders will include a representative from the customer who has knowledge and understanding of the solution, the IT PM, a representative from HFE group, and a representative from IT Finance, preferably the person involved in developing the original ROI estimate for the project.

The purpose of this first checkpoint is to review the plans for the ITBV project. In the first part of the meeting the IT PM shares all relevant information on the effort and current plans. The second portion of the meeting is dedicated to the IT Finance representative sharing any ROI work done in support of the project. This server to get the team up to speed on the project, enabling next steps to be outlined, as well as the frequency of meetings and the appropriate participant list.

The BV PM is responsible for selecting appropriate business value dials to track for the IT solution in order to quantify the bottom-line impact to the customer. The customer is critical in this work. Let me underscore that this step simply cannot be accomplished without the customer. The business value dials tracked must have customer agreement. The dials lead to the dollar measure of value that the IT solution delivers to the customer.

Customer Goals Drive Business Value Forecasts. Once ROI estimates are reviewed and the business value dials are identified, the customer will need to identify expected improvements for each business value dial. For example, if an improved platform for product development is deployed, then how many days will be reduced on the *time to market* business dial? Finance can turn those days into dollars. Using information like this and guidance from Finance, the team estimates the business value that the solution is going to deliver.

Keep in mind, that depending on the stage of the project, these estimates may be very rough. For example, initially we were working with well-understood projects that had been funded and already moved through the early stages of our product life cycle (PLC). As time went on, we engaged with more projects that were early in the PLC and necessarily less well understood.

When working with projects in the earliest stages of development, plan on using an iterative process that uses available information for coarse estimates and gathers additional information to improve the precision of the business value forecast. The techniques and the overall process remain the same, but less precise early results must be understood, tolerated, and improved.

Sharing the Costs

The results of business value studies are primarily funded by the IT organization. However, in certain situations, the results of these business value studies may be especially useful to one of the company's business units. Evaluating the productivity improvement when deploying a customer relationship management solution, for example, is likely to be of keen interest to the sales and marketing organization. In these cases, it makes sense to seek a cost-sharing agreement. Although the business unit contributes to the cost and shares the results, the IT organization must remain in control of the study.

Metrics Plan and Timeline Documented. In conjunction with the HFE representative, the BV PM should verify that all data collection methodologies and plans are documented in the metrics plan and available for team members to review. A data collection timeline is necessary.

It is this process, defining how and when data is going to be collected, that is the heart of a solid the ITBV program. The guidance provided in Chapters 4 and 5 and examples in Appendix C fit into the business value analysis process right here.

Checkpoint 2: MRC Review

The next step in our Business Value Analysis process was to ratify the metrics plan with our MRC. Early on we spent time measuring projects without getting the project approved by the MRC. In these early months of the program, we found that some projects appeared to fit the intent of the program but didn't always qualify based on various interpretations by the MRC members. Recall that we developed questions as part of the screening process to avoid this type of problem, but those questions were developed during the first 6 months of the program. As a result, we worked on programs that ultimately didn't count toward our goals and objectives.

We recommend that as part of your process the BV PM should prepare a one or two slide summary for MRC ratification describing the project, the business value dials with a forecast value, overall measurement plan, and a timeline. The MRC should then either approve the metrics plan for the program or rejected it. If rejected, the team could take the MRC feedback and run through the process a second time or decide to abandon the project. The outcome of this second checkpoint should be MRC approval of the metrics plan in concept before the team expends time and energy quantifying a project that might not be included in the program. It is best to include this step in the initial months of the ITBV program and to revisit its usefulness periodically as the program matures.

Execution of the Metrics Plan

With plans in place and checkpoints successfully passed, the ITBV team executes their plans. We know from Chapters 4 and 5 that metrics plans describe data collection methods, identify surveys and other materials that need to be developed or adapted. Field observation and laboratory experiments may be a part of the plan. The guidance provided in those chapters fits into the business value analysis process right here.

Be sure to document all deviations from the metrics plan. This is done so that as the final business value is assembled, a solid record of exactly how the data was collected is available. The forecasted business value proposition has been documented and checkpointed including all the assumptions that influenced the metrics plan. Changes in the metrics plan could have a significant impact on that original estimate.

Assessing the Results

It is important to monitor the metrics plan and review the data as it becomes available. The ITBV team, including the HFE representative, the BV PM, and Finance analysts should conduct initial reviews of the results. Once these team members are in agreement that the data is reliable and valid, then these findings are presented to the key stakeholders.

Our BV PMs also report the incremental results to the MRC on a monthly basis. Frequency will vary due to differences among enterprises and IT organizations, and the overall scope of the IT investment. After several years of ITBV infrastructure development, we report the results on an IT Indicator Dashboard, which was available to all Intel employees. When results are assessed and findings communicated, the business value process shown in Figure 6.3 on page 164 comes to an end.

> In March of 2001, Intel IT delivered an IT Dashboard that displays key organizational business indicators. Starting in early 2000, Intel IT identified indicators on which we could and should base staff-level decisions. Business unit managers worked with their staffs to discover the key indicators of organizational health within their areas, and then collect those indicators.

Consulting Process

Projects will emerge that just don't fit within the IT business value program, but are still worthy of being measured. To support the measurement process, we designed a Consulting Process to provide training, general advice, tools, templates, and review of proposed metrics plans.

To support these projects, we developed an intranet Web site that contained all the materials for the program, as well as, case studies and other examples to help make our IT professional more self-sufficient when they could not get support from the experts. Figure 6.4 shows the process we used to determine if a project would enter the consulting process.

In a nutshell, the consulting process provided support and training to IT PMs and their Finance colleagues so that they could assimilate elements of our ITBV methodology as they wished. We provided training on the basic principles of ITBV assessment, including the concepts of traditional ROI, business value ROI, and the overall measurement

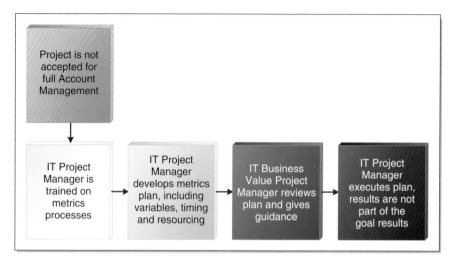

Figure 6.4 The IT Business Value Consulting Process

processes. In essence, we offered them the information that is in this book.

As consultants, we offered to review the business value dials and accompanying financial calculations and make suggestions. Our goal was to encourage IT PMs to develop plans for forecasting and measuring the business value of their IT solutions using the tools provided by our ITBV team.

Business Value and IT Governance

This section covers the final state of the program with respect to governance processes used within Intel IT. For others who are seeking to build an ITBV program, this section provides a conceptual overview of how our program fits within one type of IT governance process, the product life cycle, as shown in Figure 6.5. I also speak to how the data collected by an IT Business Value program can be used to better manage IT to maximize the value delivered to the company by getting the right data into the investment decision-making process.

Our IT organization uses a program governance approach based on one used by many of our product divisions to develop Intel's microprocessors and communications products. Intel's program governance revolves around a product development life cycle called the PLC. The three major components to the Intel PLC are phases, decisions, and program information. The phases for creating a product or service, shown in Table 6.3, are exploration, planning, development, and deployment. We also use a stage-gate approach in which an IT investment is funded in incremental stages, with subsequent funding contingent upon meeting designated critical success factors for each stage. The IT investment is tracked as it moves through the pipeline. This approach gives us the ability to accelerate, slowdown, or halt programs based on progress and ongoing business alignment.

Table 6.3   Key Tasks and Work Products within the Product Life Cycle

Product Life Cycle Phase	Key Tasks and Work Products
Explore	Complete the Business Value Index (BVI) Apply ITBV program criteria Transfer knowledge to the BVPM, an ongoing task Generate a preliminary estimate of business value
Explore + Value	Update the BVI analysis Complete 25-50 percent of the BV ROI spreadsheet Outline the metrics plan using existing data sources
Planning + Commit	Complete 50 percent of the BV ROI spreadsheet Update metrics plan Collect baseline data
Development + Go/No Go	Complete 75-100 percent of the BV ROI spreadsheet Update the metrics plan Collect post-implementation data
Deployment	Complete the BV ROI spreadsheet Close the metrics plan Archive all documents Publish business value results
Deployment + Closure	Track actual business value delivered Update the BV ROI spreadsheet with tracking data (Tracking continues until IT system removed or significantly modified.)

Our ITBV program coordinated effort with the team that controls changes to the PLC process used within our IT organization. Together we developed and embedded ITBV steps into the process. We called these embedded steps *overlays*. An overlay is a set of specific tasks and work products, shown in Table 6.3, that is carried out as part of the PLC management process. An important function of the PLC team is controlling the standard templates and methods for each of the stage-gate review processes. By working with the PLC team and developing an overlay for the IT Business Value program, we increased the overall impact of the program. The end result is that programs within the IT organization can take advantage of the work done by the ITBV team, even if their program is not being formally tracked and measured.

For IT solutions that were tracked as part of the ITBV Program Office, the BV PM assigned to a project was responsible for ensuring that the information used by the ITBV program for each project was updated throughout the PLC process. Many of the associated documents for projects were tracked and updated based on reviews at each control point shown in Figure 6.5. In many cases, the BV PM just needed to make sure our tracking system reflected any updates.

We defined a set of expected work products or tasks that should be done at each of the control points. Many of these work products or tasks are steps that we determined need to be done or updated at each phase of an IT solution's implementation. For example, we wanted to get the BV ROI forecast started as early as possible in the process, many times

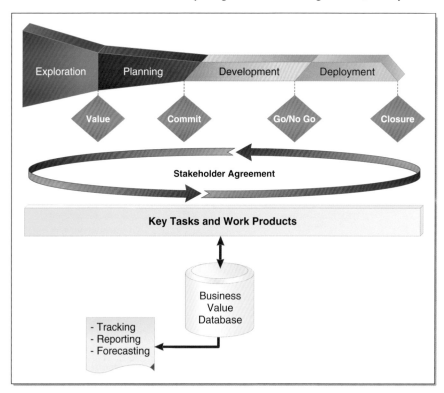

Figure 6.5 IT Business Value Processes Within the PLC

the work was estimates and we would refine the data as we learned more about the IT solution. The refinement of work products is shown in Figure 6.5.

Summary

We have built and refined our ITBV program over the last three years and we continue to evolve the program. This chapter offers up the lessons learned, the processes we have standardized, and the concepts we have developed to provide better estimates of the business value impact of IT on our company.

I expect readers to use these ideas to jump-start business value programs tailored to their own organizations. While our terminology is shared, I would expect most organizations to create their own. It is the deep structure that I believe is common. For example, a link to upper management is key regardless of whether it happens to be called a MRC.

The most important lessons in building an ITBV program are as follows:

- Build business value dials that are stable over time, and only changed when necessary.

- Describe business value dials in the customer's language, and not in the language of IT.

- Measure and track business value systematically so that pre- and post-solution assessments can make the connection between IT solutions and your company's bottom-line.

- Aim for an ITBV program with an enterprise-wide shared vocabulary. IT projects are best measured with the same set of value dials and operationally defined metrics.

- Standardize templates, tools, and processes to gain efficiencies and improve precision as the business value program matures.

- Work incrementally down the value chain starting with solutions promising the highest business value contribution potential. Gain efficiencies to make the assessment process less costly.

- Keep all stakeholders at the table, particularly the customer and senior management. Use checkpoints to anchor and stabilize a young business value program.

Developing a business value program is a sea change for most IT organizations. Expect resistance and stress communication because the business value message is relatively new to the IT organization, Finance, and customers.

Chapter **7**

Launching the ITBV
Program at Intel

*"The critical task ... is to create an organization capable of infusing
products with irresistible functionality..."*
—C. K. Prahalad and Gary Hamel

In order to appreciate the nature of the efforts that went into creating the ITBV program within Intel, it is important to understand the environmental conditions that existed for Intel and in the IT Industry at large.

This chapter is organized along the timeline of the program's creation and links in other relevant programs that contributed to the direction of the ITBV program. It is not intended to be a history of IT within Intel, but merely a summary of the important events that helped determine the formation of the ITBV program. Moreover, by summarizing the conditions that led up to the creation of the program, this chapter provides a proof point for the entire book.

As IT departments are increasingly required to justify increased IT spending by meaningfully illustrating IT's ROI and demonstrating to the entire enterprise how IT's contribution impacts the bottom line, this chapter focuses on the financial perspective of the ITBV program. It reviews some of the current Intel activities in this space, reports some of the program's weaknesses, and draws implications about what should be done next.

The Intel Finance Perspective

Intel has maintained and nurtured a customer-focused vision over the years and the ITBV program is a direct reflection of this outlook. I believe that without the support of Finance coupled with Intel's customer-focused behavior, there wouldn't be an ITBV program at Intel. Finance at Intel is organized in a way that is designed to preserve an independent voice from the business unit. There is solid-line reporting to the CFO for business unit controllers, with a matrix relationship to the business units. Business unit controllers are expected to work as partners with the staff, but also need to play a devil's advocate role to ensure that all important business decisions and investments are made with due diligence.

From the perspective of an IT finance controller, creating an ITBV program was necessary and apparent. Intel IT intended to create a program that would increase self-discipline, focus efforts on high customer impact projects, and create a culture of measurement. In short, as the ITBV program strongly reinforced the agenda of Intel Finance, it was no surprise that the program gained Finance's immediate support.

IT in the Fall of 2000

The seeds for Intel's ITBV program were planted in the late 1990s, when we re-centralized our information technology capabilities. As with many other large IT enterprises, the personal computer (PC) revolution at Intel had resulted in the proliferation and *de facto* distributed ownership of Intel's IT function during the 1980s and early 1990s. This proliferation allowed individual departments and business groups to create information technology tailored to their specific needs and to do so at a more rapid pace than had ever been possible in the era of centralized data processing.

While some core business applications—for example, the general ledger—remained managed by the IT department, there were literally thousands of small applications created at the department level using spreadsheets or simple programming tools. Furthermore, these applications collectively ended up being mission critical for Intel because the most vital business functions at the company would stop if this multitude of applications were unavailable.

Several important forces emerged in general IT environment of the 1990s to led to a reversal of Intel's "distributed IT" trend. The most important of these forces were:

1. The emergence of Enterprise Resource Planning (ERP) systems, which held the promise of improving our ability to manage what had become a highly complex supply-chain network.

2. Fear and uncertainty surrounding the looming Y2K transition.

3. The emergence of security threats, such as viruses.

4. And—perhaps most importantly—the emergence of the Internet as an economic force, which both exacerbated the other three factors and, at the same time, created a sense of urgency, as all enterprises rushed to stake out their new territory in the world of eCommerce.

Driven by these environmental changes, which emerged between 1995 and 2000, Intel implemented several major decisions that led to re-centralizing the bulk of our IT functions:

1. We centralized financial ownership of personal computer assets to the IT department.

2. We introduced server-based email, standardized office productivity software, and managed both as corporate-wide deployments.

3. We made major investments in a corporate intranet infrastructure and imposed architectural standards on applications that needed to use the network.

4. We moved line of business (LOB) application groups into a single organization that was known as the eBusiness Group or eBG.

With this organizational change, the General Manager of eBG and the General Manager of IT became co-CIOs and were charged with keeping the two organizations aligned. The end result of the combination of the forces and decisions outlined above was that Intel's IT function once again became highly centralized.

As can be expected, the transition came with a price. Seeing that the cost of Intel's IT function was growing rapidly, it didn't take long for Intel's business units to perceive a lack of responsiveness from these newly formed centralized groups and to begin demanding accountability for the rapid growth in overall IT spending.

In the summer of 2000, Intel IT began preparing its annual plan for 2001. It was now clear that a business-as-usual plan would not be acceptable to the corporation, so Intel launched an activity called *Business Plan 2001*. Despite the prosaic name, this program had a trans-formative purpose at its core: We were determined to run Intel IT like a real business, marrying the advantages of scale that centralization offered with the responsiveness and accountability that decentralization had provided.

Business Plan 2001: IT as a Business

In the year 2000, Intel IT was singularly unprepared to have a productive "customer-vendor" discussion. We understood and managed our costs according to our general ledger structure. However, we did not understand these costs either in terms that were meaningful to our customers or in terms of products and services that our customer understood and valued. In fact, prior to 2001, Intel's IT costs were allocated to the Intel business units primarily through a lump-sum "citizen charge" that simply took total IT spending and divided it by the number of employees in the corporation. This allocation methodology reflected the deep-seated mentality within IT that our job was essentially to provide the infrastructure. Under this paradigm, the annual budget for IT was set almost entirely on the prior year's cost, with a relatively small growth or decline based on a projected growth in Intel employee headcount, and with some adjustments made for particularly visible programs.

Needless to say, this approach did not result in meaningful or data-driven discussions about the right level of IT spending for Intel. While the annual budget-setting exercise was often emotional on both sides, it generally created little value. It was nearly impossible to say with any level of conviction that IT was optimally funded going into the next year.

The goal for Business Plan 2001 (BP2001), then, was to enable real business dialog about the appropriate funding for IT at Intel. This program had 4 major elements:

1. Creating discrete products and services to represent the customer-touchable outcomes of all IT activities.

2. Creating a demand forecast/capacity planning function for managing the growth or decline of each product or service through time.

3. Mapping all IT costs to the identified products and services to create a credible IT cost-accounting system.

4. Creating the IT Business Value Program, which was intended to be a proxy for the revenue created by the IT function at Intel.

Each of these elements was a significant program in its own right. A brief overview of each key element in the first three programs is outlined in the sections below and is followed by an in-depth discussion of the creation of the ITBV Program.

Creating IT Products and Services

While on the surface it appeared to be a simple task, the foundational step of expressing the work of everyone in IT in terms of a customer-touchable product or service proved to be a daunting one.

The first obstacle was cultural in nature: many of the employees in IT had a mind set not unlike that seen in the regulated utility industry. IT, in their view, was similar in nature to electricity. Our job was essentially to keep the lights on at Intel and they didn't see any value in dividing our efforts into discrete products. This camp was never convinced otherwise. The program proceeded with strong executive sponsorship, but it never had strong support from those who had embraced the utility paradigm. This, however, was not a major problem for Business Plan 2001. The utility model slowed our program down, but it did not influence the outcome.

The second obstacle, however, was more deeply problematic. Most IT products and services are composed of a solution stack of technologies, services, and an implied or explicit business process design. Various functions inside a typical IT department tend to specialize in delivering layers in that stack. Different groups were responsible for network transport, management of servers, development and maintenance of a business applications, customer support, and so on.

BP2001 aimed to market a complete solution stack as a discrete product that solved a business problem. IT groups competed to provide these "end products." The desired outcome was eventually reached, but it was at the cost of bruised egos and significant ill-will for the overall BP2001 program.

Ultimately, this program settled on a catalog of roughly 150 products and services. Most of these product-line items were retail products, such as messaging and office productivity software, provided directly to end-users. A few items were wholesale items, where a partial solution stack was provided to one of the few IT groups remaining in the Intel business units. Though arrived at through a bottom-up methodology, this retail/wholesale distinction represented an important step in the maturation of our IT-as-a-business concept.

Demand Forecast/Capacity Planning

Perhaps the most complex of the four elements of BP2001 was implementing a robust set of processes for understanding Intel's internal IT customer demand for each product and service, and for planning the capacity required to support that demand. This program started with an embarrassing scarceness of data. While our asset tracking was adequate on an aggregated basis for corporate financial reporting purposes, we lacked the required specific mapping of servers, network bandwidth consumption, and even engineering workers, to individual services. We were essentially managing a factory without understanding how much of that factory's capacity was being used to produce each of our products.

It was no better on the demand side of the equation. We knew how many "accounts" existed for large items like network access and messaging, but had a poor understanding of how many employees were using many of these services. In addition, even with account-based services, it wasn't clear that an "account" was an appropriate unit of measure. Our need for factory capacity was not generally driven by account setup; it was driven by the change in use per account over time. For example, the number of email accounts scales linearly with employee headcount growth. However, the use of those accounts has grown much more rapidly, with messages sent and received per account growing at an ever increasing rate. At the next level down in the analysis, the average message has become larger over time, with attachment of large files becoming common.

What did all this mean? For each of the newly defined products and services, the following information was needed:

- Develop and understand a "factory floor" model of support for that product and service.

- Develop a "unit of work" for that product and service that most closely mapped to required capacity.

- Develop processes for forecasting future product and service demand.

Immense progress has been made in each of these areas, but 5 years later this work remains an ongoing program at Intel IT. The rapid rate of change in IT product mix, usage models for those products, and in the underlying technology required to support them, makes this area a "moving target." The effort remains worthwhile, however, and our progress has enabled significantly better management of our IT factory and has correspondingly improved our credibility with the rest of Intel.

IT Cost System

An immediate deliverable of BP2001 was the creation of a working cost accounting system for IT, allowing periodic calculation of the total and unit cost for each of the newly defined products and services. The solution developed was patterned from the system used by Intel for calculating the cost of semiconductor components, reducing the time required to design it. In using this system we also hoped to improve the credibility of the cost data with our internal customers. Ironically, the IT system was implemented using standard spreadsheet software, although we certainly pushed that software to its limits.

The basic design of the system was simple and intuitive:

- List all departments in IT by cost code in along the top of the spreadsheet.

- List all 150 products and services as the rows in the spreadsheet

- Input a "percent of effort" for each department for each of the products.

- Multiply period spending per department by those percentages to calculate total product cost for that accounting period.

- Divide total product cost by actual units of work for that product to calculate unit cost.

- Divide total product cost by forecast units of work for that product to calculate future product cost.

This basic design did not capture the complexity of what we were modeling, resulting in some important enhancements:

- Several large "cost pools" were created, representing items such as network connectivity and data center hosting, which roughly equated to the "wholesale" IT concept mentioned above. We also created an overhead cost pool to capture shared services such as information security and our procurement function. Many department cost codes were mapped in whole or in part to one of these cost pools, greatly reducing the initial input and maintenance required for department to product mapping.

■ The cost calculation then became multi-phased:

  - First we calculated values for each aggregate cost pools.

  - To the unburdened cost of products and services, we added a share from each wholesale cost pool, in proportion to usage of the pool by the product or service.

  - Finally, we burdened the costs of products and services with overhead based on percentage of overall IT cost.

This enhanced design became an enormously complex spreadsheet, known as the *MOAT*, or the *Mother of all Templates*. However, the complexity was largely hidden from users, with the main burden being the initial population of mappings. Within a few months IT had a functioning cost system and a credible calculation of unit cost for each product. This was a major win for IT.

A side benefit of the design of the MOAT was realized shortly after implementation: it allowed for reverse operation. Inputting a demand forecast for each product, and calculating, would provide a proposed funding level for each department. While this data was not seen as accurate enough for final budgeting purposes, it did prove useful as a sanity check during the budget process, providing for the first time a dynamic input to a budget process dominated by run rate.

The IT Business Value Program

Although each of the prior 3 elements of BP2001 presented difficult challenges, we consider the revenue side of running IT like a business to be the toughest problem. Despite cultural storming and missing data, we had basic concepts in play. Thinking in terms of products, forecasting demand, modeling a factory, and performing basic cost accounting are standard activities in business with well-understood methodologies.

Our goal with ITBV was more challenging, however. We wanted to understand the actual dollar value Intel was receiving in return for its investment in IT capabilities. There were of course various methods available for estimating this value. We considered the following approaches:

1. We could use the our cost system as a foundation for estimating the unit cost of a product or service offering.

2. We could offer products and services on a pay-per-view basis to let our market accept or reject the price.

3. We could look outside to see whether third-parties could compete with our price for the same product or service offering.

While these methods are a reasonable starting point, they all basically beg the question of real value delivered. All the market method really does is to transfer the question of determination of value from the IT organization to the customer the IT organization supports. While this is appropriate for final decision making, it does nothing to put better data into the mix. The customer is the right person to make the decision, but the decision would still get made from gut feel. Perhaps IT will be a mature enough discipline one day so that value is understood and price is a good proxy for value.

Our view of the market method was that it was primarily useful at setting a minimum "bar" of value. In other words, for IT to be considered successful, we needed at a minimum to be returning our cost plus a normal rate of investment return. But an agreed upon method was needed to calculate that return.

The second major family of methodologies available for value calculation are standard project valuation tools covered in any introductory finance course, with the central concept of discounted cash flow at their core. (See *Principles of Corporate Finance* by Brealey and Myers, 2002.) These methodologies are well-established and easily adapted to a wide variety of business contexts. Their use in the ITBV program was an obvious choice. However, simply having the tools was the least of our problems.

The biggest issue we had to deal with was the credibility of the data. Although a minority of IT programs had obvious measurable outcomes, such as the outright automation of jobs or reductions in product inventory, it was more often the case that IT program outcomes were "soft", or difficult to associate with a single change. These data problems were far from unique to Intel. As work began to address this issue, the team reflected on Alan Greenspan's observations that IT contributes to economic productivity and that quantifying the contribution is difficult. The ITBV credibility challenge came to be known as the "Greenspan Value" problem: our design goal was to develop a body of valuation data that would satisfy even Alan Greenspan.

Key Design features of the IT Business Value Program

With this background in mind, I will describe the major design elements of the ITBV program from the perspective of the IT Controller, and ultimately that of the Intel CFO.

Program Goals

As mentioned above, the overriding success metric for the ITBV program was to prove that the IT function at Intel was, at a minimum, paying for itself and also delivering the expected minimum return expected for an Intel investment. Naturally, everyone wanted to see more than that minimum level of attainment, which would give us a Net Present Value of exactly $0, but it was a good first goal.

The ITBV program also had important secondary goals:

1. Change the mind set within Intel IT, focusing management and employee attention on projects with the highest expected value to Intel's business.

2. Improve IT's credibility inside of Intel, making it clear that we had an understanding of the real needs of the business units, and that our priorities were shared, or at least aligned.

3. Develop a generalized methodology for valuing investments in information technology. This goal was seen as potentially helpful to Intel's core business, putting a valuable tool in the hands of CIOs worldwide as they sought to justify continued IT investments at their respective companies.

We did not expect that the measurement program would be mature enough immediately to show full payback of IT spending. So, in the first year we established a relatively modest goal of identifying $100M dollars in demonstrable business value. Although that financial goal was considered important, the underlying objective in the first year was to establish the program, to develop the measurement methodology, and to start a cultural shift within our IT organization.

These objectives received a dramatic boost in attention when it was agreed with corporate headquarters that the ITBV program would be directly linked to Intel's annual Employee Bonus (EB), a bonus paid to all Intel employees. EB varies as a percent of employee compensation, ranging from small percent in entry-level jobs, to a very large percentage at the executive level. But, at all levels, it has historically proven to be a powerful incentive for focus and performance. So, going forward, the business unit objectives for Intel IT would include hitting our ITBV target—a big win as we sought to launch the program.

This win was not merely on the incentive side. Establishing the results of the ITBV program as an EB objective helped to establish credibility outside the immediate program team. To get our program added as an EB item, approval from IT senior management and the Executive Office of Intel was required—no small accomplishment for what was to date a program only on paper.

Program Staffing

Program manager.   At the time the program began to come together, we had a strong program manager who was available in the IT department. This person had an Intel Finance background and a strong network in the corporate finance department. Her strong leadership along with her belief that and ITBV program was the right thing to do provided instant credibility.

Project managers.   A small but strong team of project managers (PMs) was recruited from across the origination. These PMs were eventually assigned to cover various IT functional units, sought programs for tracking within the ITBV program, worked to prioritize the programs that were tracked, and ensured that all aspects of the work were consistent with the rules of the ITBV program.

Human Factors Engineers.   A distinctive aspect of Intel's ITBV program was our strong emphasis on HFE as a core discipline for measuring results. The program was determined not to shy away from difficult measurement problems or to indulge in "gut feel" estimation of productivity benefits. It was our intent at the outset to use objective and disciplined experimental design and measurement methodologies to gather credible data on employee productivity gains associated with new IT solutions. A forward looking senior member of IT involved in the BP2001 program pulled in a senior HFE to help address this issue.

Finance.   Naturally, we also needed finance skills on the team. This was primarily driven by the need to perform rigorous analysis of each program's forecasted and actual business value and to roll up cumulative results in a way which avoided cross-program double-counts. There was also a secondary need to ensure the unassailable credibility of program data. Finance's independent voice was essential for that purpose, especially when discussing program results with corporate or with Finance representatives from other Intel departments.

Oversight

It is typical for programs at Intel to have multiple layers of supervision, the ITBV program was no exception. Supervision and Management Review Committees are often seen as a mixed blessing, as they are frequently accompanied by a certain level of bureaucracy. In this case, oversight was essential to our purposes because one of our goals was to shift management thinking towards business value delivery. Their direct involvement helped accomplish this goal.

Oversight for the ITBV program started with the direct supervisor of the ITBV program manager. This manager was well respected and had considerable Intel Finance experience before joining the IT department. His role was to assist in program development, ensure adequate resources to accomplish its mission, and to ensure the integrity of the program.

The second layer of supervision came from a management review committee (MRC). The ITBV MRC was chaired by the IT Finance Controller and consisted of a handful of IT Senior Staff members. The MRC was also attended by the ITBV program manager, her supervisor, the ITBV research manager, and other key stakeholders. At the outset this MRC met monthly, ratifying proposed goals, operational processes, and program methodology. As the program matured the MRCs focused on approving specific IT programs toward the new EB goal.

The third layer of program oversight came from the Intel's CIO and VP of IT. He ratified program goals and would be responsible for presenting the program results as part of the executive office review of IT's EB package of results.

The final layer came directly from the executive office, comprised of Intel's CEO, COO, and CFO. While not directly involved in operation of the program, they paid detailed attention to the results when presented as part of IT's EB package, it was expected that these individuals would ask difficult questions about specific programs. Knowledge that this level of scrutiny would be applied was well-known to everyone involved, helping ensure execution and program integrity.

Program Scope

The scope of the ITBV program included the whole Intel IT organization, with the ultimate intent being an IT organization that more than paid for itself with proven business value results. However, after significant consideration, an important reduction in scope was decided on for the early years of the program: we were to focus only on programs which were bringing new business value to Intel.

This decision ruled out measuring deployed solutions delivering ongoing value to the company, such as the corporate messaging system. While there was no debate that these systems were valuable, even indispensable, the measurement problem was deemed too difficult to be part of our starting point. It was more important to focus on what was getting done now, not congratulating ourselves for last year's work.

Projects for the benefit of IT were highly debated. For example, re-engineering of an application to reduce network or support costs, should this count toward the goal set for the program? While it was argued that Intel would ultimately benefit for this reduction of IT costs, the program needed strong and focused energy on measuring the direct benefit to Intel's business. The program was not to focus on cost reduction activity within the IT organization. These activities were seen as critical for Intel's competitiveness, but this decision went directly to the intended IT culture shift. The entrenched, inward-looking focus of many IT staff members resulted in heated discussions as angry managers were informed their programs would not count toward the ITBV EB goal.

Finance Approach

The detailed measurement methodology of the ITBV program is dealt with throughout the book, however, four items are worthy of calling out with respect to the Financial aspects of the ITBV program.

1. Using discounted cash flow is the core of our financial approach. While IT programs often generate many soft returns, our intent was to force out the softness. By insisting that all business value measurement be reduced to cash flow impact, we hoped to force development of new techniques for credibly gathering data and quantifying it. This was critical to program credibility and our goal to develop a generalized methodology which could be used industry-wide.

2. A 3-year ROI horizon is standard. While many IT investments have returns extending beyond 3 years, it is also true that our ability to forecast those returns is immature due to variability in business processes, organizations, and the market in general. Furthermore, many new capabilities can require significant additional investment 3 to 4 years after initial deployment, including items like functionality upgrades and security patches. Using a 3-year horizon

was seen as a good compromise in light of these other considerations.

3. Business value dials are our key indicators when returns on an investment are measured. These dials ranged from direct impact on Intel revenue, to reduction of inventory, to improvements in employee productivity, as discussed at length in Chapter 2. In establishing these categories in partnership with our customers, we focused the program on the types of real business return we wanted from IT and catalyzed valuable discussion on measurement and methodology.

4. We require dual measurements that match forecast ROIs with actual ROIs to drive accountability. While a forecast ROI is required to enter the process and to estimate financial returns for the ITBV program, an actual ROI is required to exit and for IT to receive credit towards the EB goal. The impact of this requirement is that no program contribution is counted prior to production implementation and that our ITBV team would spend the bulk of its time measuring real-world human performance.

The dual measurement requirement should not be confused with the rule of not double counting business value benefits. Each project needed a forecast and actual ROI, and, in addition, business value contributions must be independent between the projects to avoid counting the same value twice.

Program Marketing

The ITBV program developed a significant marketing campaign. Marketing the program was seen as essential to achieve the ITBV program goals. The ITBV marketing campaign targeted several internal and external groups. Internal groups included IT program and functional managers, IT senior management, and business unit and corporate management. Among the external groups were IT industry influencers, IT industry leaders, academia, and large-enterprise IT organizations.

Marketing materials were developed for all aspects of the ITBV program and program leaders invested significant personal time in traveling to support the communication goals of the program.

Our marketing campaign proved extremely successful. Our initial efforts with marketing focused on gaining support within Intel for the program. Almost by accident we found that our own field sales teams were very interested in the work we were doing. Our sales teams recognized that we were producing valuable real world measurements for the benefits of information technology, and not the usual "speeds and feeds" or generic data, that our field sales teams were used to. As a manufacturer of technology components used by IT shops all over the world, our ability to illustrate the bottom-line benefits of technology had been limited, the ITBV program however assisted in filling this gap.

An effort that started out to prove to internal management that Intel IT was delivering bottom-line value began to attract interest beyond the walls of Intel. Consequently our stakeholder groups were expanded to external audiences who continue to track our progress today and in some cases, contribute to the further development of the ITBV program.

Intel ITBV Program Accomplishments

The first year of the ITBV program was a solid success. We achieved all the program goals, exceeded our financial goal, and also delivered a well-rounded program methodology and structure with buy-in received from all key parties. In 2002, the ITBV program successfully documented over $180 million in new business value across 15 programs, against a goal of $100 million.

With success in hand, 2003 was set to be a tougher year. Our financial goal was increased to from $100 million to $250 million, and the novelty of the program had worn off. We were now in execution mode. Halfway through the year, the ITBV program was forced to escalate to IT management our concern about a dramatic fall-off in program submissions. This escalation resulted in action from all IT departments, and after a few nervous months we began to see the pipeline fill with projects. Now our measurement machine was put to the test; we had a major backlog of programs to process with an acute constraint in the number of HFEs available to the program. However, by the end of the 2003 we again beat the financial program goal, documenting $419 million in new business value across 17 programs.

In 2002 and 2003, the ITBV program capped the maximum business value any one program could contribute to the goal, at $20 million and $40 million respectively. This was done to prevent any one project from accounting for the majority of the business value goal for that year. With the caps removed, the new business value documented was $602 million and $440 million respectively.

The following year brought new challenges and a much higher business value goal. The goal for 2004 was set at $400 million. The ITBV program was seen as mature enough that it no longer needed the brute force incentive scheme of being an IT Employee Bonus item and so the incentive connection was removed, as well as the cap on programs. Intel IT had several other key programs needing EB-level focus that year. The program was facing a critical test: had we penetrated deeply enough into the way IT did business to hit our goals once again?

The year proved to be the most challenging for the program, complicated by a major reorganization which combined IT with enterprise applications organization, eBG. With solid execution by all teams within IT, the program once again managed to beat its goal. In 2004 the program documented $479 million in new business value.

Post-reorganization, the ITBV program was combined with a similar program being run in parallel by eBG. Although the programs had been distinct from each other and had some methodological differences, the programs had been sharing liberally from the start. The new program promises to continue the ITBV program's work, remaining as a key institution of the way Intel does business. This work is analyzed in a Stanford Business School case study (Stanford University, 2004).

Another program which co-existed with ITBV was an effort charged with developing a tool called the Business Value Index (BVI). The BVI team shared many elements of development and governance, and collaborated extensively with the ITBV team. Put simply, the BVI is a tool used to identify and prioritize IT projects which have the greatest potential return on investment. BVI is a prioritization methodology designed to help balance quantified and soft returns when deciding on IT investments.

BVI is used early on in the invest prioritization process and the ITBV tools are used subsequent to those activities. We see BVI as a vital tool for enterprise IT organizations. Detailed measurement of all quantifiable program returns is not feasible. Intermediate methodology is practically necessary when prioritizing large numbers of programs against each other. See Curley (2004) for an expanded discussion of the Business Value Index.

Business Value Documented from 2002-2004

In three years of tracking the business value that IT delivered to Intel, the ITBV program documented in excess of $1.3 billion dollars. This number represents the total combination of the three-year NPV for projects that qualified for the program. There are many reporting methods that can be used to summarize the total business value documented by the ITBV

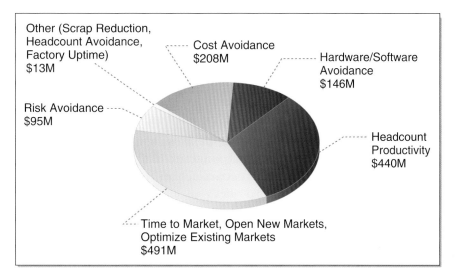

Figure 7.1 Bottom-line Impact by Business Value Dial

program, over the first few years of the program changes were made in how we calculated the business value delivered.

Taking these changes into account and applying them consistently across all the programs measured between 2002–2004, with the reporting caps removed, the total business value is $1.39 billion. This result provides the best estimate of shareholder value created over this time period for projects tracked by the ITBV program. Figure 7.1 summarizes how the $1.39 billion in value delivered breaks out across the business value dials.

IT Business Value Program Accomplishments

The ITBV team worked with numerous technology owners and dozens of Intel business groups and their respective finance representatives, to review and qualify projects within the program. The following are a few of our program's key accomplishments:

■ We investigated over 300 projects to determine whether to include them in the program and selected a subset to review in depth. Out of the 300+ programs, over 60 clearly delivered new business value. Each of these programs was validated by Finance and the respective business units.

■ The team documented business value in 11 categories. These categories are defined as business value dials (see Chapter 2).

- The ITBV team developed standard measurement methods, standard valuation methods, training materials, and evangelized the program across the IT organization.

- We provided data to support data-driven investment decisions to maximize the business value delivered.

In the process, we learned several lessons:

- We realized that linking business value concepts and milestones into the Product Development Life Cycle used extensively within IT was critical for IT to realize the full value it is delivering.

- We learned that identifying the key business value dials for each program and focusing on that subset was critical to quantifying business value.

- We found that employee productivity measurements required extra analysis, data collection, and partnerships from Finance and participating business units to verify the business value.

- We saw that using a common language of business value based on the needs of our customers helped build a stronger partnership between the organizations.

Other outcomes from the program include published case studies and documentation of many of our methodology innovations. White papers and case studies are available through Intel's IT@Intel program and posting of best known methods (BKMs) on Intel's IT Share Net. Our ITBV program is also engaged with academic institutions, industry forums, and other organizations to help establish industry standards for measuring the business value of IT.

Program Weaknesses

Although appropriate at the launch of the program, our decision not to attempt measurement of business value contributions from existing IT capabilities continues to be a gap in our measurement capability. Like many IT organizations, Intel IT spends the bulk of its annual budget in maintaining operations of existing capabilities, it is deeply unsatisfying to our IT organization and IT Finance not to see offsetting quantified business value. Although, in general, the importance of these existing systems is not questioned, it is perfectly legitimate to wonder about their value relative to newer innovations, and to want to see a more data-driven approach in deciding relative levels of investment in innovation vs. maintenance. The practical effect of continuing to evaluate the business value of new programs, but not of old ones, might even perversely be to bias investment towards the old, since we have effectively created an extra hurdle for new programs to jump.

More broadly, we face ongoing work to make business value focus a key thread in the cultural fabric of Intel IT. IT employees are engineers and technical contributors who are passionate about IT in its own right. Although progress has been made in building awareness of business needs, we have by no means finished in this area. Getting everyone in the game is a requirement in the quest to move from being a technology-focused organization to becoming a customer-focused organization.

Future Enhancements

While we have accomplished a great deal already, two significant enhancements to the ITBV program are in our sights for the future.

First, our current methodology, as outlined above, is applied to *selected projects*. While the value of those projects can obviously be aggregated to a total, that total by no means represents the total value of IT at Intel. Yet it would take a tremendous investment to attempt to scale our current methodology to encompass all of the thousands of individual projects undertaken by IT in any given year. What is needed is a complementary top-down measurement methodology for estimating ITBV contributed at the level of the enterprise. The development of this methodology is of keen interest to the IT Finance organization and will certainly require the same level of involvement that we provided to the development of the present set of methods.

Second, we have a great deal of work to do in our extension of the use of the ITBV results. While the results are currently used both inside Intel's IT organization as a tool to prioritize competing investments and outside of IT as a tool for evaluating our effectiveness as an organization, it is our strong belief that the ITBV data could also be used to directly increase our business value.

The business returns from IT system implementations frequently lag the initial investment. This is often because management is uncertain that forecast efficiencies will, in fact, materialize and prefers to "wait and see" before taking actions such as redeploying staff. Unfortunately, by the time it becomes clear that the forecasted business value is real, it is often the case that investment resources have found their way into other activities that may or may not support their highest and best use. With delay, the company loses the time value of money.

It is our belief that, as ITBV forecasts continue to gain credibility, operations management will be increasingly confident to take action more quickly and thus significantly increase the total ITBV contributed by each implementation.

Summary

The future of Intel's IT investment decisions demands proven economic justification. We expect senior management to question every solution we deliver to Intel's employees. Precision, accuracy, and continuous measurement must remain a standard process for valuing IT. Though the extra scrutiny creates more work for IT professionals across the enterprise, it also strengthens the benefits that our businesses receive. Even if economic conditions improve in the upcoming years, IT investments must continue to measure business results, improving competitive advantage and recognizing that IT delivers bottom-line value. It is critical to adopt metrics and measures of IT's value as part of the approval, development, and implementation process of IT solutions. Focusing on the data and keeping the customer involved encourages the line-of-business owners to invest.

Although the ITBV program is judged by all involved to have been a major success, much work remains to be done. Inside Intel IT, we continue to need to march forward. Ongoing project measurement, attainment of annual BV goals, and incremental methodology improvements, comprise a large sustaining program which continues to help align IT's priorities to those of the Intel's business units, and to gradually shift IT's culture towards a business focus.

We also continue with advanced research on the topic of information worker productivity measurement. For example, current research is examining in detail the impacts of information overload and workplace distractions on employee productivity, and promises to point us towards future information solutions which reduce these negative impacts.

Outside of Intel, we also continue to work to proliferate what we have learned, hoping to put better tools in the hands of CIOs everywhere, which will help them to focus their investments on the areas of greatest business return.

Finally, we continue to work with academia to develop core methodologies for productivity measurement, and to promote human factors engineering as a core discipline. From a Finance perspective, HFE is absolutely critical to quantify some of the most important economic impacts in the modern workplace. Working without HFE data is to a large extent like flying blind; it has become a priority at Intel and elsewhere to make the HFE discipline a core capability of the modern IT organization.

Chapter 8

What's Next in IT Business Value

In theory, theory and practice are the same; in practice, they are not.
—Yogi Berra

In this final chapter, we look ahead and examine questions that do not have straightforward answers. Practitioners beware: this is a look into the future. Let's begin by reviewing business value research in the academic community, and reflecting on how this research both informs and ignores the practical needs of the ITBV program team.

Intel has been collaborating with the faculty of MIT's Sloan School of Management in investigating the use of activity-based performance measurement (ABPM) to determine the business value of IT solutions. First, we provide an overview of this next-generation methodology and illustrate the concepts with a business value study underway at Intel. Then, in closing this chapter and the book, we offer an introduction to next-generation human factors engineering: user experience design.

Academic Approaches to IT Performance

Two key characteristics can be used to distinguish academic studies on the business value of information technology. The first is the unit of analysis that is the focus of the study; the second is the nature of the variables—both inputs and outputs—that are examined.

The Unit of Analysis

The unit of analysis can vary from the very large (macro) to the very small (micro). Some studies, typically those undertaken by economists, consider the national economy as a whole or entire industry sectors. Others, more often those undertaken by researchers in management studies, look at the firm or organizational entities smaller than the firm, such as a business unit, a functional group (*e.g.*, a firm's finance department) or a project team. And some recent studies have begun to examine IT business value at the process level (Laubacher et al., 2005) and individual worker level (Van Alstyne and Bulkley, 2005).

Variables—IT inputs and performance outputs

Studies that focus on IT value typically examine an input that represents the level of information technology usage or investment. The exact nature of the input examined can vary widely. Many studies look at the dollar value of IT spending, with some even breaking that spending out into various categories (Aral and Weill, 2005). Other studies consider a broader input, examining IT spending in conjunction with other spending that is associated with it, such as training or process re-engineering (Brynjolfsson and Hitt, 2000). Still other studies focus on the effects of a particular technology or bundle of technologies, such as automated teller machines in banking (Dos Santos and Peffers, 1995) or numerically controlled machinery in manufacturing (Kelley, 1994).

The outputs measured in these studies are similarly varied. Some studies examine productivity, defined as the amount of production generated by a given unit of input. Others measure changes in the market value of firms, considering market value either on its own or benchmarked against a market or industry index. Some look at the impact of IT on profitability or examine the return on IT investments; others look beyond initial technology procurement costs and focus on the total cost of ownership over the entire life cycle (MacCormack, 2003). Still other studies examine operational improvements generated by information technology, such as faster time to market or increases in the number of inventory turns per year. Still others take into account the way that benefits generated by information technology are transformed into benefits for the consumer—what economists call *consumer surplus*—in the form of lower prices or higher quality (Brynjolfsson, Smith, and Hu, 2003).

Productivity Paradox Resolved

The most continuous stream of academic work on information technology and business value has been the debate among economists on whether IT enhances productivity at the national, sectoral, and firm levels. This debate began in the 1980s when the personal computer revolution drove a substantial increase in technology spending by business, especially in the United States. Economists observed large increases in spending on an important capital investment item—computer hardware and software—and hypothesized that such investment would lead to increases in business productivity. They were initially surprised to find that economy-wide productivity measures were seen to remain at the same levels that had been registered during the relatively stagnant 1970s. This counter-intuitive finding came to be known as the *IT productivity paradox*. Its best known formulation came from Nobel laureate Robert Solow, who wrote in 1987, "You can see the computer age everywhere but in the productivity statistics."

One of the difficulties with these early studies was that even though IT spending was growing rapidly, it still comprised only 1 to 2 percent of firm revenues. As a result, its impact was difficult to measure, and the early data sets that were examined were simply not large enough to pick up the effects within acceptable error ranges. Another problem was that these early studies examined productivity at the level of the national economy or industry sectors. Intra-sectoral competition tends to convert increases in firm productivity into consumer surplus, an effect that could confound the findings of gains achieved by IT in studies based on economy-wide or sectoral data.

In the mid-1990s, MIT's Erik Brynjolfsson and Lorin Hitt assembled a very large data set on company IT spending and performance. With this data, they were able to demonstrate that information technology had a significant positive effect at the firm level, with IT strongly correlated with increases in revenues and market capitalization. In fact, the effect they detected was so large that it could not be explained by IT hardware and software investment alone. To account for the gains, Brynjolfsson and Hitt posited that technology spending was typically accompanied by complementary spending in organizational changes that also generated substantial benefits.

By the late 1990s, the labor productivity statistics published by the U.S. Bureau of Labor statistics began to show a significant increase. Labor productivity in the U.S., which had grown at only 1.3 percent annually on average throughout the 1970s and 1980s, doubled in the late 1990s. By the year 2000, U.S. labor productivity was growing at nearly 4 percent per year. There was widespread agreement among economists that information technology was a major factor driving this jump in productivity.

Ironically, even as economists were coming to a consensus on information technology's role in improving firm performance and productivity in the U.S. economy as a whole, management writer Nicholas Carr published a widely influential article warning that IT was on its way to becoming a routine input that could no longer enable firms to achieve strategic advantage (Carr 2003). The divergence of these two opinions, however, can be attributed to the differing perspectives held by Carr and the economists. The economists were seeing evidence that IT created value when looking at data that described conditions at hundreds of firms or across an entire economy, while Carr and other writers on strategic management were focused on whether IT could enable a particular firm to achieve a distinctive position within its unique market and competitive environment.

Brynjolfsson and Hitt's subsequent work has clearly shown that IT alone is not enough. Firms that invest in IT without making the requisite organizational investments actually do worse than firms that don't make an investment (Brynjolfsson, Hitt, and Yang, 2002). The real gains are achieved when firms couple IT investment with a series of IT-enabled organizational practices—what Brynjolfsson calls "invisible factories." To put this in the words of two consultants who wrote a book rebutting Carr's claims: "IT doesn't matter—business processes do" (Smith and Fingar 2003). In short, the IT ecosystem has to be managed to achieve the desired productivity gain.

Other research streams

Other streams of academic work on IT and business value are not as coherent or as focused as the economists' research on the productivity paradox. These studies are undertaken by researchers in many disciplines, and they employ a wide variety of approaches and perspectives. They include case studies of technology implementations at individual organizations and surveys across multiple organizations.

A small stream of work combines the IT business value lens with the resource-based view of the firm taken from the strategic management field. The resource-based view of strategy arises from the premise that firms achieve competitive advantage by assembling combinations of resources that are scarce and difficult to replicate. In the case of IT and business value, the resource-based perspective suggests that IT, when deployed creatively and strategically, can allow firms to develop or enhance a distinctive and defensible strategic position. For more information on this, see Bharadwaj (2002).

An important larger point is that no stream of academic work connects the project perspective—where practicing IT managers must make decisions—with the convincing evidence on firm-level and economy-wide performance gathered by economists. A robust academic theory, joined with empirical evidence, on whether and how IT creates value at the business-unit and workgroup level remains elusive.

ITBV Programs and Academic Research

In general, the academic studies cited use relatively large units of analysis (*e.g.*, the company is the unit of analysis) and use indirect or diffuse measures of IT deployment (*e.g.*, overall IT spend) and business value (*e.g.*, gain in enterprise profitability). While positive findings are reassuring, research of this type raises important issues for ITBV programs about alternative techniques and, most distinctly, the ITBV program's goals and objectives.

Direct vs. Indirect Measurement

Chapter 4 advocates using experimental methods, business value dials based on operational definitions, precise system bundles, and random assignment of employees in laboratory situations to produce a trustworthy estimate of employee productivity gain for specific IT solutions.

In contrast, academic studies most often collect aggregate indicators of IT input and business value output and use statistical machinery such as multiple regression to measure interrelationships among these variables. However, while multiple regression is a trustworthy indicator of association or correlation, it does not provide evidence of causality.

Our experiments aim to show whether a specific investment in IT is, in fact, the cause of a specific and measured improvement. Experiments are typically conducted in isolation to establish the value of a specific investment in IT and are generally not done within a larger context of similar work or within an overall framework for multiple experiments. Consequently, the results derived from case studies can be very limited with respect to their ability to be reused outside of the context under which the data was originally collected. Finally, direct measurement methods, such as laboratory experiments, can be time consuming and interfere with routine work processes.

Units of Analysis

In terms of the research unit of analysis, we have argued in favor of micro units—individual employees performing specified tasks with different IT bundles to support their work. Using a unit of analysis that is at the sector level may be useful to show the overall impact of IT, but will not help IT professionals make a business decisions for specific IT investments. At the other end, using a unit of analysis that is at too low a level might result in showing the impact but in a way that can't be used for any purpose other than the exact outcome measured.

Considering work on the productivity of IT along these two dimensions presents interesting implications for IT professionals and academic researchers in terms of understanding how to bridge the gap between academic theory and empirical evidence.

For example, work focusing on the higher units of analysis

- Will not provide information on the business value returned from individual investments in IT.

- Will not provide cumulative information on the business value returned from a planned series of investments in IT.

- Will not provide differential information to IT strategists looking for the best return among competing investments.

- Will not provide hard data to show CFOs what they are getting for the specific investments they have already made or are going to make in IT.

In short, understanding the business value of a portfolio of specific IT investments aimed at different employee segments and tasks is lost if the portfolio is averaged and treated as a single unit of analysis.

In addition, many of the correlational techniques used for larger units of analysis are not readily usable for the ITBV team. Large samples are needed with measures taken consistently across an industry. Moreover, correlational research is necessarily retrospective; the trends and interrelationships are among historical data and thus are looking backward. Merely knowing that IT investments, on average, lead to business value benefits—even if we add in that the effect is greater when IT governance is stronger—still doesn't tell us which of the next-generation IT systems to invest in, when to invest, and who would benefit most.

Tightly controlled experiments, however, that focus on low-level, direct measures can produce trustworthy results that can be highly specific to the IT solutions and employee populations under investigation. Thus, generalizability is a challenge for us. If one looks closely enough, every situation will look different.

In summary, both experimental and correlational approaches have merits and limitations as to the conclusions that can be drawn from their results. Direct measurement favors hands-on experimental measurement of business value indicators. Given the goals and objectives of our ITBV program, we focus on outcomes that inform investment decisions.

Bridging the gap

With these ideas in mind, one path we are taking is melding the systematic approaches used within our ITBV program with approaches used in academics, economics, and correlational studies. Our assumption is that we can use systematic ITBV assessment processes over time to generate *proxy* metrics that capture the business value associated with IT investments across an organization. Over time, correlations with this proxy metric will provide us with aggregate, firm-level estimates of the overall impact of investments in IT.

The creation of an IT Business Value program within Intel resulted in the following key characteristics that can help bridge the gap caused by deficiencies in the current approaches:

- A common language—*i.e.*, the use of business value dials—for discussing the business value of IT that enables comparisons across projects and organizations

- An extensible technology-neutral framework focused on systematically measuring the business value of information technology

- A standard method—*i.e.*, the BV ROI template—to determine the business value of information technology

- Processes and procedures to develop a portfolio of both forecasted and realized business value delivered by IT solutions

- Defined guidelines that feed data into key processes to maximize and manage the business value of information technology investments

These elements of an ITBV program contribute to developing a more direct and data-driven firm level metric with respect to IT performance. Furthermore, in doing this, a powerful conceptual approach emerges.

When these activities are carried out in the same way over time, the result is the development of a firm-level proxy metric of the impact of information technology. As more IT solutions are measured and stored in the business value portfolio, the more the total IT contribution to the business is captured. Over time, the amount of IT spending captured within IT solutions that are measured as part of an ITBV program will increase, and as this happens, a more accurate indicator of the IT contribution emerges.

We are realistic about this approach and we do not assume that every dollar of IT spending will be accounted for. Some IT projects are just part of doing business—for example, measuring the business value of WAN maintenance is not really required or desirable. Taking into account these types of projects, only a percentage of the total IT spends will get represented in the business value portfolio. The difficult question is determining what percentage of the IT spend has to be covered before a reasonable level of confidence in the proxy metric is established.

In addition, as IT organizations systematically track the business value delivered by IT solutions, the potential for re-using previously documented results for early business value estimates increases, as new IT solutions can be expected to impact similar business value dials. The IT solution still has to be measured, but the process is streamlined and the estimates are likely to be quite accurate.

To help drive reuse across the IT industry, we are exploring the concept of a public repository for sharing selected projects from business value portfolios in order to reduce work across a larger number of IT organizations. When the business value of an IT solution is not deemed confidential, it could be entered into this public repository for use by other IT organizations. When evaluating a new IT solution for business value, IT organizations could review the benchmark data set for similar work and reduce the time to develop early estimates of the opportunity. For a concept like this to be effective, various control points are required to ensure the quality of the data that is represented within the system.

Extending this line of thinking, the same approach could be used to get industry benchmarks on IT organizations relative to their peers. Various types of analysis could be performed to investigate the business value delivered vs. the ratio of IT spending across the business value portfolio.

Collaborating with Academia: Intel and MIT

In 2004 and 2005, Intel joined forces with the activity-based performance measurement (ABPM) team at MIT's Sloan School of Management and worked on a study of the smart device implementation at Intel's

Sales and Marketing Group. This collaboration provided opportunities for both Intel and MIT to share thinking about the measurement of IT value. This work, combined with the systematic efforts developed by Intel's ITBV program, represents another possible way to bridge the gap between theory and practice.

Activity-Based Performance Measurement (ABPM) at Intel

Activity-based performance measurement is an MIT research program that is developing new tools to measure performance at the activity level and to connect the resulting activity-based metrics with business unit and enterprise-level measures of performance. One important application of ABPM is to assess the impact of IT investments, which typically must be undertaken at the activity and process level, on a firm's bottom line. ABPM can enable more intelligent consideration of IT investment decisions and a clearer understanding of IT's contribution to a firm's financial results.

A key insight that serves as the basis of ABPM is that there are common patterns in the types of benefits associated with activities that have similar underlying characteristics. In other words, if the same IT solution is applied to two firms with similar business processes, a similar type of benefit will result.

This principle provides considerable leverage in the challenge of measuring benefits and enabling generalizations about the types of benefits associated with particular technologies when applied to similar classes of processes. In practice, ABPM works by measuring benefits using traditional ROI calculations in the first instance. While this is time consuming, this first instance of measurement generates insights into the type and magnitude of benefits that can then be used to make measuring proceed more quickly and easily in later cases.

Firms already use this principle in assessing the business cases they assemble to justify investment decisions. For example, imagine an IT professional who develops a business case that argues for implementing a new technology for a firm's customer support group. Now consider that the proposal was approved, and the implementation was successful. If a similar technology were then proposed to further enhance the customer support group's operations, the firm's managers and finance people would no doubt refer to the prior successful business case and would more than likely readily accept a subsequent business case based on the same assumptions as the first one.

People inside firms have been doing this sort of intuitive comparison of similar business cases for a long time. ABPM's approach is to do the same basic thing, but just do it more rigorously and systematically.

To compare across different business cases in a systematic and rigorous way, firms must keep track of benefits associated with relevant sets of activities. To do this, they will need a place to store knowledge about the benefits associated with each key type of business process. One useful tool is a process repository that MIT has been developing for the last ten years, called the MIT Process Handbook (Malone et al., 1999). This is a repository of knowledge about business processes that can be thought of as a periodic table of processes, as the way the processes are arranged in the repository is based on an underlying conceptual framework that takes into account the key characteristics of the processes and how they fit together. An on-line version of the MIT Process Handbook is available at *http://ccs.mit.edu/ph*.

MIT–Intel Smart Device Study

The objective of the smart device study is to calculate the costs and benefits to Intel's Sales and Marketing Group (SMG) of integrated cell phone-wireless email devices among its population of road warriors— field staff who spend more than half their time traveling. The study followed a three-phase methodology similar to the one employed in the RFID study described on page 205: identification of processes affected by the smart device, mapping of processes before and after, and comparisons of costs and revenues with and without the smart device.

We gathered data through a series of in-depth interviews with sales and marketing staff who were receiving the new devices. This included the following types of Intel employees:

- Marketing staff who serve large customers
- Marketing staff who work in regional sales organizations serving smaller customers
- Marketing staff who engage in ecosystem enablement of Intel products
- Technical experts who support sales and marketing staff

A baseline was established through conducting interviews before the smart device was deployed to identify key business processes and existing use of IT tools. Follow-up interviews were conducted several

RFID case study

The first ABPM case study examined the impact of radio frequency identification (RFID) technology in the retail supply chain. The key functionality of RFID in retail is that it enables the counting of tagged items present at key junctures in a supply chain with less work, with greater accuracy, and in less time than can be accomplished by prior methods, such as manual counting or bar code scanning. The MIT team undertook initial field work at a large consumer goods manufacturer and large retailer. The study employed a three-step approach:

1. Identify processes that would be affected by RFID
2. Map those processes before and after RFID
3. Estimate difference in costs and revenues before and after RFID.

The study identified seven types of general benefits that can be achieved through RFID implementation in the retail supply chain:

- Greater responsiveness to customers
- Labor savings in counting
- Reduction of theft
- Reduction of disputes with trading partners
- Reduction of excess inventory
- Reduction of spoilage/obsolescence
- Reduction of out-of-stocks

In addition, there were other kinds of benefits that could be achieved under particular circumstances. For example, firms that rely on expensive containers to ship their goods can benefit from RFID-enabled asset tracking, and companies that are victimized by counterfeiting, such as makers of luxury goods, can benefit by using RFID to validate the genuineness of their products.

In the course of this study, the MIT team developed a model that estimated costs and benefits of RFID for a generic manufacturer and retailer. More importantly, the team developed a systematic framework that firms could use for identifying and estimating costs and benefits of planned future RFID implementations (Laubacher et al., 2005).

months after users received their smart devices to identify how business processes and tool usage had changed.

The study identified five key business processes in which Intel's sales and marketing personnel are engaged:

- Providing customer input to Intel product development
- Winning contracts
- Supporting customers' product development
- Helping customers sell to end users
- Providing after-sales support

Different groups within SMG placed greater or lesser emphasis on each process. For example, supporting customers' product development efforts is a major activity for SMG teams that serve large accounts, but is much less important in the regional sales groups.

The study found three major types of benefits from the smart device implementation:

- *Increased employee productivity:* SMG field staff self-reported an average gain of 1-2 hours of additional productivity per week through use of the smart device. In particular, they were able to track and respond to email messages and note schedule changes during times when they had previously been out of communication—for example, while waiting in line at airports or in transit between meetings.

- *Greater effectiveness at critical moments:* Sales staff reported that the always-in-touch feature of the smart device allowed them to be more effective during critical moments, such as during the final stages of a large computer maker's design process, or when customers need help in addressing supply or technology problems. While this impact is incremental, small changes across large accounts can represent substantial business value. Similarly, the smart device would likely play a key role in solving a critical supply or technical situation at a customer site. These problems, however, can be expensive for Intel, so the benefit here can be considerable as well.

- *Stronger customer relationships*: SMG staff also noted that the smart device allowed them to be more responsive to their customers in their daily interactions, and they expected that this greater responsiveness would contribute to stronger relationships.

Past customer surveys have shown that a better relationship with the customer is likely to translate into larger orders in subsequent years. To test this assertion the study team plans to use customer survey data from before and after the smart device implementation to determine if a positive correlation exists between smart device usage and customers' rankings of their account managers in their survey responses.

While the study findings are not yet finalized, preliminary analysis suggests a strongly positive return on investment for the smart device. It also demonstrates the extensibility of the ABPM method into another business process domain.

Promise of ABPM

In the long term, ABPM has the potential to lead to the development of a broad framework that would allow firms—and possibly even cross-firm entities, such as industry associations or professional organizations—to leverage prior measurement work. It could save companies from having to reinvent the wheel each time a business case needs to be written or return on an IT investment is being calculated. ABPM thus aspires to gather, and then store and reuse, knowledge gained while measuring IT business value. This principle of reusing knowledge from prior measurement efforts is closely akin to the ideas about reuse being implemented in the ITBV program.

Gaining a Competitive Advantage through User Experience Design

I have been a Human Factors Engineer for more than 15 years, and I teach the subject at Arizona State University Polytechnic. I've established and managed Human Factors Engineering (HFE) and User-Centered Design (UCD) groups at large and small companies across a number of business sectors. Within Intel, I have taken HFE/UCD work from tactical observations when a group has ease-of-use issues to dedicated teams embedded within the organizations focusing on large scale strategic initiatives.

You might be wondering why a trained HFE wrote this book and managed an ITBV program within one of the largest IT organizations in the world. The answer is that a well-run ITBV program is user-centric. This approach gets the whole IT organization focusing on the customer and end user and assists in getting everyone moving towards a user-centric mind set. As a result, the HFE/UCD agenda is driven as an outcome of focusing on the business value delivered as it was defined by the customer.

User Experience Design

User experience design has its roots in UCD, a philosophy that places the end user at the center of all design activities. UCD and other related areas (such as Human Factors Engineering, Human-Computer Interaction, Interaction Design, Usability Engineering, and so on) all seek to humanize our interaction with technology. Figure 8.1 shows the relationship between UCD and UED.

IT delivers the greatest business value when it understands what end users need to do to accomplish work-related activities that are linked to their business objectives, and then designs a user experience that directly supports those objectives. The solution must be designed to bridge the gap between the end users and their business objectives from the start. From an ITBV perspective, solutions designed to enable scenario-driven ROI from the beginning help deliver strategic results for the supported organizations.

UCD focuses on the usability of a product or service. Graphics and other design elements aim to facilitate the end user's interaction with the product or service. UED is a process that extends the UCD philosophy to incorporate all aspects of the end-user's interaction with the product or service. Experience begins with an awareness of the product or service and includes all aspects of the end user's interaction to achieve their goals.

Commonly accepted definitions of User Experience Design include at least these five components of experience:

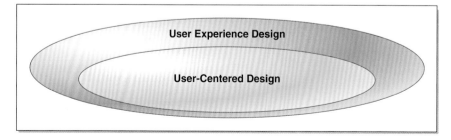

Figure 8.1 Relationship Between UCD and UED

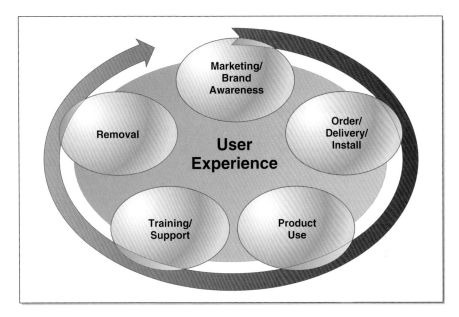

Figure 8.2 Five Components of User Experience

- ■ Marketing and brand awareness
- ■ Order, delivery, and install
- ■ Product or service use
- ■ Training and Product support
- ■ Removal or end of life

Figure 8.2 shows the components of user experience that the user encounters once a solution is deployed. Each component refers to a particular aspect of the end user's experience, and the importance of each aspect to the user will vary throughout the life of the solution.

- ■ Marketing and Brand awareness focuses on the image portrayed to end users before they interact with the IT solution. This includes advertisements, staff interaction, aesthetics, word of mouth, and so on (Rubinoff 2004). These items need to be aimed specifically at the intended end user and match the overall desired experience, as they are the foundation for what is to come. It is important that this component be consistent, comfortable, intuitive, and trustworthy in order to create a solid brand image (Goto 2004).

- ■ The second component that impacts user experience is Order, Delivery, and Install. This is typically the user's first encounter with the IT solution. Depending on the type of solution, it can include a number of elements, including packaging, first-time setup, integration with other solutions, registration, billing, and so on. As the user's initial hands-on experience, it should be straightforward and accommodate both new and advanced end users.

- Product or Service Use, is the heart of user-centered design. The International Standards Organization (2000) provides an excellent definition with respect to the concept of usability as it relates to this component: a solution should be effective, efficient, and satisfactory to the end-user within the context that it is used.

- Training and Product Support is a component that could entail a large portion of the end-user's experience. This component can include training, support, updates, problem resolution, warranties, and ongoing maintenance.

- The last component is Removal/End of Life—the final interaction the end user has within the experience and possibly the first experience with a replacement solution. This interaction is often overlooked, and it can be extremely damaging if not proactively managed. Moving from one version of a solution to another should be straightforward, and the IT solution should be easy to remove or transfer to a new IT ecosystem.

User Experience Design within IT

IT organizations who already recognize—from support calls, quality indicators, and surveys from end-users—that their end users have ease-of-use issues with deployed IT products might have support from key senior managers or might already have a staffed HFE/UCD team managed by senior UCD professionals.

If a UCD effort is already established, the next step in its evolution is establishing a User Experience Design program. If a UCD team is not in place, one should be formed before trying to tackle UED.

The User Experience Design Program should focus on these key processes:

- Developing standard metrics for user experience with products, services, and solutions

- Developing metrics for the overall experience IT delivers and manages

- Delivering a consistent user experience through extending processes and guidelines
- Making user experience a core element of the business through developing a user-centric innovation process
- Measuring the user experience with all IT provided solutions
- Measuring the user experience provided by the IT organization across all solutions provided

For example, Lindgaard (2004) explains how a competitive analysis project resulted in a solution that management hadn't asked the team to consider. The effort started as a study on warehouse management in the form of an analysis between two competing technologies for use in grocery distribution. The warehouse was roughly five acres in size, with aisles and shelves from floor to ceiling. Assemblers collected goods ordered by supermarkets, placed them on a pallet, and wrapped them in plastic before placing them at one of 18 loading bays. Management was dealing with two issues: incomplete orders and damaged goods at time of delivery. It was felt that introducing a hands-free device during order assembly would address the issues.

The team was asked to evaluate the usability of two competing technologies. What the team discovered through solid end-user analysis was that the root cause of the two issues was the warehouse management system. As a result, management did not invest in either of the two competing solutions, and the effort resulted in changes in the warehouse management system to resolve the issues.

This is the core of user-centered innovation: to understand what the end users need to accomplish and deploy the right IT solution to allow them to meet those objectives.

User Experience Design in IT solutions

It is critical to understand that for an IT solution to have a good user experience, necessary activities must be performed during all stages of design and development (see Figure 8.3 on page 212). In effect, the user experience must be built into an IT solution using a multi-disciplinary team that represents all the components of the experience.

The user's first experience with an IT solution occurs at deployment. Users will not encounter every aspect of the experience at that time; the experience unfolds through multiple interactions.

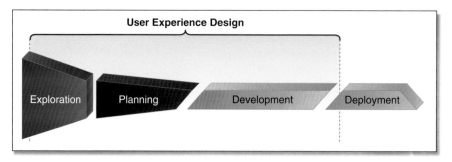

Figure 8.3 User Experience Design and the Product Life Cycle

Another way to envision the goal of a User Experience Design program is shown in Figure 8.4 and Figure 8.5. Figure 8.4 depicts a generic IT organization with each support group deploying products or solutions, and each managing or not managing the IT user experience that results. In this case the user's experience with IT is fractured; it is unlikely that it will be a singular, cohesive, compelling user experience.

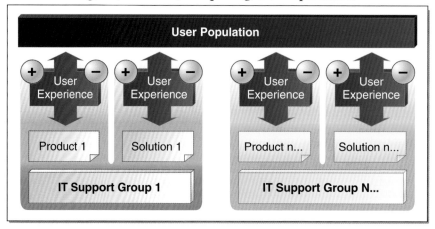

Figure 8.4 Unmanaged IT User Experience

Figure 8.5 shows the desired state, in which IT delivers a user experience that is managed across all support groups. In this case, the user's experience with IT is consistent across the entire IT organization.

To achieve this state, the user's experience with IT has to be designed, deployed, and managed. It is important to note that this is much more than delivering consistent user interfaces or standards applied to internal Web sites or applications. Consistent user interfaces may influence the user experience, but they do not and cannot define it.

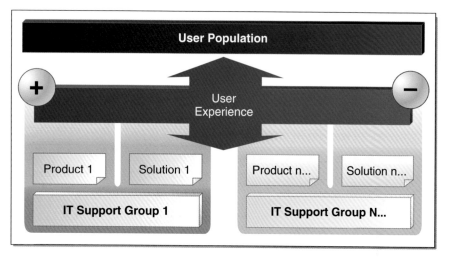

Figure 8.5 Managed IT User Experience

Delivering Compelling User Experiences

There are three essential stages to realizing the goal of delivering a competitive advantage through compelling user experiences.

Stage 1: Creating an ITBV Program

This has been the focus of this book. The outcome that should result from having implemented an ITBV program that is focused on measuring the impact of IT solutions should be the following:

■ Moving IT thinking from techno-centric to user-centric (*i.e.*, the culture change to a user focused organization)

■ Defining value based on the end-user/customer, not on IT (*i.e.*, creation of business value dials based on what the end-user/customer values as important)

■ Measuring projects within the business value dials to help create connective tissue between IT and the strategic objectives (SO) of the groups IT supports. Think of this as scenario-driven ROI.

Stage 2: Establishing a User Experience Design (UED) Program

Implementing a User Experience Design program to continue the transition from techno-centric to user-centric started by the ITBV program. It is at stage 2 that the culture shift starts to manifest itself in how the IT organization thinks about supporting the end-users. The IT User Experience Design program is focused on designing, developing, and measuring the user experience delivered and managed by an IT organization. The desired outcome at this stage is to:

■ Make user-centered innovation the norm that will be carried out throughout the IT organization

■ Continue extending the user-centric foundation developed in the creation of an ITBV initiative

■ Design solutions to enable scenario-driven ROI from the beginning and align the solutions with the strategic objectives of the support organizations

Stage 3: Embedding User Experience Design in the Business

In order to continually grow skills and abilities, IT organizations need to understand how capable they are at engaging in UED. Measuring the user experience delivered and managed provides insight in to how well it is being managed, but will not answer how capable an organization is at UED. With this concern in mind, development has begun within Intel on an IT User Experience (UE) Capability Maturity Framework (CMF), as shown in Figure 8.6. The outcome of this stage is:

■ Systematic measurement of the ability of IT to engage in user experience design

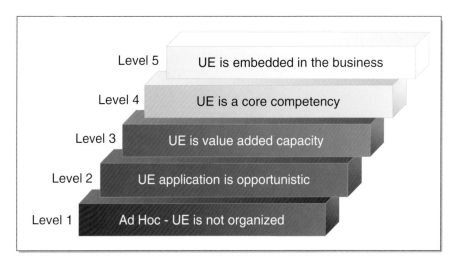

Figure 8.6 IT User Experience Capability Maturity Framework

Source: Intel, modified from SEI CMM

■ Deployment of the right IT solutions to enable compelling and innovative user experiences

■ Increased business value delivered by progressing towards the upper levels of the framework

The IT UE CMF will be a formal approach to assessing an IT organization's capability to engage in UED. It is based it on a solid foundation of existing work in usability maturity models (UMM) by researchers like Earthy (1998), Jokela (2001), and Jokela, Siponen, Hirasawa, and Earthy (In press). All are recognized experts and have published extensively in this area.

However, existing approaches tend to focus solely on UCD, with an emphasis on how well a product team engages in the process and have an implicit assumption that a product or solution is already selected. They also have a bias toward an outsider in view of the development process with respect to HFE/UCD involvement.

Measuring User Experience

Intel is in the process of developing a standard methodology for measuring user experience. Due to the scope of Intel's IT installed user base, surveying—rather than usability testing—was selected as the most efficient assessment method. The metric itself will be developed in a series of stages.

Stage 1: Establish Usability Metric. We have settled on using the System Usability Scale, or SUS (Brooke, 1996), which is freely distributed as an online survey. It is easy to administer and score, and with only 10 items, the SUS has the added advantage of being relatively short, compared to other usability inventories.

Stage 2: Validate and Expand. During this stage we will validate our SUS findings by comparing subjective data to objective data gathered in usability tests. In addition, other elements will be examined beyond usability data to map onto the other components of user experience. Candidate items from training, marketing, and other disciplines will be evaluated for inclusion in the overall metric.

Stage 3: Measure User Experience. Soon the complete user experience survey will begin to take shape. All relevant user experience components are in place and will be validated as results come in. By the end of this stage, Intel has a fully developed and validated user experience metric for use across IT applications.

The IT UE CMF is an attempt to systematically extend this solid foundation of work to take the entire user experience into account and to evaluate how well the organization does in selecting the right IT solutions to enable compelling and innovative user experiences. An underlying assumption of this model is that the business value created increases as IT organizations progress through the framework. Demonstrating how capable an IT organization is at UED is central to the overall effort of delivering compelling user experiences that result in competitive advantages.

Business Value vs. Cost Justifying Usability

Business value is similar to HFE/UCD concepts of cost justifying usability (Bias and Mayhew, 1994). Cost justifying usability differs from business value in the following ways:

- Focus on justifying usability-related project activities done by HFE/UCD professionals
- Tactical in nature, not strategic, focusing on justifying the existence of HFE/UCD professionals on a project
- Rarely a part of a larger systematic effort
- Isolates the return on usability related activities, not the return for the entire project
- Not directly linked to the strategic objectives of the organization.

Work by Lund (1997), Rosenberg (2004), and Lindgaard (2004) summarize a number of limitations with the cost justifying usability approach.

I believe a series of tactical justifications will not result in a fundamental change in how HFE/UCD is employed in organizations. Cost justifying usability is not a long-term strategy to drive systemic change within organizations. It is more important to understand cost justifying usability as a subset of the total business value a solution delivers. The focus of these efforts should be on measuring the total business value delivered in the language of the customer/end user.

To execute this vision, it is important to do the following:

- Establish an IT Business Value program to systematically link IT to the bottom line

- Establish a User-Centered Design group to focus on deploying more usable IT solutions

- Establish a User Experience Design program to take UCD to the next level in this evolution

- Evaluate how well the IT organization is delivering compelling user experiences for IT solutions

IT organizations must demonstrate their bottom-line impact as they continue to battle for budgetary resources and must work to enable a competitive advantage by expanding their focus from what is dictated by TCO to include delivering compelling IT user experiences. As companies realize the business value of optimizing the user experience, they will come to expect IT to deliver on this front.

Establishing an ITBV program makes explicit the connection between what an IT organization delivers and what the customer or end-user has defined as valuable. It forces an organization to adopt a user-centric view of the world, as their value is determined and measured by the customer or end user who receives those solutions in a structured systematic fashion.

As this foundation starts to change the culture and enables the subsequent work that needs to happen with respect to user experience design, it starts to resemble the core of any market-driven organization. When pushed to the edge, it looks a lot like marketing. A truly market-driven organization defines this as maximizing the link between what they make and what the customer and end users want.

Summary

Formalizing the measurement of business value is one approach to changing corporate attitude toward the value of investing in IT. Project owners will be more willing and more equipped to document, measure and objectively demonstrate the value of their projects in customer terms. Creating an ITBV program is one way to encourage and develop better alignment with groups that IT supports. Investments in IT will continue to require proven economic justification and must contribute to a company's competitive advantage. It is critical for IT organizations to adopt metrics and measures of business value as part of their approval, development, and implementation processes. Focusing on data and keeping the customer involved encourages the line-of-business owners to invest the time to evaluate their project's impact on the company's bottom-line. In short, an ITBV program supports managing IT for business value.

I encourage every IT organization, large and small, to establish a program that measures the bottom-line impact of the IT solutions they deliver. While there are no silver bullets when measuring the business value of IT, creating or adapting business value dials and taking measures is certainly the place to start. For those who want to go down this road, here are some parting thoughts:

- Develop a common definition of business value based on what your customers and end-users see as valuable.

- Work closely with your customers and end-users to develop a set of business value dials that are defined in their language. Use a standard measurement framework and a standard valuation process.

- Develop a business value process that links organizational activities together and gives them a common purpose.

- Participation by Finance is critical to an ITBV program. Let Finance own the selection of the appropriate financial metrics and final results.

- Measure twice and count once. That is, measure both forecasted and actual business value, and never count the same value contribution for more than one project.

- Use a standard metrics plan to drive objective data collection across all business value dials.

- When launching an ITBV program, start small and grow the process. Focus on new business value, dedicated resources, and make sure senior management supports the effort.

- Integrate the results into your organization's IT governance system to manage IT for business value.

- Use the program to enable a culture shift that focuses on business value in all aspects of running the IT organization, including a shift from techno-centric thinking to user-centric thinking.

As I come across new ideas or examples of great approaches that others use to measure the business value of IT, I shall post them at the *Measuring the Business Value of IT* Web site located at *www.intel.com/ intelpress*.

Appendix **A**

Case Study

Well done is better than well said.
—Benjamin Franklin

Measuring the business value of IT investments is a process of making multitudes of decisions on a variety of business, technical, and usability issues. While white papers often document successful outcomes, I developed this case study to examine the business value appraisal process and identify the alternatives that IT planners considered on their way to success in putting new technologies to work.

Prepared in the style of a business school case, this example brings readers to a critical judgment at its midpoint. I encourage you to pause and consider what you might have done, had you been in the decision-maker's shoes. The second half of the case reveals the decision taken and its consequences. I am indebted to the individuals named in this study who took the time to explain not just what they accomplished, but also how they accomplished it.

Improved Throughput at St. Vincent's Hospital

"St. Vincent's has a throughput problem," CIO Tim Stettheimer concluded six months after he arrived at St. Vincent's Hospital in January of 2003. "The hospital's Executive Committee is looking for operational changes to gain efficiencies. If we could be more efficient, then we wouldn't have to redirect patients to other hospitals as often. And, if we turn people away at the door, I suspect they will be less likely to come back to St. Vincent's in the future."

Called *diversion* in the hospital industry, redirecting patients to other hospitals incurs an opportunity cost. At St. Vincent's Hospital, a 338-bed acute care facility located in Birmingham, Alabama, patients are turned away when emergency care resources are fully tapped and when critical care and medical-surgical unit beds are unavailable.

"We know our utilization is at 86 percent and so there is room to improve," Stettheimer reasoned. "And, we know from satisfaction surveys that some of our patients are unhappy that they have to wait in long lines for services such as radiology. I wonder how many patients are in the queue in radiology right now?"

The opportunity cost of diversion is high. Executives at St. Vincent Hospital formed the Throughput Committee to study the problem. This task force estimated that in 2003, the hospital lost $13,300 per hour in revenue when patients were diverted to other facilities and measures indicated that the hospital was in a state of diversion for over 1,500 hours that year. Thus, over $19 million in potential revenue was lost on a annual basis.

Seeking a Solution

The Throughput Committee identified a number of indicators of the problem with hours of diversion at the top of the list. Other indicators were patient time spent waiting, time to clean rooms after patient discharge, and percentage of patients discharged before noon. This last measure is important because, like a hotel, when patients are not discharged before noon, a gridlock occurs when new patients arrive in the afternoon. Patients arriving in the morning for tests often need a bed in the afternoon.

"Slowly the nature of the solution emerged," Stettheimer explained. "We had indicators that could guide us to greater throughput, but these indicators weren't available in a timely fashion. What we needed was a real-time system where we could watch over the operations of the hospital. We really did need to know how many patients were waiting at radiology, and a lot more."

"We know how to track patients," Gary York said to Stettheimer in a brainstorming session, "with location sensing and RFID technologies." York is an IT strategist familiar with health care industry requirements.

"And we want a real-time system where hospital staff can see where their patients are and what needs to be done. Visualization is going to be a key part of this project," Stettheimer responded.

"I agree that visibility is the key," York replied, "We know that there is a lot of useful information already captured electronically at St. Vincent's Hospital, but it's in silos that prevent it from being widely known. We can retrieve this information through the health care communication standard, HL7."

"I think we can improve throughput if we can combine patient location with clinical and process information and make all this information visible at the same time to hospital staff," Stettheimer concluded.

York and Stettheimer outlined their ideas to the Executive Committee using the diagram shown in Figure A.1.

"With RFID added to our technical foundation, we will be in position to provide more current information to hospital operations groups such as transport and custodial services," Stettmeier explained. "We can help

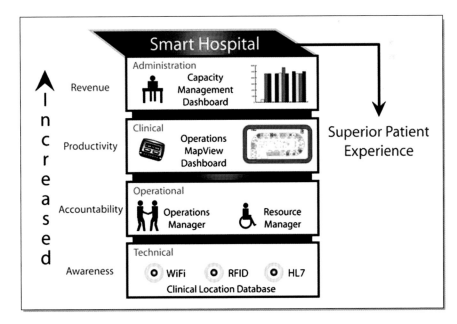

Figure A.1 Throughput Improvement Architecture for a Smart Hospital

clinical services by providing a real-time view of where patients are in the hospital and we can display other information, such as instructions from our new physician order entry (POE) system."

"Based on information stored in our clinical location database (CLD), we can gain synergy between clinical and process data gathered together from separate departmental systems," York added, noting that the CLD is an element in the foundation layer of the smart hospital architecture. "And we can provide administrators with dashboards to monitor how the hospital is doing on key indicators such as "% Discharge before Noon.""

Investment Decisions for Innovative Technologies

St. Vincent's Hospital is a member of the Ascension Health organization and is the identified flagship for deploying new technologies. St. Vincent's Hospital has been the site for prior experiments in digital imaging and electronic patient records. Their overarching objective is to create a *digital* hospital and to field point-of-care systems to both streamline operations and optimize the quality of care.

Excited by Gary York's vision, Tim Stettheimer began to think through the way forward. "Investing in new technology has its risks," Stettheimer reminded himself. "With greater risks come greater rewards, of course. What we need to do is find ways to manage those risks."

"We also need to understand the return on this investment. We will want to put measures into place so that we can make informed decisions about deployment to other units at St. Vincent's Hospital and for other Ascension Health hospitals," Stettheimer concluded.

The Way Forward

"What we need is a pilot study that will test the technology and provide us with the information we need to evaluate further deployment," Tim Stettheimer explained at a coordination meeting with his IT staff. "A pilot study will put less capital at risk, simplify technical deployment, and provide the opportunity to measure the effects our investment has on patient throughput and staff productivity."

"We chose the medical/surgical unit because we knew that it triggered a diversion problem, but we were unsure exactly why," Stettheimer explained. "Also, if medical/surgical throughput improved and beds were more often available, then that would relieve pressure on Emergency Services. Emergency Services goes into a diversion state when that department has nowhere to turn. And, finally, medical/surgical beds represent the most common resource at our hospital and other hospitals. So, a pilot use of RFID and other technologies has the potential to make a big difference for St. Vincent's Hospital and for other hospitals as well."

Designing the Business Value Study and the Solution

Gary York founded a company called Awarix and set out to build this vision of a better patient management system into a real solution. To better understand throughput issues, St. Vincent's Hospital and Awarix staff first conducted an observational study.

"We needed to know more about what we were about to measure and where the IT solution could be most helpful," said Gary York in a technical briefing in late 2003. "We needed to know whether data about when rooms become available is accurate, for example. We decided to focus our attention on the key transitions, which are admissions, discharge, and transfer (ADT). Identifying and eliminating ADT wait time should improve throughput."

"We honed in on key indicators as well," York continued. "We found out that our baseline percentage of discharges before noon was 48 percent. We knew from our observational study that it takes an average of 39 minutes to record ADT changes."

Working with the Throughput Committee members representing different stakeholders, York and the St. Vincent's Hospital IT staff worked out the high-level requirements for the solution. The system was to provide visible, accurate and timely data available at a glance to users without requiring any technical competency. For practical reasons, the

RFID device would travel with a patient's medical charts, which travel with the patient in all cases. Information available in St. Vincent's Health care Information System would be integrated with the new system, which was to be called Awarix.

If It's Brown, Wash It Down

"Awarix is very easy to use," explained Theresa Meadows, R.N., who oversees the training process. "It takes about 10 minutes for doctors and nurses to understand how the system works. While we provide a 'cheat sheet,' many of the icons are quite obvious to the eye." Figure A.2 shows this diagram.

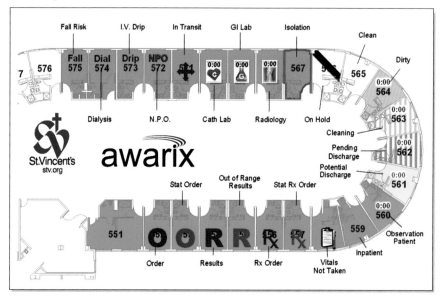

Figure A.2 Awarix View of Unit Status

"Green rooms are rooms with patients," Meadows went on. "And the letters and colors signify events. An 'R' means that a test result has become available and it is blue when normal and red when it's not. A blue 'O' indicates that a doctor has left an order to be carried out for this patient. Rooms with patients who are off to radiology are tagged with an x-ray icon. As soon as a patent is discharged, the room shifts to brown, which is a signal to the custodial staff to clean it.

"Our staff members find this solution very helpful. In the past, hunting for and fetching patients has been a hit-and-miss proposition. It was not uncommon to walk the length of the unit only to find that the patient was elsewhere in the hospital, perhaps at physical therapy. With Awarix, a nurse can glance at the display and make sure the patient is available."

"Empty, clean rooms are marked in white and are easy to spot," Meadows pointed out. "Before we launched Awarix, we had what we called 'hidden beds.' These are beds that actually are available for patients but unknown to the admissions staff. As many as five or six beds could be hidden. This could trigger a diversion when, in fact, it was not necessary."

Business Value Results

"We are pleased to report significantly positive results from this pilot study," a spokesman for the Throughput Committee said in reporting to the hospital's Executive Committee. As Table A.1 shows, the accuracy with which St. Vincent's hospital now captures ADT events had improved by over 85 percent and the variability had been reduced to 1 Sigma due to a significantly reduced range of values. The wide fluctuation in accuracy observed before introducing Awarix suggests that the hospital had no process at all. These results show that St. Vincent's hospital has vastly improved the ADT process simply by providing visibility to those responsible for reporting ADT data.

"We are making significant headway on discharging patients before noon," the committee also reported. The 21 percent improvement was likely to improve throughput and increase overall revenues to St. Vincent's Hospital. And, with Awarix in place, IT can provide hospital administrators with a dashboard that displays this metric and hospital managers can focus on ways to improve it further.

Table A.1 Two Process Improvement Metrics

Indicator	Before	After	Improvement
ADT Accuracy	39 minutes	6 minutes	> 85%
ADT Range	-38 minutes to 7.9 hours	1 minute to 45 minutes	1 Sigma
Discharges by Noon	48%	58%	21%

Cost Benefit Analysis

St. Vincent's Hospital invested $523,341 directly in developing and deploying the Awarix pilot system. Hospital variable costs increased during the the pilot testing, due to increased patient volume, leading to a total pilot cost outlay of $1,709,529. Net revenue increased by $2.58M, also due to increased patient throughput. The contribution margin, which is the net revenue generated from treating patients less the expenses incurred, was on the order of $876,791, indicating a 151 percent return on investment over the term of the pilot study.

Metrics including those in Table A.1 led St. Vincent's Hospital analysts to conclude conservatively that capacity would be increased by one additional patient per week per nursing unit and that the average length of stay for patients would be reduced by about a quarter of a day. The increase in gross revenue for St. Vincent's was $5.5M for the first five months after Awarix went live. Annualized, this would result in a $13.2M increase in gross revenue, which is about 70 percent of the estimated $19M in lost revenue.

"I expect a cumulative effect as we continue to roll out this technology," Stettheimer said when reflecting on the pilot study's findings. "Namely, we are building a platform to accomplish specific throughput objectives and, at the same time, we are establishing an IT infrastructure that will support incremental improvements at relatively low costs. Other hospital processes will likely be improved using the Awarix investment as a foundation."

Epilogue

Before the full deployment of the Awarix patient tracking system, St. Vincent's Hospital was constantly on diversion and could only hold a maximum of 2,231 patients per month. As shown in Figure A.3, after

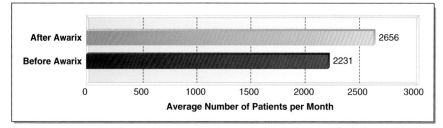

Figure A.3 Improved Throughput at St. Vincent's Hospital

Awarix was in place, the capacity of the hospital rose to 2,656 patients

per month, a 19 percent increase. This change took place over a five month period. Before Awarix was in place, the average length of stay (ALOS) for patients was 50 hours. Three months after Awarix was in place, ALOS dropped to 24 hours. Since health insurance ordinarily covers only 24 hours of care in many situations, this change in ALOS had both positive financial and capacity consequences for the hospital.

Another benefit of Awarix is that the hospital staff likes it. Often, new technology brings more work to the nursing staff, but in this case, their work was made easier. They could save steps and time by glancing at the status boards to see exactly what needs to be done. At a review of the system with nursing directors, the IT team received a round of applause for what the nurses thought was the best technology ever deployed at St. Vincent's Hospital.

Appendix B

Business Value Studies

Send me photographs from time to time so that I can see how you draw the bow.
—Eugene Herrigel, *Zen and the Art of Archery*

This appendix reviews work done on two specific projects that represent the type of work done by the ITBV team over the years to capture the business value of IT. Each case study contains:

- A brief project description
- The business value dials used
- The scope of the evaluation
- The overall design of the evaluation
- A discussion of how we determined what to measure
- Issues encountered during the evaluation
- A summary of the business value from the evaluation

The first study measured the impact of our e-Workforce solution. The e-Workforce program is a set of software applications and business processes designed to support collaboration. The second study is based on the use of IT in manufacturing and reviews how the use of IT assisted in greater tool utilization for testing and helped avoid purchasing millions of dollars worth of new test equipment.

Measuring Changes in Workforce Productivity: Gauging the Impacts of Intel's e-Workforce program

Project Description

To further our evolution into a 100 percent e-Corporation, Intel IT launched a multi-year initiative called e-Workforce. A major element of our e-Workforce program is increased support for collaboration. We embedded core business processes, such as meetings, team planning, and document management, into new and existing technologies. The goal of e-Workforce is to overcome the limitations of time and distance as globalization defines Intel's corporate landscape, the program focuses on enabling people, no matter where they are located.

For a complete write up of the e-Workforce measurement work, please visit Intel.com/IT.

Business Value Dials

This evaluation focused on two business value dials: employee productivity and cost avoidance. The method used to determine the business value for employee productivity is provided in Chapter 4

The cost avoidance business value dial was defined as the reduction in travel-related spending that resulted from e-Workforce. We determined the number of travel-related events that user said they avoided as a result of the functionality provided by e-Workforce. This data was then combined with data we obtained form our corporate travel office to determine the financial impact of travel reduction.

Scope of Study

We compared new methods of collaborating using a new office productivity application and a document management system with the old methods of accomplishing those same tasks with an earlier version of the office productivity application and when file sharing was accomplished with operating system commands, shared drives, and other data repositories. We kept the hardware platform constant, using identically-configured notebooks for the lab study. We only changed the software bundle loaded onto the notebook. In the field study participants used their current hardware and the software that corresponded to either the baseline or post implementation condition.

The lab study was restricted to sites where we had usability labs. Participants were randomly selected and we selected employees from a variety of job types. The field study was limited to locations where had human factors engineers on site to talk with the participants in person and make the necessary observations. Activity log were sent to users in Asia, Europe and the United States for baseline and post implementation data collection.

Data Collection Techniques

To determine the impact of the e-Workforce solution on the workforce we used six data collection techniques:

- Surveys done before and after implementation

- Semi-structured interviews done before and after implementation

- Field observations done before and after implementation

- Self-report activity logs done before and after implementation

- Lab-based user performance tests to measure specific user tasks

- Database review for travel-related costs

We employed surveys to collect satisfaction data and to analyze the impact of the solution on travel behavior for face to face meetings. Surveys are easy to administer and can be collected efficiently from a large number of users. However, surveys can be impacted by a participant's willingness to respond and other user reporting biases.

We employed semi-structured interviews to gather open-ended responses, allow for follow up questions, and to uncover unanticipated information. At the same time we conducted semi-structured interviews we also conducted field observations to measure user performance on tasks that could not easily be reproduced in the lab user performance test.

We had users fill out activity logs to determine the frequency with which tasks are performed and to determine adoption rates. To make this approach work, we defined a core set of activities with clear starting and stopping points.

We asked participants to perform a core set of tasks in a lab setting, allowing us greater control in establishing user performance metrics. Representative participants executed predefined tasks and we collected completion times and user satisfaction with the solution.

We used a company database to extract data on the air travel, hotel stays and car rentals for both international and domestic travel. We used a survey to understand the reasons for employee travel and to determine if the e-Workforce solution contributed to travel reduction.

Study Design

The evaluation lasted for a total duration of 9 months, of this time roughly 3 months was spent collecting data. There was a 6 month waiting period between the baseline data collection and the post implementation data collection. The delay was designed to allow users to become familiar with the functionality of the new solution.

Sampling and Baseline Data Collection

We recruited hundreds of Intel employees to participate in various aspects of the evaluation. Not all participants completed each part of the evaluation. We recruited these participants from a pool of employees targeted to receive the solution and used a stratified random sampling plan to get a representative set of participants.

The baseline field observations measured tasks that were not well suited for our lab study. We measured the time to complete these tasks before participants upgraded to the e-Workforce suite of software. Fifty participants completed the baseline field observation. We waited six months and then collected the data for the same tasks from for 46 of the original 50 participants.

Activity Logs

To understand the value of differences between tasks measured, we needed to understand what percentages of users were adopting the new task methods supported in e-Workforce. We collected data from 437 participants who completed a baseline activity log over a one day period. We followed up six months later with a post-implementation activity log. We had 303 of the original 437 participants fill out this second activity log.

Travel Cost Reduction

One of the benefits of the e-Workforce solutions is that it enables employees to have virtual meetings. These virtual meetings are assumed to reduce the need for travel and hence the travel cost. To test this assumption, we performed a survey and an analysis of our travel cost data.

We used a company database to collect the data on the air travel, hotel stays and car rentals for both international and domestic travel. Though employees traveled using both commercial airlines and an Intel provided air shuttle service, we only analyzed data on travel using commercial airlines.

We used a survey to understand the reasons for employee travel. We selected a representative set of 300 employees who traveled in the 6 month period after the e-Workforce solution was implemented and sent them a survey request. We got survey responses from 39 employees. The survey was designed to find the proportion of the employees who traveled for specific activities. The survey asked the employees if the e-Workforce solution helped them to perform those activities virtually, and if so, did it help them to avoid making any trips.

Laboratory Testing

We did a lab study, asking 30 participants to complete a 2 hour lab based user performance study. We selected a cross-section of user types to best represent typical Intel business users. The study followed standard experimental protocol (*e.g.*, introduction, participant briefing, data collection activities, and a debriefing) and used standard procedures to reset each platform at the end of the test session. We provided familiarization activities for tasks that were not performed regularly. We counterbalanced the order of the test platforms to minimize potential learning effects. Just as many participants started with the baseline system as those who started with the post implementation system.

We conducted t-tests on data collected during the evaluation. A t-test evaluates the statistical significance of the difference between sets of observations and returns a likelihood that the observed difference occurred by chance. Likelihoods less that $p = 0.05$ indicate significant findings.

Determining What to Measure

We teamed with experts and did early field work with the program office that was deploying e-Workforce to determine the task to measure. We also did a preliminary review of documentation and conducted interviews with team members and subject matter experts to determine other tasks and business processes that the solution would support.

We used this information to identify tasks that were well structured and could be reproduced. These tasks would be in our lab study. Other tasks had more variability, and we were concerned that creating a specific scenario for them and testing them in the lab would not provide representative results. We decided to measure these tasks using field observation.

We knew we wanted to measure the impact of the solution on travel activities. This required determining the best approach to get the data from the participants. We also needed to determine who had data we could use within our own systems and what data was the right data for what we wanted to measure.

Issues Encountered

During the course of the evaluation we encountered a number of issues that made data collection difficult.

- We needed to work with various stakeholders to get employees recruited from across the company. On a number of occasions the group was slow in getting names and had incomplete or inaccurate data. This created extra work for the ITBV team when trying to get participants for the baseline condition, many people contacted had already installed components of the e-Workforce solution or didn't fit the segment required by the sampling plan.

- Most business value studies assume an adoption rate of 100 percent for the new task methods, averaging data used to develop the frequency estimate and the total population that engages in the task. We determined in this evaluation that some situations were more complex and that assuming a 100 percent adoption rate would overestimate the business value of the solution. We also determined that this would require us to generate multiple baseline conditions to account for various adoption rates of the current tasks. We developed additional data collection tools to address these issues.

- When measuring productivity improvements we found that the baseline method used can vary. In previous work, only one baseline method was assumed to be utilized, when in reality, multiple baseline methods might be in use. We needed to understand what percentage of the population used each of the baseline methods when doing a task.

- Employee productivity can be measured at two levels: process improvements and task improvements. Process improvements are at the macro level, and task improvements are at the micro level. We took the approach of first measuring productivity at the task level.

- The e-Workforce program differs from past ITBV team efforts in that it's a multi-year program being rolled out in phases. This required the team to develop and extend previous methods to ensure proper measurement across multiple deployments. Productivity improvement can be viewed along a continuum: as a single implementation in time or as multiple deployments. If the solution spans multiple products or projects, the productivity improvement for the solution is the cumulative impact of all the products or projects.

BV ROI and Results

The financial value of increased employee productivity to the company is calculated in dollars per year and was calculated using data collected in Phase II. We followed the processes for determining employee productivity gains that are outlined in Chapter 4.

To determine the time saved we needed the following parameters: task frequency, difference between baseline and post implementation user task times, and the adoption rate of the new tasks. We determined using an adoption rate of 100 percent was not justified by our data. We used a baseline adoption rate and determined the expected yearly increase in adoption rate each year based on data we had collected during the evaluation.

We do not report the average cost an employee outside Intel, so we reported timed saved as a percentage of an employee's work week. Using data collected during the evaluation, deploying e-Workforce would save each employee that used the solution on average 12.8 hours per year.

In addition, one of the benefits of e-Workforce is that it enables employees to have virtual meetings. We assumed that these virtual meetings would reduce the need for travel and lower travel related costs. We determined that e-Workforce reduced the amount of travel required to meet face to face with other Intel employees by $6.8M per year.

Using the data from travel cost reduction the value of increased employee productivity, we calculated the 3 year NPV of the e-Workforce program. We determined that the 3 year NPV was over $55M for the first phase of the e-Workforce program.

The Business Value of Increased Throughput Time on Flash Test Fixtures

Project Description

Flash memory is a low-cost, high-density, highly reliably memory used in many different products today. This memory is non-volatile and can be programmed and re-programmed as needed.

One of the primary goals of our flash memory test engineering group is to improve test times and processes, ultimately improving throughput time (TPT). The goal of this project was to increase the number of flash products tested in parallel by mating existing memory testers to an off-the-shelf materials handling system. The existing test cells, the handler and tester combination, can test 64 chips simultaneously. By using a handler with a 128 chip capability, the number of chips tested at the same time can be improved.

The majority of tests performed on flash memory products are serial, so there was little opportunity to improve overall testing time. However, one test that takes approximately 40 percent of the total test time can be done in parallel. Parallel testing of chips still requires 40 percent of the overall test time but is not affected by the number of chips being tested.

- For illustration, assume that the test time for 64 chips is approximately 100 seconds. Since 60 seconds of the total test time is spent on serial testing of 64 chips, doubling the number of chips would increase the serial test time to 120 seconds.

- The remaining portion of the test can be performed in parallel and takes 40 seconds to complete regardless of the number of chips being tested.

- Thus, the total time spent testing 128 chips would be 120 seconds for serial testing and 40 seconds for parallel testing leading to a total of 160 seconds.

Business Value Dials

The business value dial used for this evaluation was cost avoidance. While the solution targeted increasing the TPT on individual testers, the business value was realized by reducing the number new testers that needed to be purchased to test additional product.

In other words, using the new solution would allow additional product to be tested, but would allow it to be done without purchasing as much new equipment. The difference between the cost of additional equipment required using the old testing process and the cost of new equipment required using the new process is the cost avoidance for the program.

Scope of Study

This study was limited to one step in the flash memory testing process. Data was collected in a single factory and we assumed that the results would transfer to other assembly test facilities running the same testing processes.

Data Collection Techniques

For this project the data collection was relatively straightforward. Using existing information on the testing process and baseline data on test time, we established a baseline. To determine the post-implementation improvement, test time measures were captured using existing tools and processes.

Study Design

For this study the design simply required comparing the baseline test process to post-implementation test process. The difference between the two test processes was used to determine the increase in TPT for the tools. Since test tools are consistent across tests, data collected from the baseline and post-implementation was reliable and valid.

Determining What to Measure

Since this was a manufacturing test process, determining what to measure was not the issue; it was the test process time. The real issue was in determining that reducing the TPT was not the primary source of business value, but instead the value came from reducing the purchase of new equipment.

Issues Encountered

A long-range issue emerged about obsolescence. Would new testing devices be available to handling the increased testing capability or would they simply disappear, leaving the factories with equipment they could no longer use.

BV ROI and Results

The gain in TPT per tester enabled the test areas to provision less equipment while maintaining the same level of TPT. Using the forecasted reduction in capital expenditures from avoiding the purchase of new equipment, the business value for this project was $22.5M.

Assessment Tools

*One validates not a test, but an interpretation of
data arising from a specified procedure.*
—Lee J. Cronbach

This appendix contains examples of some of the tools and procedures that Intel has used in developing its ITBV program. It includes the following:

- An outline for developing a metrics plan

- Samples of communication with customers

- A sample of a weekly activity log form

- A description of the process Intel uses for creating collateral materials for a Lab Study

- Job descriptions for key ITBV team members

- Intel's Business Value Data Dictionary

▭The Metrics Plan

Table C.1 Anatomy of a Metrics Plan

Description of the IT solution
Business Value Dials
Study scope and objectives
Data collection techniques
Measurement timeframe, baseline and post-implementation
Data source and data owners identified and verified
Dependencies: Possible risk factors for data collection
Study locations
Study design
Methods description
Detailed study design
Employee segments
Sampling plan
Participant recruitment process
Time frames for collection
Product features or vectors for testing
Tasks
Identification
Categorization
High vs. low structure
Ability to measure
Measurement techniques
Prioritization
Team members
Exceptions that should be noted

Request for Participation

Request for Participation - Sample

By Invitation Only -- Please do not forward
Action Required by <insert date>

Help Information Technology (IT) Evaluate <insert platform description>

Do you use your IT-provided <insert platform description> notebook as your primary work PC? If so, you will soon be eligible for a system upgrade as part of the refresh program and you may also be eligible to participate in an evaluation of the <insert platform description> notebook.

Note: If you do not have an <insert platform description>, please update your asset information as noted in the question and answer section below and disregard this message.

How can I participate in the evaluation?
Read the evaluation participation rules. If you are interested in participating in the evaluation program, **complete the questionnaire <linked to the survey> by <insert date>**. The survey is not first-come first-served. Everyone that has an eligible notebook will be considered for the evaluation. If you need to stay on the <insert current platform description>, you are ineligible to participate in this evaluation.

Individuals selected to participate will be contacted by <insert date> with additional information. If you are not selected to participate in this evaluation there is no impact on your eligibility for the refresh program. The refresh program team will be contacting eligible employees at a later date.

Evaluation Participation Rules
This evaluation is geared at understanding the user experience and productivity enhancements of the <insert platform description> wireless notebooks. Results of the evaluation will help IT make decisions regarding deployment and support of these systems.

If you are selected to participate in this evaluation, you will receive a new <insert platform description> notebook that you will retain at the end of the evaluation. For the duration of the evaluation, you will also receive an account with <insert provider description> for use with Public HotSpots* and access to the <insert company name> wireless network.

The evaluation will run through <insert date>. During this time, you will be required to participate in the following activities:

- Complete Web surveys sent to your e-mail inbox.
- Attend two one-hour interviews covering your experiences.
- Complete a weekly log of activities related to using your notebook.
- Participate in a one-hour focus group.
- Attend a two-hour usability lab study.
- Attend the refresh migration training class.

Information you provide as part of the evaluation remains confidential. The information collected is not associated with individual users at the end of the evaluation.

The Human Factors team will contact selected individuals who are interested in assisting in the evaluation. We appreciate your support and participation in completing our initial survey. For those selected to participate, we look forward to working with you in the months ahead.

General Questions and Answers

Q: I don't have an <insert platform description> notebook. How do I update my asset data?
A: To validate your asset data and ensure asset accuracy, periodically run your <insert process description or application description> to update your information. Only employees with <insert platform description> notebooks that are part of the refresh program are eligible to participate in the evaluation. We do not have the ability to make exceptions.

Q: Why did I receive this message?
A: You received this e-mail message because asset records indicate that you have an <insert platform description> notebook that will be eligible for the refresh program.

Q: Should I forward the message to people I think would like to participate?
A: No. Please do not forward the message. This evaluation is by invitation only. Only employees that have <insert platform description> notebooks are eligible. This work is being done as part of the regular refresh program.

Q: What will the survey be used for?
A: The survey will be used to see which eligible employees are willing to spend additional time to participate in the evaluation.

For further assistance please contact <insert contact information>

<insert any required copy right information>

▭ Customer Communication

Customer Communication - Sample

Action Required by <insert date>

Notebook Usage Survey

The Human Factors team would like to thank everyone for their participation in the <insert description> evaluation. As we approach the end of the evaluation, we'd like to understand how you are currently working with your <insert platform description> notebook. **This survey is independent of the weekly activity logs which will continue through <insert date>.**

Click the link below to open the survey. The survey takes 15-20 minutes to complete. Your responses are an essential part of the evaluation; please take time to answer the questions as accurately as possible.

<insert link to survey that has been requested>

It is important that you complete the final survey for our analysis efforts. Again, thank you for your time!

<insert contact information>

<insert any required copy right information>

▭▭▭▮Interview Script

Interview Script for Notebook PC - Sample

Interview Script for <insert project description>
Last updated: <insert date>

Introduction:
Hello. I'm <insert name> in <insert organization name>. I'm helping IT understand how <insert platform description> is adopted at <insert organization name>. I'd like to take about 30 minutes to talk with you about your mobile computing experiences and your new <insert platform description> notebook.

The information you provide is recorded for internal use only. What you say will not be personally linked to you unless your consent is given in advance. You can stop this interview at any time if you need to. Do you have any questions?

Relating to Job Role and User Profile

Could you please describe for me your job role?

How long have you been working in this particular role? How long have you been working at <insert company name>?

Could you tell me a bit about a typical day at work?

Does your job require you to travel much? Where do you usually go for work-related travel?

How much time do you spend at your desk? Do you spend time away from your desk while you are working at an <insert company name> location? If so, how much time do you spend and where do you usually go? (Prompts: meetings, café, manufacturing, lab, colleague office, etc.)

About the system

How many computers do you have when you combine both work and personal use? Are your additional computers notebooks, desktops, or something else?

So what do you think about your notebook computer?

Do you use your notebook quite a bit after working hours? If so, what do you tend to do with it?

Is there anything you've noticed you do with your notebook computer that might be interesting? Why is that?

Mobility

So, have you been carrying your notebook PC around more or less frequently than a previous system you've used? Why do you think that is/isn't?

Do you feel like you work differently when you are with your notebook PC when compared to how you worked with previous notebooks?

How does your notebook PC make you feel?

Can you tell me about your thoughts on the form factor of the system?

Does your notebook PC help you communicate with your coworkers and family members more effectively? How so?

Do you use real-time communication software? If so, what situation prompted you to use it?

Is there an interesting location you've taken your notebook PC? Is that a situation you wouldn't normally think to take your PC with you? If you worked with your notebook in that location, how long did you end up using your system while there?

How often do you think you used the PC in place of PDAs or pagers or Cell phones to communicate with others?

When you moved from place to place, did you place the laptop in the standby mode, shut down mode or online mode?

Connectivity

What was the typical connectivity method you used to connect to the Internet from public places? Wireless or phone line?

If you had wireless or modem, who was your wireless provider?

If by phone line, what was the speed of modem? Would you prefer moving to wireless and why?

What are the public places you have used your notebook to connect from and how frequently?

Have you ever attempted to connect to a hot-spot? What happened? What types of hotspots were they?

How many different hotspot providers have you used? Are you subscribers to those or did you access them for free? How do you know where to connect to a hotspot?

Do you plan to stay in a hotel or visit a specific venue because it has broadband with wireless?

If you knew you had access to a wireless connection at the following locations <insert locations>, how likely is it that you would connect and take advantage of that opportunity?

Are there places you wish you really could connect to hotspots but can't currently?

Battery Life

How do you feel about the battery life of your system?

How much battery life would you estimate you are getting?

Do you feel there is a need for improvement with the battery life of your notebook PC?

Do you charge your notebook as frequently as you used to?

How has the battery life helped you in your job role?

Do you think battery life is an important factor in working from places where there is no plug-in facility available such as when flying, while traveling long distance in train/car, being in public places during games etc.

Performance

Are you able to accomplish more things with your new notebook PC? Why do you think this is?

Do you notice a significant performance increase or decrease after moving to a <insert platform description> notebook?

What kind of applications do you typically use and how many of them do you have open at any given time?

Describe ways in which you multi-task. Do you regularly use background-processing applications such as disk defragmenter, disk cleaner, virus check etc.? If yes, do you multi-task while they run on the background, or do you typically run them stand alone?

Summary

How easy has it been to make the transition from you previous system to the new <insert platform description>?

If you could improve on anything, what would you ask for?

 What do you envision as the dream PC 10 years from now? What features would it have?

Survey

Questionnaire for Hard Drive Backup Solution

<u>Background Information:</u>

1. What is your job title?

2. What is your business group?

3. Which is your field site?

4. How often do you travel in a week?

5. Where do you spend your typical week:
   - At the fields sales office: _____Hours
   - At the customer site: _____Hours
   - Working from home: _____Hours
   - Working from airport/hotel: _____Hours
   - Other: _____Hours

<u>Previous Hard Drive Failures:</u>

6. Did you ever experience any hard drive related issue? If yes, list the nature of the problem.
   - _____
   - _____
   - _____

7. How many times did you experience that problem in the last two years?

8. How did you resolve those hard drive problems? Check the one that applies.
   - ☐ Sending the notebook to the Technical Assistant Center (TAC)
   - ☐ TAC walked me through and resolved the problem
   - ☐ Rectified it by myself

9. If you sent the laptop to TAC, how many days were lost without the laptop each time on an average?

10. While the hard drive was being repaired or replaced, did you use any other avenues to maintain your productivity?
    - ☐ Used phone calls to interact with customer: Yes   No
    - ☐ Used the Traveler workstation more often: Yes   No
    - ☐ Took the help of Admin: Yes   No
    - ☐ Took the help of Field Applications Engineer: Yes   No
    - ☐ Used PDA for emailing and calendaring   Yes   No
    - ☐ Other avenues: _____
    - ☐ None of the above

Impacts of Hard Drive Failures:

11. List the key impacts of the hard drive failure.
    List them in the descending order of their impact severity:

    1. _____
    2. _____
    3. _____
    4. _____
    5. _____

12. Was your productivity affected due to hard drive failure? If yes, what tasks were affected?

    ❏ Emails
    ❏ Calendaring
    ❏ Task list
    ❏ Preparing the presentation or a document
    ❏ Net meeting
    ❏ Browsing
    ❏ Other _____

13. Did you feel the aftereffects of the lost productivity in terms of catching up after your received the laptop from TAC? If yes, how much time did it take to catch up with lost productivity?

    _____ Days, or
    _____ Hours

14. Did you lose data? If yes,

    What kind of data?
    ❏ Emails,
    ❏ Files,
    ❏ Other: _____
    How much data was lost? _____ %

15. Did the downtime result in any missed sales targets?

    ❏ Yes
    ❏ No
    If yes/no, explain why and how much: _____

16. Did the downtime result in missed customer meetings?

    ❏ Yes
    ❏ No
    If yes/no, explain why: _____

17. Did you fail to return customer calls during the down time?

    ☐ Yes

    ☐ No

    If yes/no, explain why: _____

18. Did the down time result in missed deadlines or deliverables?

    ☐ Yes

    ☐ No

    If yes/no, explain why: _____

19. Did the down time result in loss of credibility with the customer?

    ☐ Yes

    ☐ No

    If yes/no, explain why: _____

<u>Current Back Up Solutions:</u>

20. Do you have any back up solution currently?   Yes   No

    ☐ CNB (Connected Network Backup)

    ☐ External drive

    ☐ Other solutions: _____

21. How often do you use the back up solution?

    _____ Times per month, or

    _____ Times per year

    ☐ Never used it

22. Did having a back up solution reduce the severity of impact during subsequent hard drive failures?

    ☐ Yes

    ☐ No

    ☐ Cannot say, as I never experienced a failure ever since.

23. What do you think are the potential benefits of having a Hard Drive Back Up Solution? List them in their descending order of significance.

    1._____

    2._____

    3._____

    4._____

    5._____

Activity Log

Weekly Activity Log – Sample

For <insert date>

please enter your ID# [   ]

Wireless Connection

Please specify how often you used your wireless connection last week in the following locations. Also, please let us know how much time you spent using your wireless connection last week at the following locations.

	Frequency per Week	Duration (Hrs. and/or Mins.)
Home	[ ]	[ ] Hrs [ ] Min
Cube	[ ]	[ ] Hrs [ ] Min
Campus	[ ]	[ ] Hrs [ ] Min
Client	[ ]	[ ] Hrs [ ] Min
Airport	[ ]	[ ] Hrs [ ] Min
Cafe	[ ]	[ ] Hrs [ ] Min
Other Public Place	[ ]	[ ] Hrs [ ] Min

Check all that apply:

☐ I consciously opted to stay at a hotel with wireless broadband access.

☐ I carried my notebook outside without a bag.

☐ I used my notebook's battery power continuously between 3 and 4 hours.

☐ I used my notebook's battery power continuously for more than 4 hours.

☐ I had difficulty connecting to or using a public hot spot.

Success: Describe something you did with your <insert platform description> notebook during the week that you wouldn't have done if you were using your old system <insert platform description>.

[   ]

Criticality: How critical was this success in supporting your computing needs?

☐ ☐ ☐ ☐ ☐ ☐ ☐   ☐

Not Critical   Very Critical   N/A

Difficulty: Tell us about problems with your <insert platform description>

```



```

Criticality: Please rate the criticality of this difficulty.

☐ ☐ ☐ ☐ ☐ ☐ ☐   ☐

Not Critical   Very Critical   N/A

Any other comments?

```



```

Employee Performance Measurement

Table C.2   Employee Performance Measures

Category	Performance Measurement*	How to Achieve It
Efficiency	• Amount of the user takes to complete a task • Number of tasks, or proportion of a large task, of various kinds that can be completed within a given time limit • Ratio between tasks that were completed vs. not completed • Amount of dead time when the user is not interacting with the system;	• Reduce the time it takes to perform a task • Restructure the nature of the tasks
Accuracy	• Ratio between tasks that were successful vs. those that resulted in errors • Amount of time spent recovering from errors • Number of user errors	• Reduce the costs associated with making an error • Remove a task that a person performs • Remove or reduce errors • Reduce the number of end-user processes to achieve the same goal, lowering the probability of errors
Time to Proficiency	• Number of features used vs. not used by the users • Number of features that a user can remember or recall • Frequency of use of job aids such as user manuals or user help wizards • Amount of time taken by the user to achieve an acceptable level of performance • How frequently the manual or help tool solved the user problem;	• Design product so that it reduces testing time+Provide adequate training materials and help tools
Employee Satisfaction	• Number of times the user expresses frustration in completing the task • Number of times the user has to work around a difficult work procedure	• Improve the overall user experience

*Adapted from Nielsen, J. (1993). *Usability Engineering*. San Francisco: Morgan Kaufmann.

Creating Collateral Materials for a Lab Study

Before we begin a lab study, we go through a process of creating collateral materials that we will be using.

Creating Tasks and Scenarios

We first choose a list of representative tasks from among the tasks that participants typically perform as part of their work. We select only tasks that participants engage in frequently. We gather information on the types and frequency of tasks from several sources, including surveys, studies done by our suppliers, third-party research, and research from various consulting groups. We also design our tasks based on feedback from participants during pilot studies.

We develop scenarios that must take place in a prescribed order. Counterbalancing and randomization in task presentation isn't possible, since test materials depend on progressive scenarios.

Collateral Materials for the Test Tasks

Creation of the collateral material begins when we create the network test accounts and e-mail accounts, install the appropriate security software for each account, and create any other accounts that the test scenarios require. Test accounts must be created for each location.

Once we've determined tasks and scenarios, the next step is to create the appropriate collateral material for completing each task. For example, a task might require using different documents stored in different folders, sending an e-mail response to an existing e-mail, sending a saved e-mail, using shared drives and folders, using networked printers, using book-marked Web sites, using a wireless network, using remote access or local area network connections, using shortcuts for launching applications from the desktop, and so forth. We create and save all task prerequisites for the entire infrastructure before beginning.

For tasks that involve sending or receiving emails, we create a private e-mail folder, then configure the e-mail application to open into the personal folder inbox. This avoids the tedium of creating and saving new e-mails for each participant at the session's start. All other folders, such as sent items, outbox, deleted items, and calendar are also created in the personal folder.

Familiarization Activities and Collateral Material

Participants perform the majority of test tasks so frequently during work that it's reasonable to assume that they already know how. However, for infrequent or more complex tasks, we want to bring all participants to a standard level of familiarization. To do this, we've adopted two methods: familiarization tasks and familiarization videos.

A familiarization task simulates a test task; we have a participant complete it just before performing the actual task. That helps participants understand the actual task's features, screen controls, and navigation between screens. We model the familiarization tasks from the test tasks without duplication. That gives the participants an overall understanding of the steps to complete the task, but without providing details. We create the collateral material for the familiarization tasks with the same process we use for creating the test tasks themselves.

A familiarization video shows a presenter completing the tasks. The presenter reads a task and scenario, then steps through it while explaining navigation and details. We capture the audio and screen navigation using a software program, convert it to an executable file, and place it on the test system bundles as part of system preparation. During the test session, participants play back each video before the appropriate test task.

Test Monitor and Participant Packets

To ensure that lab tests are conducted consistently across all locations, after all the collateral material is ready, we prepare a test monitor packet with instructions to the test monitor. The role of a monitor is to prepare the test system bundle and to manage the participant session. The packet tells the test monitor how to:

- Configure the systems before each test session.
- Welcome and introduce the participant to the study.
- Administer the skill assessment matrix.
- Obtain the signed video consent form.
- Allocate the participant to one of the test systems, per the study design.
- Bring the system to the correct state before beginning a task.
- Follow the criteria for starting and stopping the watch.

- Determine the various paths participants might adopt to accomplish the task.

- Determine if passing criteria have been satisfied.

- Administer the post-task questionnaire.

- Administer the post-test survey.

- Start the imaging process to reset the machine.

The participant packet contains instructions to be followed during the test, along with the tasks and scenarios, surveys to be completed during and after the test, sheets for recording task completion time, and instructions for the familiarization activities.

Creating Test System Images

All collateral materials for the test and familiarization tasks are created and saved on a test system using a test account. We also save copies of the collateral in a shared drive as a backup. We prepare a configuration document to trace all the steps required in creating the collateral and the system's base image. In addition, we create an acceptance test plan with a checklist of configuration settings and required files that must be present on the system bundle, which serves as the passing criteria for final system configuration.

Once all collateral materials are created and saved to a shared drive, we reformat or re-image the hard drive with a standard Intel IT build. The materials are then copied back from the shared drive and all configuration steps are repeated on each test system bundle, as outlined in the configuration document.

Through this image conditioning process, we want to end up with a system that works exactly like whatever production system has been in use.

Once we've captured a stable image, we make a dry run for each task to verify that all collateral material works correctly: that participants can log on to the system, that various applications launch, and that all tasks can be completed successfully in all the various ways possible.

We compare the results of the dry run with the acceptance plan, note any issues, and update the configuration document accordingly. We also note and resolve any gaps in the materials. We iteratively repeat this process of conditioning the image until we've created a clean and complete set of materials and all configuration steps have passed the acceptance test plan. The system is now ready for creating a final image that includes the operating system, applications, and the collateral materials.

Creating a Final Image File and a Bootable DVD

To obtain a final image, we first re-image the test machine with a standard build. We then reboot, connect to the network, and log on using the test account. After a successful logon, we copy all collateral materials from the shared drive to the system in the appropriate folders, and all required configuration steps are completed. This involves creating a personal folder in the e-mail system for each participant, and pointing it to the appropriate local file where e-mail is saved. The e-mail folder is synchronized, so the offline database is updated locally.

Once we've completed the configuration steps, the system is ready for final imaging. We use a standard disk imaging application to create an exact replica of the test system, creating the image as a single file and saving it in a shared drive.

The final image file is then copied from the share to a DVD and labeled with the appropriate machine and test account. As the image created for one system bundle and one test account shouldn't be used later for loading on a different machine using a different test account, it's essential to create test systems individually for each combination of test participant and system. We repeat this process for each pair of test accounts and test systems, resulting in one DVD for each pair.

We then copy the DVD back and test it on each test machine for which it was created. If all the tests complete per the acceptance plan, then we consider the collateral material creation process complete. However, if we notice any small gaps, they're captured and a list of configuration steps is created. These steps are copied into the appropriate section of the test-monitor packet; the test monitor applies these fixes as part of preparing the system prior to test sessions. The test system is now ready to be used in a lab session.

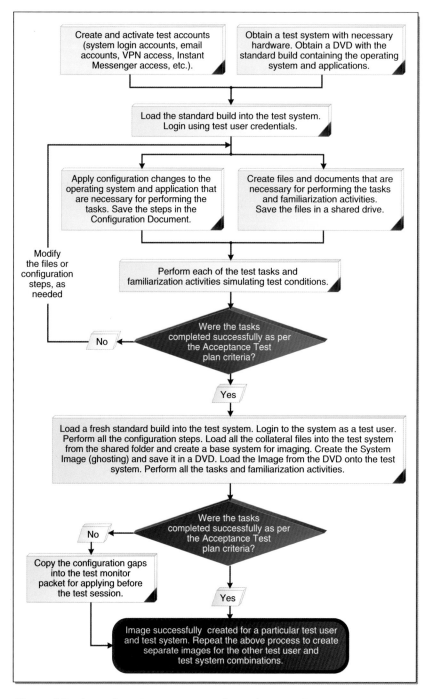

Figure C.1 Flow Chart for Creating Collateral Materials

▭ Job Descriptions

IT Business Value Job Descriptions - Samples

ITBV Program Manager:
Individual is responsible for developing, managing and marketing a program to be designed to measure the return on investment (ROI) for IT-driven projects specifically focused on the end user organizations. Responsibilities include recruiting participants in the initial definition and setup stages of the program, scoping the program, gaining senior IT management support for the program and rolling it out corporate-wide. In addition, this individual will manage a team of 3-4 Project Managers who will drive specific measurement projects and the Research team including the Research Manager who, in turn, will manage a team of Human Factors Engineers.

Successful candidate will have excellent verbal and written communications skills, strong people management with 5+ years of experience in people and program management and experience in marketing using electronic media. Requires a graduate degree in Finance, Marketing, Statistics or other related field, 8+ years of experience, 2-3 years IT experience preferred.

IT Business Value Project Manager:
Individual will develop metrics methodologies, manage metrics plans, and perform ROI analysis for projects within IT. Responsibilities include working with IT divisions to forecast value (ROI) of overall productivity gains expected with roll-out of new or updated IT solutions to business units. In addition, individual will manage coordinated project tracking and ensure all projects are fully documented across the group. The individual will be responsible for cross-functional coordination of metrics programs with business units and among IT divisions. Development and dissemination of best practices is also a core requirement of the job. In addition, individual will manage the development and operation of a Resource Center web site to support all business value metrics activities.

Successful candidate will have experience in project management and measuring actual performance against forecast. Must have strong analytical and project management skills. Excellent written and verbal communication skills. Requires Bachelor's degree in Finance or related field, 3-5 years experience, 2-3 years of IT experience preferred.

Human Factors Engineer
Job Description: This position is responsible for Human Factors Engineering support in the areas of application development, system definition, internal processes, and user productivity. This position is engaged in a wide range of usability engineering activities and works closely with other Human Factors professionals, technical writers, software engineers, business analysts, finance analysts, and graphics designers to support Information Technology (IT) products and services. The successful candidate must be capable of defining system requirements, specify interaction models, defining user interfaces, develop/evaluate UI simulations and conducting lab and field-based usability testing. The successful candidate will have proven experience working in the area of user productivity, the ability to define and measure user productivity, and a strong background in statistics and experimental methodology.

Degree and experience requirements include: PhD + 3 year industry experience, MS + 5 years industry experience, or BS + 7 years industry experience. Degree should be in an experimental social science (e.g., cognitive psychology) or from a focused Human Factors Engineering program.

Business Value Data Dictionary

The business value project database has grown and developed over the years as the program has developed. The data elements are primarily used for project reporting, dollars counted toward our stated goal, number and percentage of projects within each value dial, and various forecast reports. Another use that has developed from this database has been project tracking for the different BV project managers; to follow and keep up with the many projects each may have in various stages and statuses throughout the year. The database has become an integral part of the program and all team members rely on it for reporting, status updates, and as a method for sharing project information with other team members in order to get help with more complex projects.

Below each data element is listed and described within the context of the ITBV program.

Field Name:	Date Submitted
Description:	Automated date entry reflecting record creation date.
Field Entry:	N/A
Comments:	8 character date field

Field Name:	Project Name
Description:	Actual known/common name of project for easy reference.
Field Entry:	Required - Alpha Numeric
Comments:	Field is limited to 40 alpha- numeric characters.

Field Name:	Status
Description:	The status reflects where the project is in relation to completing the business value package.
Field Entry:	Required - Limited to drop-down menu choices (In Progress, Pending, Closed/Rejected, Closed/Future, Accepted

Comments:	Once a project has started and the data gathering is underway its status becomes "In Progress." If a project is on hold waiting on an event, decision or an external task to be completed it is given a "Pending" status. If at any time a project is determined not to be acceptable under the program guidelines or a decision has been made not to pursue the business value component (*i.e.*, value is too low), then it is given a "Closed/Rejected" status and is no longer included in reporting. In some cases projects will be delayed or pushed out until a future time, in these cases they are classified as "Closed/Future" and will be re-visited at some given interval of time (*i.e.*, new calendar year). If the project is approved, the numbers are included in goal tracking and the project is flagged as "Accepted."

Field Name:	ITBV Project Manager
Description:	This is the IT Business Value team project manager responsible for completing the business value package for the project.
Field Entry:	Alpha-Numeric
Comments:	

Field Name:	HFE Contact
Description:	In cases where productivity or usability gains are being measured, a Human Factors Engineer resource is assigned to project to conduct the appropriate measurements and ensure the data is gathered, analyzed, and reported using approved methodologies.
Field Entry:	Alpha-Numeric
Comments:	

Field Name:	Financial Analyst
Description:	A financial resource is assigned to each project. It is their responsibility to create the financial Return On Investment (ROI) that will later be used as part of the Net Present Value (NPV) calculations.
Field Entry:	Alpha-Numeric
Comments:	

Field Name:	IT Project Owner
Description:	This is the actual business unit project owner , that is, in most cases, the project manager responsible for the project completion.
Field Entry:	Alpha-Numeric
Comments:	

Field Name:	IT Business Unit(s)
Description:	This is the Business Unit that owns project , and is responsible for all aspects of the project including. The IT Project Owner is typically a member of this business unit.
Field Entry:	Alpha-Numeric
Comments:	

Field Name:	Customer Business Unit
Description:	Reflects the customer's business unit, primarily used for reporting back to each business unit GM and staff which of their projects has been accepted and tracking of total dollars delivered to a stated goal .
Field Entry:	Alpha-Numeric
Comments:	

Field Name:	Project Description
Description:	Free-form text describing the project, limited to a one paragraph description
Field Entry:	Alpha-Numeric
Comments:	

Field Name:	ROI
Description:	A "Yes/No" field indicating whether or not there is an existing ROI for this project.
Field Entry:	Limited to Yes/No
Comments:	

Field Name:	Initial ROI (in $M)
Description:	Initial ROI for the project. Once the ROI is entered, it is not updated through the life of the project.
Field Entry:	Numeric only - single decimal
Comments:	This number is used for comparison with the Projected ROI and the value ultimately approved for the program.

Field Name:	Projected ROI (in $M)
Description:	Projected ROI as the project progresses. This number is updated to reflect the latest ROI figures.
Field Entry:	Numeric only - single decimal
Comments:	This number will be compared to the "Initial ROI" numbers to see how much the numbers fluctuated during the project. Large differences are investigated to understand the source of the discrepancies and if any process updates are required.

Field Name:	Confidence in projected ROI
Description:	Reflects the Business Value PM assessment of the ROI.
Field Entry:	Limited to drop-down menu choices (High, Medium, Low)
Comments:	Early on in the project, confidence in this number may be low and move higher as the project progresses and the ROI becomes more stable. Toward the end of the project this field will be changed to high to reflect the current status.

Field Name:	NPV Status
Description:	Status of NPV being readied to submit /present to MRC
Field Entry:	Required - Limited to drop-down menu choices (In Progress, Accepted, Ready)
Comments	Used by the overall ITBV program manager to schedule reviews with the MRC

Field Name:	Approved NPV in $M
Description:	This will be the final number as presented/accepted by the MRC.
Field Entry:	Numeric Only - single decimal
Comments:	

Field Name:	Timeline for rollout
Description:	Indicates a specific month, day, year, quarter, or week the solution is anticipated to be implemented.
Field Entry:	Alpha-Numeric, limited to 25 characters
Comments:	

Field Name:	Confidence in Timeline
Description:	ITBV PM's assessment of the confidence in the solution being rolled out on time.
Field Entry:	Limited to drop-down menu choices (High, Medium, Low)
Comments:	This field was used to help develop an overall picture of when business value would be delivered.

Field Name:	Comments
Description:	Used by the ITBV PM to document meetings, decisions, deliverables, etc. This is an on-going update of the project.
Field Entry:	Alpha-numeric, free-form text
Comments:	

Field Name:	Year
Description:	This is the calendar year the project is expected to deliver in.
Field Entry:	4 digit numeric
Comments:	Used for forecasting and reporting purposes.

Field Name:	MRC Ready
Description:	A "Yes/No" field that reflects whether a project is completed, documented, and ready to be presented to the MRC for final review and approval.
Field Entry:	Limited to Yes/No
Comments:	

Field Name:	Disposition
Description:	Any project that has entered into the BV program, regardless of final status, has a disposition. This field indicates what the final outcome of the project was. It is strictly an informational field. Choice ins
Field Entry:	Limited to drop-down menu choices (Value Below Minimum, Customer Cancelled, Reduced Funding, MRC Rejected, Not Measurable, Completed)
Comments:	

Field Name:	Archive Date
Description:	Each year projects from the previous calendar year are archived, along with all associated documentation, presentations, etc. This date references the archive year for each project.
Field Entry:	Date field (mm/dd/yyyy)
Comments:	

Field Name:	Content
Description:	This reflects any white papers, presentations, etc. that were generated from this project for future reference or use.
Field Entry:	Alpha-numeric
Comments:	

Field Name:	Value Dial(s)
Description:	Reflects under which value dial(s) this project delivered value. This allows easy reporting by value dials and an overall view of how many projects and dollars were delivered under each respective value dial.
Field Entry:	Limited to drop-down menu choices, listing all recognized value dials.
Comments:	This also provides a good reference for looking back at previous projects for BKM's and methods for getting projects measured.

References

Alreck, P. L. and Settle, R. B. 2004. *The Survey Research Handbook, 3rd edition.* New York: McGraw-Hill/Irwin series in marketing.

Apfel, A., Smith, M., and Viviano, A. 2002. Return on Investment and Business Value of IT: An Analysis and Survey of Current Approaches. White Paper: Gartner Measurement. March 25.

Aral, S. and Weill, P. 2005. IT Assets, Organizational Capabilities and Firm Performance: Asset and Capability Specific Complementarities. MIT Center for Information Systems Research Working Paper.

Bharadwaj, Anandhi S. 2000. A resource-based perspective on information technology capability and firm performance: an empirical investigation. *MIS Quarterly* (24) 1, 169-196.

Batzer, S, Desai, A., and Mason, J. W. 2003. Modeling the Cost Avoidance Potential of a Structured Approach to IP Reuse at Intel. Intel Design and Test Technology Conference.

Bias, R. G. and Mayhew, D. J. 1994. *Cost-Justifying Usability.* Morgan Kaufmann Publishers, Academic Press.

Brannick, J. 1999. Decreasing the staggering costs of turnover in your organization. *www.brannickhr.com/decreasing%20_staggering_costs.html.*

Brealey, R. and Myers. S. 2002. *Principles of Corporate Finance.* New York: McGraw-Hill.

Brooke, J. 1996. SUS: a "quick and dirty" usability scale. In P. W. Jordan, B. Thomas, B. A. Weerdmeester, and A. L. McClelland (eds.) *Usability Evaluation in Industry*. London: Taylor and Francis.

Brown, M. G., and Svenson, R. A. 1998. Measuring R & D Productivity. Research-Technology Management. Industrial Research Institute. November, 1, 30.

Brynjolfsson, E. 1992. The productivity paradox of Information Technology: Review and Assessment. *Communications of the ACM*. December 1993.

Brynjolfsson, E. and Hitt, L. M. 1993. Is Information Systems Spending Productive? New Evidence and New Results. *Proceedings of the International Conference on Information Systems*.

Brynjolfsson, E. and Hitt, L. M. 2000. Beyond Computation: Information Technology, Organizational Transformation and Business Performance. *Journal of Economic Perspectives* 14 (4), 23-48.

Brynjolfsson, E. and Hitt, L. M. Manuscript: Beyond Computation: Information Technology, Organizational Transformation and Business Performance. Portions of this manuscript appear in *MIT Review* - 2000. The Puzzling Relations Between Computer and the Economy. MIT Press.

Brynjolfsson, E., Hitt, L. M., and Yang, S. 2002. Intangible Assets: Computers and Organizational Capital. Brookings Papers on Economic Activity: Macroeconomics (1), 137-199.

Brynjolfsson, E., Smith, M., and Yu (Jeffrey) Hu. 2003. Consumer Surplus in the Digital Economy: Estimating the Value of Increased Product Variety at Online Booksellers. *Management Science*, 49 (11), 1580-1596.

Business Value of Information Systems at Intel - Copyright © 2004 by the Board of Trustees of the Leland Stanford Junior University. All rights reserved. To order copies or request permission to reproduce materials, email the Case Writing Office at: cwo@gsb.stanford.edu or write: Case Writing Office, Graduate School of Business, Stanford University, Stanford, CA 94305-5015.

Carr, Nicholas G. 2003. IT Doesn't Matter. *Harvard Business Review* 81 (5), 41-49.

Chapanis, A. 1996. *Human Factors in Systems Engineering*. New York, NY: John Wiley & Sons, Inc.

Coelli, T., Prasada Rao, D.S. and Battese, G. E., 1998. *An Introduction to Efficiency and Productivity Analysis.* Boston: Kluwer Academic Publishers.

Colkin, E. 2002. Getting Tough on ROI. *Information Week.* October. *www.informationweek.com/story/IWK20021017S0013.*

Curley, M. 2006. An IT Value Based Capability Maturity Model. Working Paper #0601, IVI. National University of Ireland, Maynooth. April.

Curley, M. 2004. *Managing Information Technology for Business Value. Practical strategies for IT and Business Managers.* Intel Press.

Dedrick, J., Gurbaxani, V., and Kraemer, K. L. 2002. "Information technology and economic performance: A critical review of the empirical evidence." University of California, Irvine, Center for Research in IT and Organizations (CRITO). November.

Dixit, A. K. and Pindyck, R. S. 1994. *Investment Under Uncertainty.* Princeton, NJ: Princeton University Press.

Doherty, W. J. and Thadani, A. J. 1982. The Economic Value of Rapid Response Time. IBM. November. *www.vm.ibm.com/devpages/JELLIOTT/evrrt.html.*

Dos Santos, Brian. L. and Kenneth Peffers. 1995. Rewards to investors in innovative information technology applications: First movers and early followers in Aims. *Organization Science* 6(3), 241-259.

Dumas, J. S. and Redish, J. C. 1999. *A Practical Guide to Usability Testing.* Intellect Ltd.

Drucker, P. F. Productivity in Knowledge and Service Work: The New Priority for the Information Society. Productivity: Key to World Competitiveness. Report Number 1039, 9-12.

Earthy, J. 1998. Usability Maturity Model: Human Centredness Scale. INUSE Project deliverable D5.1.4(s). Version 1.2. London, Lloyd's Register of Shipping.

Epstein, M. J. and Rejc, A. 2005. Evaluating Performance in Information Technology. Strategic Management Series. Management Accounting Guideline. AICPA. CMA Canada, 1-29 (Epstein, Marc J., Adriana Rejc. 2005. "Evaluating Performance in Information Technology." Society of Management Accountants of Canada and American Institute of Certified Public Accountants)

Epstein, M. J. and Rejc, A. 2005B. Measuring the payoffs of IT investments. *CMA Management*. December/January, 20-25.

Fitz-Enz, J. 1997. It's costly to lose good employees. *Workforce*, 76, 50-51.

Fitz-Enz, J. 2000. *The ROI of Human Capital. Measuring the Economic Value of Employee Performance*. AMACOM American Management Association.

Garrett, J. J. 2002. *The Elements of User Experience. User Centered Design for the Web*. New Riders Press.

Goodhue, D. L. and Thomson, R. L. 1995. Task Technology Fit and Individual Performance. *MIS Quarterly*, June, 213-236.

Goto, K. 2004. Brand Value and the User Experience. *Digital Web Magazine*, July. *digital-web.com/articles/ brand_value_and_the_user_experience*.

Hactos, J. T. and Redish, J. C. 1998. *User and Task Analysis for Interface Design*. New York, NY: John Wiley & Sons, Inc.

Harbour, J. L. 1997. *The Basics Of Performance Measurement*. Productivity Press.

Harvard Business Review. 1999. *Business Value of IT*. Harvard Business School Press.

House, C. and Price, R. L. 1991. The Return Map: Tracking Product Teams. *Harvard Business Review*. January - February, 92-100.

House, C. 2004. IT Under Siege. Internal Intel Document, May.

Intel Corporation. Boosting Employee Productivity: Measuring the value of system upgrades. Santa Clara: Intel Corporation. IT@Intel white paper, November 2002. *www.intel.com/it/alpha.htm*.

Intel Corporation. Defining the Value of e-Business: Seventeen Standard Measures. Santa Clara: Intel Corporation, May 2003. IT@Intel white paper, *www.intel.com/it/alpha.htm*.

Intel Corporation. Effects of Wireless Mobile Technology on Employee Productivity: Wireless mobility changes the way employee work. Santa Clara: Intel Corporation. IT@Intel white paper, November 2003. *www.intel.com/it/alpha.htm*.

Intel Corporation. IT Business Value Metrics Program: Capturing technology value through business metrics. Santa Clara: Intel Corporation. IT@Intel white paper, April 2003. *www.intel.com/it/alpha.htm*.

Intel Corporation. Putting a Value on Productivity: Measuring IT-enhanced employee productivity. Santa Clara: Intel Corporation. IT@Intel white paper, May 2003. *www.intel.com/it/alpha.htm*.

Intel Corporation. Measuring Employee Productivity: Data collection and analysis methods for productivity studies at Intel. Santa Clara: Intel Corporation. IT@Intel white paper, June 2004. *www.intel.com/it/alpha.htm*.

Intel Corporation. St. Vincent's Hospital Enhances Patient Throughput with RFID and Greater Visibility of Patient Flow. Santa Clara: Intel Corporation. IT@Intel white paper, 2005. *www.intel.com/it/alpha.htm*.

Intel Corporation. The Workplace Hits the Road: Intel IT finds its field employees save time, improve productivity using Intel Centrino Mobile Technology. Santa Clara: Intel Corporation. IT@Intel brief, February 2004. *www.intel.com/it/alpha.htm*.

Intel Corporation. Business Benefits of Wireless Computing: How wireless improves productivity and return on investment. Santa Clara: Intel Corporation. IT@Intel white paper, September 2004. *www.intel.com/it/alpha.htm*.

Intel Corporation. Intel Communicates Globally through Instant Messaging. Santa Clara: Intel Corporation. IT@Intel white paper, May 2004. *www.intel.com/it/alpha.htm*.

Intel Corporation. 2006. Intel SMB IT Makeover Program Helps New Swan Derive Business Value From Information Technology. Case Study.

ISO 9241. 2000. Ergonomic Requirements for Office Work with Display Terminals, International Standard Organization.

Jokela, T., Siponen, M., Hirasawa, N., and Earthy J. 2006. "A Survey of Usability Capability Maturity Models: Implications for Practice and Research." *Behaviour & Information Technology*, Vol. 25, No. 3, May-June, 263-282.

Jokela, T. 2001. *Assessment of user-centred design processes as a basis for improvement action. An experimental study in industrial settings*. Oulu, Oulu University Press.

Kaipia, R., and Saarineen, N. 2001. Measuring the value of collaboration. Working Paper. *www.tuta.hut.fi/*

Kay, R. L. 2003. Untethered Computing: Feasible, Economic, and Desirable. White Paper. IDC. Sponsored by Intel Corp. January.

Kaydos, W. 1999. *Operational Performance Measurement. Increasing Total Productivity.* St. Lucie Press - CRC Press LLC.

Keen, J. M and Digrius, B. 2003. *Making Technology Investments Profitable. ROI Road Map to Better Business Cases.* New York, NY: John Wiley and Sons, Inc.

Kelley, M. 1994. Information Technology and Productivity: The Elusive Connection. *Management Science*, 40, 1406-1425.

Kirchoff, S. 2002. Technology is a major part of productivity. But is that a good thing? MIT. Digital MASS. Boston.com. *ebusiness.mit.edu/news/globe_story6-11-01.htm.*

Koch, C. 2002. Why Doesn't Your ROI Add Up? You do the math. *Darwin Magazine.* March. *www.darwinmag.com/read/030102/roi.html.*

Laubacher, R., Kothari, S. P., Malone, T. W., and Subirana, B. 2005. What is RFID worth to your company? Measuring performance at the activity level. MIT Center for Coordination Science Working Paper.

Lichtman, A. and Mondolo, D. 2005. *Migrating from Dial-Up Networking to Broadband Reduces Cost.* Intel Corporation. IT@Intel white paper, September 2004. *www.intel.com/it/alpha.htm.*

Lindgaard, G. 2004. Making the business our business: one path to value added HCI. *Interactions*, May-June, 11[3].

Lund, A. M. 1997. Another approach to justifying the cost of usability. *Interactions*, May-June, 4[3].

MacCormack, A. 2003. Evaluating Total Cost of Ownership for Software Platforms: Comparing Apples, Oranges and Cucumbers. AEI Brookings Joint Center for Regulatory Studies, Related Publications 03-9.

Malone, T. W., Crowston, K., Lee, J., Pentland, B., Dellarocas, C., Wyner, G., Quimby, J., Bernstein, A., Herman, G., Klein, M., Osborn, C. S., and O'Donnell, E. 1999. Tools for Inventing Organizations: Toward a Handbook of Organizational Processes, *Management Science* 45, 3, March, 425-443.

Mark, G., Gonzalez, V. M., and Harris, J. 2005. No task left behind?: Examining the nature of fragmented work, in *Human Factors in Computing Systems: Proceedings of CHI'05.* New York: ACM Press, 321-330.

McCall, R. B. 1970. *Fundamental Statistics for Psychology.* 3rd Ed. Harcourt Brace Jovanovich, Publishers.

Microsoft Business Value. 2000. An Introduction to the Microsoft REJ Framework. *www.microsoft.com/value.77*

Murphy, T. 2002. Achieving Business Value From Technology. Gartner Symposium ITxpo. October.

Myers, B. L., Kappelman, L. A., and Prybutok, V. R. 1997. A comprehensive Model for Assessing the Quality and Productivity of the Information Systems Function: Toward a Contingency Theory for Information Systems Assessment. In Garrity, E., and Sanders, L., Editors, *Information System Success Measurement*, Harrisburg, PA: Idea Group, 94-121.

Neuendorf, K. A. 2002. *The Content Analysis Guidebook.* Thousand Oaks, CA: Sage Publications.

Nielsen, J. 1993. *Usability Engineering.* San Francisco: Morgan Kaufmann.

Norman, D. 2004. *Emotional Design: Why We Love (Or Hate) Everyday Things.* New York, NY: Basic Books.

Phillips, J. J. 1996. Measuring ROI: The Fifth Level of Evaluation. *Technical and Skills Training.* April, 10-13.

Phillips, P. P. 2002. *The Bottom Line on ROI.* Atlanta, GA: CEP Press.

Puckett, R. P. 1998. Measuring Productivity in Food Service Operations. *Dietary Manager Magazine.* February.

Robinson, P. and Foster, D. 1979. *Experimental Psychology: A small N approach.* NY: Harper & Row.

Rosenberg, D. 2004. The myths of usability ROI. *Interactions*, September-October, 11[5].

Rubin, J. 1994. *Handbook of Usability Testing: How to Plan, Design and Conduct Effective Tests.* New York, NY: John Wiley & Sons, Inc. ~~New York.~~

Rubinoff, R. 2004. How to Quantify the User Experience. Sitepoint.com, April. *www.sitepoint.com/article/quantify-user-experience*

Schlegel, K. 2001. Measuring Web Site Return. Web and Collaboration Strategy, META Group. June. *www.itworld.com/nl/it_insights/06052001/pf_index.html.*

Shadish, W. R., Cook, T. D., and Campbell, D. T. 2001. *Experimental and Quasi-Experimental Designs For Generalized Causal Inference.* Houghton Mifflin.

Smith, H. and Fingar, P. 2003. IT Doesn't Matter—Business Processes Do: A Critical Analysis of Nicholas Carr's IT Article in the *Harvard Business Review.* Tampa, Florida: Meghan-Kiffer Press.

Solow, R. 1987. We'd better watch out. *New York Times Book Review,* July 12.

Stensrud E., and Myrtveit, I. 1995. "Measuring productivity of object-oriented vs. procedural programming languages: Towards an experimental design," Proceedings of the 18th Information Systems Research Seminar in Scandinavia, Gothenburg Studies in Informatics, Gothenburg, Sweden, 7, 665-679.

Sward, D., Govindaraju, M., and Graves, S. 2005. Measuring Employee Productivity Gains from e-Workforce Solutions. Santa Clara: Intel Corporation. IT@Intel white paper, August. *www.intel.com/it/alpha.htm.*

Sward, D. 2006. Gaining a Competitive Advantage through User Experience Design. Santa Clara: Intel Corporation. IT@Intel white paper, January. *www.intel.com/it/alpha.htm.*

Tallon, P., Kraemer, K., and Gurbaxani, V. 2000. "Executive perspectives on the business value of information technology." *Journal of Management Information Systems,* 16:4.

The Changing World of the CIO. Prepared for Microsoft by Knowledge@Wharton. *knowledge.wharton.upenn.edu/microsoft/042402.html*

Van Alstyne, M. and Bulkley, N. 2005. *An Empirical Analysis of Strategies and Efficiencies in Social Networks.* Academy of Management Conference.

Ward, T. 2001. Toby Ward's Intranet Buzz: Measuring the Dollar Value of Intranets. *www.intranetjournal.com/articles/200104/ pii_04_25_01a.html.*

Wen, H. J. and Sylla, C. 1999. *A Road Map for the Evaluation of Information Technology Investment in Measuring Information Technology Payoff: Contemporary Approaches* (Editors: Mahmood, M.A., and Szewczak, E.), Hershey, PA: Idea Group Publishing.

Wheelwright, S. C. and Clark, K. B. 1992. *Revolutionizing Product Development. Quantum Leaps in Speed, Efficiency, and Quality.* The Free Press. Maxwell Macmillan International.

Wickens, C. D. and Hollands, J. G. 1999. *Engineering psychology and human performance (3rd Ed.).* Upper Saddle River, NJ: Prentice-Hall.

Wolfe, P., Wetzel, M., Harris, G., Mazour, T., and Riplinger, J. 1991. *Job Task Analysis—A Guide to Good Practice.* Englewood Cliffs, NJ: Educational Technology Publications.

Yates, J.F. 1990. *Judgment and Decision Making.* Englewood Cliffs, NJ: Prentice Hall.

Index

Continuing Education is Essential

It's a challenge we all face – keeping pace with constant change in information technology. Whether our formal training was recent or long ago, we must all find time to keep ourselves educated and up to date in spite of the daily time pressures of our profession.

Intel produces technical books to help the industry learn about the latest technologies. The focus of these publications spans the basic motivation and origin for a technology through its practical application.

Right books, right time, from the experts

These technical books are planned to synchronize with roadmaps for technology and platforms, in order to give the industry a head-start. They provide new insights, in an engineer-to-engineer voice, from named experts. Sharing proven insights and design methods is intended to make it more practical for you to embrace the latest technology with greater design freedom and reduced risks.

I encourage you to take full advantage of Intel Press books as a way to dive deeper into the latest technologies, as you plan and develop your next generation products. They are an essential tool for every practicing engineer or programmer. I hope you will make them a part of your continuing education tool box.

Sincerely,

Justin Rattner
Senior Fellow and Chief Technology Officer
Intel Corporation

Turn the page to learn about titles
from Intel Press for system developers

Managing Information Technology for Business Value

Practical Strategies for IT and Business Managers

By Martin Curley
ISBN 0-9717861-7-8

Managing Information Technology for Business Value is Martin Curley's call for IT and business planners to reformulate the way they manage IT. Traditionally, IT success has been measured in terms of internal IT systems parameters, such as availability, capacity, and processing speed.

It is Curley's contention that if IT is to deliver business value, then IT should be measured in core business terms, such as customer satisfaction, revenue growth, and profitability.

At a time when some corporations are reducing IT spending and once again looking at IT as a cost center, Martin Curley's *Managing Information Technology for Business Value* provides a necessary and timely counterbalance.

The book introduces a capability maturity framework for improving the business value from information technology. The framework includes structured improvement paths and best practices from Intel and the Industry.

66 *If you're buying one book on the subject of business value from IT, this is it. Curley shines a light on the path ahead for ambitious users of IT. If you have any impact on how IT gets used in your organization, you owe it to your shareholders to read this book. It will impact your bottom line!* 99

—*John Fleming, CEO,*
Enzo Consulting

66 *IT is moving from the back room to the board room—pushing corporations through a strategic inflection point, and presenting CIO's with new and often unforeseen challenges. In this engaging book, Curley offers practical advice and insights into how to respond to these challenges. I consider this book required reading for all IT executives.* 99

—*Prof. Paul Tallon,*
Carroll School of Management,
Boston College

Enhance security and protection against software-based attacks

The Intel Safer Computing Initiative

Building Blocks for Trusted Computing

By David Grawrock

ISBN 0-9764832-6-2

With the ever-increasing connectivity of home and business computers, it is essential that developers understand how the Intel Safer Computing Initiative can provide critical security building blocks to better protect the PC computing environment. Security capabilities need to be carefully evaluated before delivery into the marketplace. Intel is committed to delivering security capabilities in a responsible manner for end users and the ecosystem.

A highly versatile set of hardware-based security enhancements, code-named LaGrande Technology (LT), will be supported on Intel processors and chipsets to help enhance PC platforms. This book covers the fundamentals of LT and key Trusted Computing concepts such as security architecture, cryptography, trusted computer base, and trusted channels.

Highlights include:

- History of trusted computing and definitions of key concepts
- Comprehensive overview of protections that are provided by LaGrande Technology
- Case study showing how access to memory is the focal point of an attack
- Protection methods for execution, memory, storage, input, and graphics
- How the Trusted Platform Module (TPM) supports attestation

In this concise book, the lead security architect for Intel's next-generation security initiative provides critical information you need to evaluate Trusted Computing for use on today's PC systems and to prepare your designs to respond to future threats.

Applied Virtualization Technology

Usage Models for IT Professionals and Software Developers

By Sean Campbell and Michael Jeronimo
ISBN: 0-9764832-3-8

Server and desktop virtualization is one of the more significant technologies to impact computing in the last few years, promising the benefits of infrastructure consolidation, lower costs, increased security, ease of management, and greater employee productivity.

Using virtualization technology, one computer system can operate as multiple "virtual" systems. The convergence of affordable, powerful platforms and robust scalable virtualization solutions is spurring many technologists to examine the broad range of uses for virtualization. In addition, a set of processor and I/O enhancements to Intel server and client platforms, known as Intel® Virtualization Technology (Intel® VT), can further improve the performance and robustness of current software virtualization solutions.

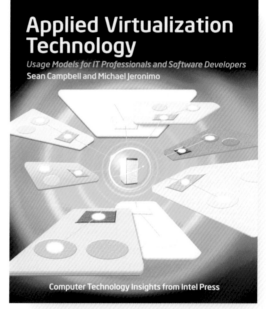

Applied Virtualization Technology
Usage Models for IT Professionals and Software Developers
Sean Campbell and Michael Jeronimo

Computer Technology Insights from Intel Press

This book takes a user-centered view and describes virtualization usage models for IT professionals, software developers, and software quality assurance staff. The book helps you plan the introduction of virtualization solutions into your environment and thereby reap the benefits of this emerging technology.

Highlights include:

- The challenges of current virtualization solutions
- In-depth examination of three software-based virtualization products
- Usage models that enable greater IT agility and cost savings
- Usage models for enhancing software development and QA environments
- Maximizing utilization and increasing flexibility of computing resources
- Reaping the security benefits of computer virtualization
- Distribution and deployment strategies for virtualization solutions

Multi-Core Programming
Increasing Performance through Software Multi-threading

By Shameem Akhter and Jason Roberts
ISBN 0-9764832-4-6

Software developers can no longer rely on increasing clock speeds alone to speed up single-threaded applications; instead, to gain a competitive advantage, developers must learn how to properly design their applications to run in a threaded environment. This book helps software developers write high-performance multi-threaded code for Intel's multi-core architecture while avoiding the common parallel programming issues associated with multi-threaded programs. This book is a practical, hands-on volume with immediately usable code examples that enable readers to quickly master the necessary programming techniques.

Discover programming techniques for Intel multi-core architecture and Hyper-Threading Technology

The Software Optimization Cookbook, Second Edition
High-Performance Recipes for IA-32 Platforms

By Richard Gerber, Aart J.C. Bik, Kevin B. Smith, and Xinmin Tian
ISBN 0-9764832-1-1

Four Intel experts explain the techniques and tools that you can use to improve the performance of applications for IA-32 processors. Simple explanations and code examples help you to develop software that benefits from Intel® Extended Memory 64 Technology (Intel® EM64T), multi-core processing, Hyper-Threading Technology, OpenMP†, and multimedia extensions. This book guides you through the growing collection of software tools, compiler switches, and coding optimizations, showing you efficient ways to get the best performance from software applications.

❝ *A must-read text for anyone who intends to write performance-critical applications for the Intel processor family.* ❞

—Robert van Engelen,
Professor,
Florida State University

Special Deals, Special Prices!

To ensure you have all the latest books
and enjoy aggressively priced discounts,
please go to this Web site:

www.intel.com/intelpress/bookbundles.htm

Bundles of our books are available,
selected especially to address the needs
of the developer. The bundles place
important complementary topics at
your fingertips, and the price for a
bundle is substantially less than
buying all the books individually.